Moving Every Child Ahead

From NCLB Hype to
Meaningful Educational Opportunity

Moving Every Child Ahead

From NCLB Hype to Meaningful Educational Opportunity

**MICHAEL A. REBELL
AND JESSICA R. WOLFF**

Foreword by Susan H. Fuhrman

Teachers College, Columbia University
New York and London

Published by Teachers College Press, 1234 Amsterdam Avenue, New York, NY 10027

Library of Congress Cataloging-in-Publication Data

Rebell, Michael A.
  Moving every child ahead : from NCLB hype to meaningful educational opportunity / Michael A. Rebell and Jessica R. Wolff ; foreword by Susan Fuhrman.
     p. cm.
  Includes bibliographical references and index.
  ISBN 978-0-8077-4850-3 (pbk. : alk. paper)
  ISBN 978-0-8077-4851-0 (hardcover : alk. paper)
     1. Educational equalization—United States. 2. Academic achievement—United States. 3. United States. No Child Left Behind Act of 2001.
  I. Wolff, Jessica R. II. Title.
  LC213.2.R43   2008
  379.2′6—dc22   2007035056

ISBN 978-0-8077-4850-3 (paper)
ISBN 978-0-8077-4851-0 (hardcover)

Printed on acid-free paper
Manufactured in the United States of America

15 14 13 12 11 10 09 08   8 7 6 5 4 3 2 1

To **Sharon and Sarah**,
whose constant candor and support
help me see when the emperor has no clothes.

—M.A.R.

To my parents, **Michael and Sara Wolff**,
true humanitarians whose values will always inspire me.

—J.R.W.

Contents

Foreword

The passage of the federal No Child Left Behind Act in 2002 was hailed as an historic moment in American education, the culmination of both the movement among states to codify learning, teaching, and curriculum standards for all children, and of efforts dating back to the Civil Rights era to secure equal opportunity for minority students and those from disadvantaged backgrounds. Its ambitious goals of achieving universal student proficiency in math and reading by 2014 were linked with unprecedented measures to ensure accountability by states, districts, communities. and schools.

Now we have reached the halfway point for achieving those goals. Is the law working as planned? With the future well-being of millions of young people hanging on the answer, the need of legislators and policymakers for quality research that paints a picture of *what is* rather than *what they wish it could be* has never been greater. Yet in the highly politicized arena of education in the United States today, obtaining answers to questions of this kind is no simple task.

In *Moving Every Child Ahead*, Michael Rebell and Jessica Wolff present precisely the kind of nuanced, fine-grained exploration of NCLB and its impact that the country so desperately needs. They begin their analysis by asking what policies and programs are needed to overcome historic inequities and current achievement gaps, rather than by asserting any set ideological or political positions. They then systematically analyze the major aspects of the law and provide telling recommendations for revising it in order to meet the actual needs of all students, and especially those from disadvantaged backgrounds.

NCLB has two main stated purposes: ensuring that all students have meaningful educational opportunities and requiring that 100% of America's students be proficient in regard to challenging standards by 2014. Currently, the mechanisms in the law stress accountability for meeting the demanding proficiency requirements and largely neglect the opportunity goals. Drawing on data from a major symposium held at Teachers College, Columbia University, by the Campaign for Education Equity in November of 2006, Rebell and Wolff show that little real progress is being made toward the mandate that all students be proficient by 2014. They then argue that the priority emphasis of the law's two major purposes should be inverted. Greater immediate emphasis on the opportunity goal will lead to higher, more rapid, and more sustained student achievement.

The authors set forth a provocative but significant concept of "meaningful educational opportunity" that is drawn from concepts developed by the federal courts in implementing the Supreme Court's 1954 decision in *Brown v. Board of Education,* congressional statutes like the Individuals with Disabilities Education Act, and from the recent rulings of dozens of state courts in school finance and education adequacy litigations that have directly considered the resources that students, and especially students from backgrounds of poverty, need to meet challenging state standards. They close by sketching a new vision of a partnership between the states and the federal government—one that gives the federal authorities a greater say in ensuring that educational standards really are challenging, and the states a much broader scope for developing the specific mechanisms and opportunities that will allow all students to meet these standards.

Not everyone will agree with the authors' recommendations. Still, *Moving Every Child Ahead* should be required reading for anyone who cares about the future of education in this country, and certainly for anyone with a serious interest in the evolution of education policy during the past 30 years. Certain findings—that no state is currently on track to achieve full proficiency as defined by NCLB by 2014, that the law's requirement that all teachers be "highly qualified" in practice means only that all teachers be "minimally qualified," and that education needs cannot be met without directly confronting the impact of concentrated poverty on most of our low-achieving students—are distressing. At the same time, Rebell and Wolff understand the critical political and educational importance of NCLB's goals—goals that represent an implicit promise to those who have historically been excluded from the benefits of education—that, at long last, America is serious about changing and including them in the future.

The book's underlying argument—that inequities related to poverty and race are the ultimate barriers to educational success, and that the emphasis of NCLB should therefore be shifted from one of universal attainment to one of universal opportunity—strikes to the heart of educational debate in the United States today. Can the nation truly guarantee a "meaningful educational opportunity" for every child, as Rebell and Wolff suggest? The answer is unclear, but the book makes a compelling case for why, now more than ever, we must devote ourselves to trying.

—Susan H. Fuhrman
President, Teachers College, Columbia University

Acknowledgments

This book and its recommendations grew out of the dynamic second annual symposium of the Campaign for Educational Equity, "Examining America's Commitment to Closing Achievement Gaps: NCLB and Its Alternatives," that was held in November 2006 at Teachers College, Columbia University, and the follow-up policy discussions with the Equity Campaign's national advisory council. The authors are grateful to all who participated for the research and insights they shared. In particular, we acknowledge the important contributions of Delia Pompa and Ted Shaw, whose passionate defense of the core goals of NCLB inspired us to try to understand and attempt to resolve the conflict between the law's vital aims and its mechanisms for achieving those aims. Although many of the symposium participants, as well as members of the Equity Campaign's national advisory council, faculty at Teachers College, and other educators, policymakers, and advocates took part in policy discussions that were seminal to our thinking, the positions and recommendations in this book are solely those of the authors and do not necessarily represent the views of participants in the symposium or of the officers, trustees, or faculty of Teachers College.

The authors are grateful to Jack Jennings and Tom Rogers for their careful review of a draft of this book and their many thoughtful and provocative comments. Tom Sobol's wise counsel has aided us throughout this project, and we also benefited from the insights of the school superintendents and other members of Public Schools for Tomorrow, who met with us at Tom's suggestion to consider and react to our concept of "meaningful educational opportunity." We also thank Douglas Ready and Richard Rothstein for reviewing Chapter 7 on standards, assessments, and progress requirements. Any errors in the interpretation of their comments are the authors' own. Susan Fuhrman's wisdom on issues of policy and on the specifics of NCLB, as well as her enthusiastic support for the symposium and for so many of the Equity Campaign's other activities, has been an inspiration. Finally, we must acknowledge Laurie Tisch for her continuing support and unwavering vision of educational equity.

We would like to thank our colleagues at the Campaign for Educational Equity and the National Access Network for the research each contributed to various chapters, and for their continuing counsel on the policy positions as they were developed: Molly Hunter (Chapter 6), Mark Noizumi (Chapter 8), and Elisabeth Thurston (Chapters 3 and 7). We thank Sherry Orbach for her research contribution to Chapter 5. We also owe a debt of gratitude to Carole Saltz, who gave us the original idea and encouragement to write this book, and to Judy Berman and all of the staff at the Teachers College Press, who shepherded this book to completion.

Introduction

In its landmark 1954 *Brown v. Board of Education* decision outlawing racial segregation in education, the U.S. Supreme Court emphasized the central importance of education in modern times: "In these days, it is doubtful that any child may reasonably be expected to succeed in life if he is denied the opportunity of an education" (p. 493). The Court then held that all children are constitutionally entitled to an "equal educational opportunity."

Providing an equal educational opportunity is, however, easier said than done. As President Lyndon Johnson (1971) put it:

> You do not take a person who, for years, has been hobbled by chains and liberate him, bring him to the starting line of a race, and then say, "you are free to compete with all the others," and still justly believe you have been completely fair. Thus, it is not enough just to open the gates of opportunity. All of our citizens must have the ability to walk through those gates. (p. 166)

To help children from low-income families to walk through the gates of opportunity, Congress, therefore, enacted Title I of the Elementary and Secondary Education Act of 1965, which provided federal funds to school districts to assist them in meeting these children's needs.

In recent years, the nation's commitment to equal educational opportunity has been bolstered by the realization that, in addition to being a moral and constitutional imperative, equal educational opportunity is also critically important to America's continued political and economic vitality. Interpreting clauses in the state constitutions that guarantee all students a basic quality education, more than a dozen state courts throughout the country have held that preparing students to function capably as voters and civic participants in our complex technological society is a vital purpose of schooling if we are to preserve our democracy. A series of national education summits—convened by Presidents George H. Bush and Bill Clinton and attended by state governors and CEOs of major U.S. corporations—and a number of high-level commission reports have argued that, for the United States to retain its competitive position in the global economy, the vast majority of our students, including the rapidly rising proportions of those from low-income and minority backgrounds, will need high-level thinking skills (Kane, Berryman, Goslin, & Meltzer, 1990; National Center on Education and the Economy, 1990, 2007). Responding to these insights, nearly every state has adopted standards-based reforms based on the premise that, with proper resources and supports, virtually all children can meet challenging academic standards. Although the actual quality of the standards varies significantly from state to state, overall these reforms have raised academic expectations for America's children.

EXAMINING THE CONTRIBUTION OF NO CHILD LEFT BEHIND

The federal No Child Left Behind Act (NCLB), signed into law in 2002, expands the equity imperatives of Title I and combines them with educational reforms emerging from the state standards movement into a potent package that promises, a half century after *Brown v. Board of Education*, that equal educational opportunity and universal student proficiency actually will be achieved. Specifically, NCLB *mandates* as America's fundamental national educational policy that

1. All children will reach academic proficiency by 2014.
2. *Proficiency* will be defined by each state in accordance with challenging state academic standards containing rigorous content.
3. All children will be taught by "highly qualified teachers."
4. States and school districts will be accountable for ensuring that all schools have the instructional capacity to make certain that their students advance in accordance with specifically defined annual progress expectations. There will be specific consequences and sanctions for schools and school districts that do not meet these expectations.
5. Student progress will be measured through validated annual assessments that are aligned with the state standards. Results will be reported in disaggregated form by racial, ethnic, disability, and income groupings in order to ensure that the needs of all students are being met.

However, in spite of this historic commitment, 5 years after its enactment, NCLB is failing to achieve any of these objectives:

1. No state is on track to reach the full proficiency goal by 2014. In fact, the number of schools that are failing to make "adequate yearly progress" (AYP) toward this goal is likely to accelerate over the next few years. Overall, progress on standardized reading and math tests has been minimal, and wide achievement gaps persist between low-income and minority students and their more affluent White peers.
2. Most states have not set academic standards that are "challenging," and a number of states have lowered their proficiency criteria in response to NCLB pressures.
3. At best, the law has ensured that more children are being taught by minimally qualified teachers, but large numbers of poor and minority students with the greatest educational needs are still assigned the most inexperienced and least qualified teachers.
4. Many of the increasing numbers of "schools in need of improvement" lack the resources and instructional capacity to bring larger percentages of their students to proficiency, and few are obtaining effective assistance from state departments of education or school districts. In many cases, state education departments and school districts also lack the required resources and capacity.
5. Many of the state tests used to measure adequate yearly progress are not valid in accordance with established psychometric standards, and most state tests are not fully aligned with the state's academic standards. These test validation issues are especially egregious as they affect English language learners and students with disabilities.

Critiques of NCLB's premises and implementation and calls for major overhaul or repeal of the act have increasingly been heard from educators, policymakers, advocates, and academics (see, e.g., American Federation of Teachers, 2006; Commission on No Child Left Behind, 2007; the Joint Organizational Statement on the No Child Left Behind [NCLB] Act, 2004; National Conference of State Legislatures, 2005; National Educational Association, 2006; Noddings, 2005; Ryan, 2004). The nature of many of their concerns can be illustrated by using President Johnson's race metaphor. It is as if, to motivate the states and local districts to train their students to run to their full potential, the federal government had decreed that, within 12 years (of which only 6 now remain), *all* children must run a mile at a challenging pace or schools will suffer penalties.

This requirement is unfair, many argue, because the law doesn't define a "challenging" pace, and, though some states have taken the directive seriously and determined that all their children should run an 8-minute mile, others have set their requirement at 10 or 12 minutes, without any objection from the federal authorities. In those states with a challenging 8-minute standard, even if their schools succeed with many of their students, when some fall short and run the mile in 10 or 12 minutes, the schools will be penalized. States that established a 12-minute requirement will be praised even if most of their students actually run at a much slower pace.

Yet, many civil rights advocates and scholars concerned with traditionally neglected groups of students still support NCLB because of its fundamental commitment to educational equity. As Melissa Lazarin (2006), senior policy analyst for the National Council of La Raza, put it, "Prior to NCLB, the [English language learner] student population was often overlooked. . . . The law has unarguably directed substantial new attention toward ELL student achievement" (pp. 3–4). Michael Nettles, Edmund W. Gordon Chair for Policy Evaluation and Research at the Educational Testing Service and an expert on African American achievement, and his colleagues write, "Despite two decades of national efforts led by the federal government to reform the U.S. education system, only since 2001 has the policy been explicit about closing gaps along race and social class lines. NCLB is a start" (Nettles, Millett, & Oh, 2006, p. 44). Similarly, Margaret McLaughlin (2006), professor and associate director of the Institute for the Study of Exceptional Children and Youth at the University of Maryland, adds that "under NCLB the concept of [Individualized Education Plans] is taking on new meaning as all students are to be held to grade-level content standards" (p. 14). For many in the civil rights community, the strength of the law's equity mandates outweighs the apparent weaknesses in the reform mechanisms for making these new rights a reality.

A key question, then, is whether it is possible to repair the apparent disconnect between the powerful equity objectives of NCLB and the law's ineffective educational reform mechanisms. Can NCLB be revised so that its core goals—eliminating achievement gaps and raising the achievement levels of all students—can actually be realized? The Campaign for Educational Equity at Teachers College, Columbia University, convened a major symposium in 2006, "Examining America's Achievement Gaps: NCLB and Its Alternatives," to answer this question. The symposium began by stepping back from the mandates of NCLB and considering afresh what actions need to be taken to overcome our nation's achievement gaps. It then carefully reviewed the structure and implementation of NCLB to determine whether the law was promoting those actions. This approach led us to conclude that the demanding national goals expressed by NCLB are largely achievable—and that the act can contribute to attaining them if the law is revised to face realistically the challenges encountered by low-achieving students and by those educators who seek to help these students.

Much of the equity muscle in NCLB comes from its demand that positive academic results be demonstrated for all racial/ethnic, language, and economic groups. But, in certain specific ways, the emphasis on outcomes has become counterproductive. The adequate yearly progress targets that schools must meet are calibrated from NCLB's mandate that all students—100%—be proficient in challenging state standards by 2014. This full proficiency objective is not motivational rhetoric as it was in earlier proclamations of national goals. In NCLB, it is a legal mandate that drives the law's whole accountability scheme. As a result of setting this mandated goal, NCLB requires rates of progress that no school system worldwide has ever achieved and the feasibility of which has never been demonstrated. For example, to meet NCLB's reading requirements at grade 4 by 2014, the annual rate of improvement would need to be 15.7 times the rate it actually was between 1998 and 2003, and at grade 8 the annual rate of progress would have to increase more than tenfold (Linn, 2004). Schools and districts that fail to meet this ultimate objective, and the associated AYP targets, suffer significant consequences.

Virtually no informed parent, teacher, administrator, researcher —or legislator—thinks this mandate can be met. Senator Edward M. Kennedy, one of the congressional architects of the law, recently acknowledged that "the idea of 100 percent proficiency is, in any legislation, not achievable" (Paley, 2007, p. A1). But politicians don't want to appear to be lowering standards, and, as a result, no one in Congress is now pressing to modify the 2014 proficiency date. If the proficiency-for-all target were merely a motivational goal, this might be an innocuous stand. But since thousands of schools around the country are being labeled "in need of improvement"—which the public reads as "failing"—because they have proved incapable of making sufficient progress toward an unempirical goal, this irrational aspect of the law is causing considerable harm.

This situation will become increasingly unworkable as we approach 2014. By that year, almost all schools in the nation will fall far short of the AYP targets and are likely to be on the "needs improvement" list (Linn, 2004). This is because the Department of Education has allowed the states to backload their AYP requirements so that the majority of progress toward 100% proficiency can be put off until the last few years. For example, under Ohio's AYP arrangement, the rate of progress required for the years from 2002–2009 is only one third of the annual rate that will be required from 2010 to 2014 (Linn, 2003).

The proficiency for all by 2014 mandate, although clearly unattainable as currently constructed, does, nevertheless, serve an important inspirational and motivational purpose. It expresses a firm national promise and public compact to further the education of *all* students— and especially of Blacks, Latinos, students with disabilities, and low-income students whose needs have been neglected in the past. For many, it serves as a rallying cry that says we must overcome the impediments of poverty and racism and finally realize equal educational opportunity. Stated in these terms "proficiency for all by 2014" is, in essence, a renewed national commitment to implement the *Brown v. Board of Education* vision of equal educational opportunity within the next few years.

We must seize on this promise to pursue thoroughgoing educational opportunity. To do so, however, the unworkable proficiency-for-all mandate should be modified before the impetus of the act is undermined by the frustration of mounting failures and either Congress repeals the act or the Department of Education ceases to enforce it. If what is truly meant by "proficiency for all" is achievement of *Brown's* vision of equal educational opportunity, then we must focus on determining what that vision actually means and how it can be realized.

The Statement of Purpose at the beginning of the NCLB lists its two primary aims as ensuring that "all children have a fair, equal and significant opportunity to obtain a high quality education and reach, at a minimum, proficiency on challenging state academic achievement standards and state academic assessments" (NCLB, 2001, § 6301). In other words, the purposes of the act are to ensure all students meaningful educational opportunities and to require that all reach proficiency on challenging standards by 2014. (The specific date was set in a subsequent provision of the law as a date 12 years from the date of its passage.) Currently, however, attainment of the proficiency goal is being stressed, with little attention to the opportunity goal. This emphasis should be inverted. Greater immediate emphasis on the opportunity goal will lead to higher, more rapid, and more sustained student achievement.

To realize its demanding equity goals, NCLB must be reconsidered from the perspective of whether it is truly promoting *meaningful* educational opportunities for all children. (As we explain in further detail in Chapter 4, we use the phrase *"meaningful" educational opportunity,* rather than NCLB's term, *"significant" opportunity,* because the former term has important judicial and legislative antecedents that give it substantive operational meaning.) This requires identifying and utilizing the concrete mechanisms for providing educational opportunities that have been developed in other contexts by Congress, the courts, state legislatures, and governmental and nongovernmental agencies, and molding them into a core concept that can give focus, direction, and coherence to NCLB.

History shows that substantial progress toward educational equity can and has been made when concrete steps are taken to provide meaningful opportunities to all students. After *Brown,* the Supreme Court was most effective in bringing about the desegregation of schools in the Southern states when it insisted on immediate, concrete desegregation plans (e.g., *Green v. County School Board,* 1968). Similarly, equal educational opportunity for English language learners got its greatest boost when the Supreme Court insisted that educational services provided to them be "meaningful," and Congress, the lower federal courts, and the Department of Education then carefully articulated in the types of services that would meet that requirement (*Lau v. Nicols,* 1974). The long history of neglect of children with disabilities ended when Congress, in the Individuals with Disabilities Education Act (IDEA), spelled out in very specific terms the types of special education and related services that would be provided to meet the individual needs of each of these children (IDEA, 1997).

We believe, therefore, that, in place of the impossible goal of 100% *proficiency,* Congress should establish as its mandatory goal for 2014 the more achievable aim of providing *meaningful educational opportunity* for all children by that time. Furthermore, the term *proficiency* should be redefined to emphasize consistent progress toward high levels of achievement, rather than absolute attainment of a concrete level of performance at a definite point in time. In addition, each state's adequate yearly progress should also be judged in terms of the extent to which the achievement gaps between advantaged and disadvantaged groups of students are reduced. This is a mechanism for ensuring that the twin goals of advancing excellence and equity are both served.

Both feasibility and credibility would be enhanced by inverting the order of emphasis between the two stated purposes and giving pride of place to the opportunity objectives over the proficiency objectives. Significant and lasting academic achievement for most low-income and minority students cannot be attained by wishing for it or by ordering it: The right conditions must be created to enable it. The bargain behind NCLB was that increased resources for education essentials would be provided in return for increased accountability (Hess &

Petrilli, 2006). Although funding for elementary and secondary education programs covered by NCLB has increased since the law's passage, states and school districts have argued that this amount does not even cover the extra costs of testing and administration. Many congressional leaders have also stated that this amount falls far short of what was promised by the president at the time the law went into effect. Fiscal equity and education adequacy litigations, which have been decided in dozens of states around the country in recent years, indicate that many schools that serve low-income and minority students lack essential educational resources and that, to narrow substantially or eliminate achievement gaps, substantial additional funding for these essential resources will be required.

The only essential educational resource that NCLB currently requires, however, is that all students must be taught by "highly qualified teachers." Under the Act's definition, most states can deem as "highly qualified" teachers with only minimum competency, since this is the operative standard in most state certification systems that are accepted as compliant with the law. These requirements have led to improvement in the availability of minimally qualified teachers, but they do little to ensure that all students will, in fact, be taught by teachers with the pedagogical skills, experience, and depth of subject-matter knowledge needed to provide the kind of instruction that will lead to proficiency in meeting challenging state standards.

In considering the extent of resources necessary to overcome the achievement gap, Congress has largely ignored the reality of the inequities of poverty and race and the enormous impact that these have on children, families, and schools. These inequities produce disadvantages and hardships that profoundly influence children's opportunities and ability to learn. There are a number of "pathways" through which these inequities exact their toll on children's academic achievement. Low-income and minority children largely attend lower-quality schools—no matter how school quality is measured. In addition, many of these children bring greater challenges to school. Many children lack adequate health care and, as a result, suffer from health-related barriers to learning. Many lack the early experiences of linguistic enrichment and cultural stimulation, "the scaffolds for learning" (Gordon, Bridglall, & Meroe, 2005, p. 322) that are the norm for most children, and these deficits account for a substantial amount of the achievement gaps among children entering kindergarten. The insecurity created by severe economic deprivation and housing instability also substantially affects children's readiness to learn.

At the end of its 2006–2007 term, the United States Supreme Court ruled in *Parents Involved in Community Schools v. Seattle School District* (2007) that although the equal educational opportunity mandate of *Brown v. Board of Education* is still the law of the land, most of the affirmative action and school assignment plans school districts have used to promote racial balancing—the primary means used by many districts to undo the impact of concentrated poverty—would henceforth be prohibited. This latest decision culminates a general trend in recent decades of the federal courts and of American society as a whole away from serious pursuit of school integration as a primary means of providing equal educational opportunity. However, the nation's strong emphasis on eliminating achievement gaps, as reflected in the enactment of NCLB, as well as plaintiffs' successes in dozens of fiscal equity and education adequacy litigations around the country, indicates that, despite the lessening of ardor for taking affirmative actions to promote racial integration, our country is still committed to achieving equal educational opportunity through other means.

We believe that the only "other means" that can substantially advance equal educational opportunity is to provide meaningful educational opportunities for all children in each of the schools that they attend. We argue in this book that, to provide such opportunities, policymakers and educators must directly confront the inequities of race and poverty and the vast barriers to learning that they create. Although we believe that our increasingly diverse nation must quickly seek new ways to promote racial and economic integration in its communities and schools, this task will be infinitely more feasible when the scandalous deficiencies in human and material resources that now exist in many of our inner-city and rural schools have been remedied.

The fundamental premise of this book, then, is that at the root of America's achievement gaps are the significant opportunity gaps endured by millions of low-income and minority students. NCLB is falling far short of achieving its ambitious goals because it mainly concentrates on accountability for results but largely neglects the resources and supports that students need to achieve these results. We spell out our concept of "meaningful educational opportunity" in Chapter 4 of the book, after setting the stage for an understanding of the concept by discussing in earlier chapters the historical, legal, and political contexts from which current concepts of equal educational opportunity arose. The later chapters apply the concept of meaningful educational opportunity to the specific provisions of the NCLB and recommend revisions that would allow the law to attain its vital core goals.

ORGANIZATION OF THIS BOOK

Specifically, we have organized our discussion of how to provide meaningful educational opportunity for all children through a revised NCLB framework into nine chapters.

In Chapter 1, we explore the history of the concept of "equal educational opportunity" as it has developed in the United States. We argue that, despite major setbacks, equality of educational opportunity has been a consistent and significant imperative throughout American history. Yet, in spite of this imperative, enormous gaps in educational achievement and in educational opportunity persist for the children of our nation's poor, of our immigrants, and of our families of color. The significance of *Brown v. Board of Education* and other federal court decisions and statutes during the civil rights era of the 1960s and 1970s and of the recent education adequacy decisions of dozens of state courts in reinvigorating America's egalitarian dynamic are the subjects of the rest of the chapter.

Recognizing our nation's largest challenge in providing equal educational opportunity, Chapter 2 examines the conditions of poverty and racial inequality in America today and explores how these conditions influence students' learning opportunities and achievement. We examine the extent to which NCLB responds to these conditions, and find that, by and large, the law fails to respond to students' major needs.

Chapter 3 describes the evolution of the federal government's involvement in education from the founding of our country, and focuses on the factors that led to Congress's passage of NCLB and its vast expansion of federal involvement in local educational affairs. A brief description of the structure of the law is followed by an examination of the problems and possibilities that have emerged during the first 5 years of its implementation.

In Chapter 4, we develop in detail the major theme of the book, the need to provide all children with a "meaningful educational opportunity." We review past attempts to include provisions for "opportunity to learn" standards in the law and broaden that concept, based on the further research and the experience of the education adequacy cases over the past 15 years, to articulate a statutory framework for revising NCLB to provide meaningful educational opportunities. This framework emphasizes broad-based educational outcomes and the availability of "educational essentials" in terms of school-based and out-of-school resources.

To illustrate the types of issues that states will need to confront in each of the resource areas that comprise a meaningful educational opportunity, in Chapter 5, we present a detailed analysis of the problems and possibilities involved in providing all students with truly effective teachers, which is probably the most important of all the resource categories. Teacher quality is the sole resource area that is presently mandated by NCLB. We argue that NCLB misleadingly labels as "highly qualified" teachers who are, in fact, only minimally qualified. We recommend emphasizing instead a concept of "highly effective teachers," the substantive definition of which would be decided by each state. States would be expected to take steps to maximize their complement of such teachers and to ensure that there is equitable distribution of these key personnel to all schools throughout the state.

Chapter 6 tackles the critical but controversial area of cost. NCLB virtually ignores the funding equity and adequacy problems that have been highlighted by the state court litigations and quantified by the many cost studies that have been undertaken by legislatures, state education departments, and advocacy groups in recent years. Although NCLB imposes numerous mandates on the states and on local school districts, and it provides some additional funding, the law neglects the need to ensure that sufficient levels of funding are in place to allow students a meaningful opportunity to make solid academic progress. We argue that the federal government needs to undertake a series of comprehensive cost analyses that not only determine the costs of the requisite school-based and out-of-school resources students but also suggest how these resources can be used in the most cost-effective manner. With this information, Congress can then determine a fair allocation of responsibility for necessary funding increases between the federal government and the states.

The political pact that led to the enactment of NCLB was premised on an understanding that in exchange for a large—but still inadequate—increase in federal funding, schools and districts would be held accountable for consistent progress toward full proficiency in terms of challenging state content standards as measured by valid and reliable annual tests. We show, in Chapter 7, that the system for establishing and assessing student proficiency standards is badly flawed: Most state content standards have not been shown to be "challenging," and many state assessment systems are not valid in accordance with applicable psychometric standards. Moreover, the current requirements for measuring progress toward proficiency impose technically impossible demands that increasingly are undermining the effectiveness and credibility of the act. In this chapter, we set forth specific recommendations to remedy each of these problems.

In Chapter 8, we turn to the critical issue of what happens to schools and districts once they have been identified by NCLB as not meeting their performance goals. We summarize the current cascade of consequences that the law imposes on such schools, and we argue that these particular mechanisms have no proven track record of success, that in some ways they actually make it more difficult for schools to improve, and that in any event they cannot be effectively imposed by a distant national government. In this area, we recommend substantial delegation of authority for dealing with capacity building of low-performing schools to the states and we cite the examples of Kentucky and North Carolina as successful models of what can be done.

Chapter 9 summarizes and crystallizes our themes by analyzing the balance of state and federal authority that results from our recommendations. Although in some areas we call for significant increases in federal authority, we also emphasize throughout the importance of giving maximum scope to the dynamic creativity that flows in our federal system from the "laboratory" of the states, whose experiences with the standards movement and the education adequacy litigations have equipped them to be prime partners in promoting both excellence and equity. We conclude by emphasizing that if NCLB is to achieve its vital objectives, we must honestly confront the two major issues that Congress seems most eager to avoid: increased federal involvement in educational policy and ensuring adequate funding to provide the resources that children from backgrounds of poverty will need to succeed.

Following Chapter 9 is an Appendix that summarizes the recommendations presented in *Moving Every Child Ahead*.

In sum, NCLB has taken on a critical, but monumental, challenge. The recent debate on reauthorization has provided the opportunity to pause and reflect on why our nation has taken on this huge challenge and to consider how it can really be met. The aim of this book is to put the important purposes of NCLB in proper historical perspective and to point out its deficiencies, but then to provide a positive prescription for putting this landmark law back on track, based on the need to provide all children with meaningful educational opportunities. We think that NCLB can make dramatic advances toward realizing the vision of *Brown v. Board of Education* in the near future, but only if we candidly confront its shortcomings and take prompt action to correct them.

CHAPTER 1

Equal Educational Opportunity: An American Imperative

Both the concept of public education and the ideal of equality in education were conceived and developed in the United States. Despite major setbacks along the way, equality of educational opportunity has been a consistent and significant imperative throughout American history, exemplified in recent times by the U. S. Supreme Court's 1954 decision outlawing racial segregation in education in *Brown v. Board of Education* and the inspiring promise of Congress's enactment of the NCLB mandate that all children reach challenging levels of academic proficiency. Nevertheless, it is clear that the America's egalitarian vision of the children of all classes, the rich and the poor, being well educated together is still far from realization. Glaring gaps in educational achievement and in educational opportunity persist for the children of our nation's poor, of our immigrants, and of our families of color. And NCLB, our most recent national effort to advance educational equity, is, at this stage, falling far short of its promise.

In large part, the persistent gap between the American ideal of equality in education and the reality of starkly inadequate schooling for low-income and minority children stems from the irony that although America's dedication to educational equity has surpassed that of any other nation, its commitment to equality in related areas of social welfare has lagged far behind that of other industrialized countries (Anyon & Greene, 2007; Wells, 2006). "As other industrialized countries built and enlarged comprehensive welfare systems to help create more equality among their citizens, policymakers in the United States invested in public schools and relatively few other supportive social services" (Wells, 2006, p. 2). The "American dream" and much of our political ideology has been based on the premise that, if given an opportunity for schooling, any individual, through hard work and perseverance, will be able to succeed (Hochschild,

1995). Unfortunately, this vision of universal and unlimited possibility has not proved true for the millions of low-income and minority children who must overcome enormous barriers posed by bad health, poor nutrition, inadequate housing, economic instability, and racism—and who are not, in fact, actually provided with the equal or adequate educational opportunities that the American dream ideology has promised them.

In this chapter, we explore the history of the concept of "equal educational opportunity" as it has developed in the United States. This will provide a legal and political context for understanding the concept of "meaningful educational opportunity" that, we will argue in later chapters, can be put into practice through specific revisions to NCLB. We give particular emphasis to attempts to implement equal educational opportunity in the years since the Supreme Court's decision in *Brown v. Board of Education*. Based on this history, we argue that true progress toward realizing equal educational opportunity has been made when concrete mechanisms were developed, often with the help of the courts, to implement abstract egalitarian concepts in particular situations.

The United States was founded as a "tabula rasa," a new world society where Enlightenment-era ideals of liberty and equality could be firmly anchored, free from the conflicting cross currents of old world traditions of monarchy, feudalism, and hierarchical social orderings. Thus, basic concepts of the essential dignity of each human being, the fundamental equality of all people, and the notion of "inalienable rights" to freedom, justice, and opportunity became the rallying cries of the American Revolution and were eloquently expressed in the Declaration of Independence, the Constitution, and other foundational documents as the organizing principles of the society (Hartz, 1955).

The egalitarian dimension of the original American experience was marked by a strong rejection of the class structure of European society. This stance was explicitly articulated in the Constitution's pronouncement that "No Title of Nobility shall be granted by the United States." Although economic differentials have always marked the American scene, the absence of a hereditary elite class and entrenched privilege has led commentators from early times to the present to emphasize the unparalleled "equality of esteem" that marks social relationships in the United States (Pole, 1978, p. 42).

In the new world setting, schools had a more significant role than in any of the old world cultures. In the United States, the shift from the extended family as the basic unity of economic production and social responsibility to an occupationally mobile economy in which the training a child received came to be of interest to all in the community—a key change that paved the way for public education—occurred much earlier than it did in Europe (Coleman, 1974). Moreover, the move to a new continent dislodged traditional cultural moorings, and, in America much sooner than in Europe, education became less a private family responsibility and more a broad communal function (Cremin, 1970).

The founding fathers of the American republic understood that schools would need to play an important role in building the new nation by "the deliberate fashioning of a new republican character, rooted in the American soil . . . and committed to the promise of an American culture" (Cremin, 1980, p. 3). They realized that, in a democracy, all citizens must obtain the knowledge and skills needed to make intelligent decisions. As John Adams put it:

> A memorable change must be made in the system of education and knowledge must become so general as to raise the lower ranks of society nearer to the higher. The education of a nation instead of being confined to a few schools and universities for the instruction of the few, must become the national care and expense for the formation of the many. (McCullough, 2001, p. 364)

Benjamin Franklin and James Madison were also vocal supporters of some form of public funding for education. They attempted to include these reforms in the Constitution, but their proposals fell victim to fears that the national government was already gaining too much power under the constitutional scheme (Hirschland & Steinmo, 2003).

The common school movement of the mid-19th century represented a delayed implementation of the egalitarian educational ideals of the founding fathers. By the 1830s, rapid industrialization and geographic expansion in America gave immediacy to the notion of forging a citizenry with common inspirational "republican" values. The common school movement was an attempt to educate in one setting all the children living in a particular geographic area, whatever their class or ethnic background. The common school "would be open to all and supported by tax funds. It would be for rich and poor alike, the equal of any private institution" (Cremin, 1980, p. 138). These schools would replace the prior patchwork pattern of town schools partially supported by parental contributions, church schools, "pauper schools," and private schools, with a new form of democratic schooling.

Although the common schools—the precursor of our modern public school system—were highly democratic and inclusive for the broad range of students whom they welcomed into their doors, from the first the movement also excluded important groups in the society. Initially, access for girls to the common schools was often limited. African Americans were totally precluded from formal learning in most Southern states during slavery, and, even after the Civil War, their education, not only in the South but in most parts of the country, was relegated to separate and generally inferior schools. In addition, the common schools sought to inculcate democratic and patriotic ideals together with basic religious values rooted in a non-denominational Protestant perspective in a manner that alienated many Catholic leaders who proceeded to establish a separate parochial school system (Rebell, 1989).

Despite these real limitations, the common school movement was a radical, democratic breakthrough for its time. Next to abolition, the political battle to establish the common schools constituted the greatest political confrontation of the 19th century (Cubberley, 1934). The advocates for common schooling, in order to cement their victory and ensure that the broad access to public education they had achieved would not be revoked in the future, codified their gains by inserting clauses into state constitutions that guaranteed in perpetuity that there would be a "system of free common schools in which all the students in the state may be educated" (Rebell, 2004, pp. 298–300).

The dramatic gains of the common schools movement were, however, followed by counterreaction. As public school systems expanded at the end of the 19th century through compulsory education laws and the absorption of large numbers of immigrants in urban centers, they increasingly became mechanisms for political acculturation and occupational sorting—at worst, dumping grounds for the poor. The bureaucratic structures for schooling created to educate masses of students in urban areas undermined the common school ideals (Tyack, 1974). In this period of rapid industrialization and economic expansion, America's ardor for individualism, the other aspect of its Lockean heritage, came to the fore, and the capitalistic ethic trumped the egalitarian dynamic. Wealthier communities and families created privileged schooling enclaves for their students or sought alternatives outside the public system, and inevitably the quality of schools attended by immigrants and other poor children waned. Black children continued to be largely relegated to separate, inferior institutions in all parts of the country.

THE PROFOUND IMPACT OF *BROWN V. BOARD OF EDUCATION*

During the first half of the 20th century, American egalitarianism was at its nadir: "inequalities of wealth, inequalities of power and associated inequalities of opportunity seemed to dominate all possible patterns for the future" (Pole, 1978, p. 214). The New Deal and the nation's fight for democracy against a racist enemy in World War II began to change this dynamic. These trends culminated in 1954 in the U.S. Supreme Court's landmark decision outlawing school segregation in *Brown v. Board of Education*. This decision reinvigorated America's historic egalitarian dynamic and initiated a new era of reform that resulted in significant institutional change and an important shift in political attitudes.

Brown's impact has been enormous. It proclaimed a broad vision of "equal educational opportunity" that has been accepted as a precedent, an inspiration, and an imperative for change in a vast range of legal and political contexts. As Senator Hillary Clinton (2005) put it, "Without a doubt, the impact of *Brown* has been so profound that it is hard to imagine how things could have been otherwise. We witness the effects of *Brown* when we ride a train, eat at a restaurant, or go to the beach" (p. 213).

Although the explicit holding of the decision was focused on terminating racial segregation in education, the decision quickly led to the articulation and implementation of new rights ensuring equal opportunities in school discipline practices, bilingual education, gender equity, special education, and a host of other educational policy areas. The *Brown* precedent also was extended beyond the school context to outlaw state-supported racial discrimination in virtually every other area of American public life.

Sparked by *Brown*, the civil rights movement of the 1950s and 1960s, manifested through the remarkable surge of demonstrations, marches, Freedom Rides, and other unequivocal expressions of the public will, revived the common school ideals, and for the first time sought to extend educational opportunity to all children regardless of race. The Supreme Court's decision in *Brown* (1954) also focused attention on the central importance of education in contemporary society:

> Today, education is perhaps the most important function of state and local governments. Compulsory school attendance laws and the great expenditures for education both demonstrate our recognition of the importance of education to our democratic society. It is required in

performance of our most basic public responsibilities, even service in the armed forces. It is the very foundation of good citizenship. . . . In these days, it is doubtful that any child may reasonably be expected to succeed in life if he is denied the opportunity of an education. Such an opportunity, where the state has undertaken to provide it, is a right which must be made available to all on equal terms. (p. 493)

The profundity of the Supreme Court's decision in *Brown* lay not merely in its outlawing of racial segregation in schools. Equally significant was the manner in which, through careful analysis of extensive evidence accumulated in the immediate case and in prior precedents, and by taking note of broader social science findings, the Court came to understand precisely how the challenged practice impeded meaningful educational opportunity for the plaintiffs.

Through a series of prior cases involving graduate school education, the Court had established the importance of educational resources and facilities to providing an equal educational opportunity and recognized that the resources and facilities provided to people of color, were, in fact, almost never equal. Moreover, the Court had previously held that even if the physical factors could be equalized, intangible factors that affected a law student's "ability to study, to engage in discussions and exchange views with other students, and, in general, to learn his profession," could not be adequately conveyed in a segregated setting (*McLaurin v. Oklahoma State Board of Regents*, 1950, pp. 641–642). This led directly to the Court's core holding in *Brown* that separate educational facilities are inherently unequal because

To separate [children in grade and high schools] from others of similar age and qualifications solely because of their race generates a feeling of inferiority as to their status in the community that may affect their hearts and minds in a way unlikely ever to be undone. (*Brown v. Board of Education*, 1954, p. 494)

Even if the physical facilities and resources could be made equivalent, the Court understood that the opportunity that would be provided in a school that was set aside from the majority culture as a matter of law could never be truly equal. To provide a *meaningful* opportunity, schools must remove the inherent stigma imposed by racial segregation.

The Court allowed about a decade to go by before it began to enforce *Brown*'s desegregation mandate vigorously. When it finally did actively confront the political resistance to desegregation, it did so by insisting on *meaningful* and not merely *pro forma* compliance. It rejected stratagems like publicly funded segregated academies and the use of a "freedom of choice plan," and it emphasized the need for a desegregation plan "that promises realistically to work and promises realistically to work *now*" (*Green v. County School Board*, 1968, p. 439). In this regard, the Court promulgated a series of specific standards that endorsed the use of busing, upheld reliance on numerical guidelines for racial balance in local schools, and advocated the redrawing of attendance zones to promote desegregation (*Swann v. Charlotte-Mecklenburg Board of Education*, 1971).

At the same time that the Supreme Court began to implement the *Brown* mandate, Congress acted to aid the courts' efforts to provide meaningful educational opportunities for Blacks and other disadvantaged children by passing the first major federal aid to education law. Title I of the Elementary and Secondary Education Act (ESEA) of 1965 provided substantial federal funding to school districts to assist them in meeting the educational needs of economically disadvantaged students. A centerpiece of President Lyndon Johnson's "war on poverty," the law was enacted specifically to expand educational opportunities for poor children:

> The Congress hereby declares it to be the policy of the United States to provide financial assistance . . . to local educational agencies serving areas with concentrations of children from low-income families to expand and improve their educational programs by various means (including preschool programs) which contribute to meeting the special educational needs of educationally deprived children. (ESEA, 1965, § 6301)

Effective enforcement of *Brown*'s desegregation mandate was also substantially aided by the passage of Title VI of the 1964 Civil Rights Act, which empowered the federal Department of Health, Education, and Welfare to cut off federal funding to any school district that discriminated on the basis of race, color, or national origin. Taken together, the ESEA and Title VI were to provide both a "carrot" and a "stick" for effective enforcement: Now that substantial amounts of federal funds were available, these funds could also be withheld if school districts were found to be in violation of the desegregation orders of the federal courts. The combination of forceful decisions by the Supreme Court and passage of Title VI and the ESEA in the 1960s had dramatic results: Although more than 98% of Black students in the states of the deep South had been attending schools that had 90% or more Black students in 1964, by 1972 less than 9% were in such segregated facilities (Rabkin, 1980).

The legal framework for educational equity was further expanded in the next decade. In addition to providing substantial funding to all economically disadvantaged students through the ESEA and codifying the antidiscrimination rights of racial and national origin minorities in Title VI, Congress also provided an extensive set of substantive and procedural rights for children with disabilities through the Education for All Handicapped Children Act of 1975 (the current version of this statute is now known as the Individuals with Disabilities Education Act, or IDEA). This new law not only set aside state statutes that had in the past excluded many children with disabilities from attending school, but it also required school districts to provide these students a truly *meaningful* educational opportunity. It did this by entitling all children with disabilities to a "free appropriate public education" that guarantees each child specially designed instruction and "related services," to meet his or her unique educational needs, at no cost to parents or guardians. The law also provides parents an extensive array of procedural opportunities and due process rights to oversee the appropriateness of the services being provided to their children.

In enforcing these congressional statutes, the Supreme Court further developed a concept of "meaningful educational opportunity." *Lau v. Nicols,* a 1974 case involving the educational opportunities of a class of students of Chinese ancestry who did not speak English, was a prime case in point. In *Lau,* the lower court had rejected plaintiffs' claim for additional educational services that would allow them to overcome their language limitations. The Supreme Court decisively rejected this stance. Applying the antidiscrimination precepts of Title VI, the Supreme Court held that "there is no equality of treatment merely by providing students with the same facilities, textbooks, teachers, and curriculum; for students who do not understand English are effectively foreclosed from any *meaningful* education" (*Lau v. Nicols,* 1974, p. 566, emphasis added).

Two decades after *Brown,* then, thoroughgoing egalitarian initiatives were taking root and principle was turning into practice. Meaningful educational opportunities began to be provided to children of color in integrated school settings, to students with disabilities in educational settings that were being shaped to accommodate their needs, and to English language learners in bilingual classrooms. Shortly thereafter, however, as the venue of the desegregation confrontations moved to northern and western locales, the Supreme Court's firm efforts to enforce meaningful educational opportunities began to wane. In litigations involving the Denver and Detroit school systems, the Court issued rulings that substantially slowed progress toward desegregation. First, it declared that nonintentional, *de facto* desegregation resulting from segregated housing patterns was not unconstitutional (*Keyes v. School District No. 1*, 1973). Second, it held that extensive urban segregation patterns could not be remedied by a mandatory metropolitan area desegregation scheme in the absence of evidence that the suburban districts had, in the past, intentionally discriminated against minority students (*Milliken v. Bradley*, 1974). In essence, in these cases, local control of education and countervailing "liberty" interests trumped the strong emphasis that the Court had previously placed on ensuring effective desegregated schooling environments for Black children.

The Supreme Court also declined to take a further necessary step toward providing meaningful educational opportunities for poor and minority children in 1973 when it refused, in *San Antonio Independent School District v. Rodriguez*, to remedy the gross disparities in Texas's school funding system, which the Court acknowledged was highly inequitable. The logic of *Brown* would seem to have implied that in order to provide meaningful educational opportunities for Black children who had attended inherently inadequate segregated schools, the schools they now attend must, at least, have adequate resources; however, the Supreme Court declined to invalidate the inequitable state education finance system. Instead, it held that education was not "a fundamental interest" under the federal Constitution and that it was outside the domain of federal constitutional law to scrutinize further the significance of the educational opportunities being afforded to residents of property poor school districts.

In the mid-1980s, the Supreme Court began to focus on the question of when remedial decrees in long-standing desegregation cases should be terminated. In a series of such decisions, the Court determined that the test for judging when a school board was entitled to be free of continuing judicial supervision would be whether the board has "complied in good faith with the desegregation decree since it was entered, and whether . . . vestiges of past *de jure* discrimination had been eliminated to the extent practicable" (*Oklahoma City Public Schools v. Dowell*, 1991, pp. 249–250). By emphasizing what is "practicable" for local school districts, rather than how to provide "meaningful" opportunities for students of color, the federal courts at this point signaled their abandonment of serious efforts to implement *Brown*'s vision of equal educational opportunity. The culmination of the Supreme Court's retreat from promoting effective school desegregation occurred at the end of its 2007 term when it invalidated the voluntary school desegregation plans in Seattle and Louisville, and made clear that future attempts to effectuate racial balance in the schools would be severely constrained (*Parents Involved v. Seattle*, 2007).

Not surprisingly, over the past decade, there has been a marked trend toward resegregation in the nation's public schools: In 2000, over 70% of all Black and Latino students attended predominantly minority schools, a higher percentage than 30 years earlier (Frankenberg, Lee, & Orfield, 2003, p. 28).

At the dawn of the new century, almost 50 years after the *Brown* decision, the contours of what was required to provide Blacks and other historically disadvantaged groups equal educational opportunities had been sketched by the federal courts, but these courts were no longer actively engaged in completing the picture. As egalitarian initiatives waned in the federal courts, however, they took on renewed vigor in the state courts and in the Congress—demonstrating the continuing power of American's egalitarian imperative and the *Brown* vision.

THE STATE COURT EDUCATION ADEQUACY DECISIONS

At about the same time that the Supreme Court's active support of desegregation remedies began to lag, legal challenges to the inequities in state education finance systems were lodged in the state courts, and these proved to be remarkably successful. This broad-based resort to the state courts was, to a large extent, triggered by the U.S. Supreme Court's closing of the gates to the federal courts in the Texas *Rodriguez* case. Although the Supreme Court held there that education was not a "fundamental interest" under the federal Constitution, education clearly is a fundamental interest under many state constitutions. State education-finance and education-adequacy cases could not ensure integrated school settings, but they did respond to the reality that most low-income and minority students attended school in property-poor urban or rural school districts that were substantially underfunded in comparison to schools in affluent, largely White suburban school districts.

The results of these efforts have been extraordinary: Challenges to inequities in state funding systems have been filed in 45 states over the past 35 years, and plaintiffs have won major decisions in most of them (National Access Network, 2006). Moreover, as the courts' emphasis in these cases has shifted in recent years from rectifying abstract fiscal inequities to ensuring that constitutionally "adequate" educational opportunities are actually available for all students, plaintiffs have prevailed in more than 70%—20 out of 27—of the major decisions (National Access Network, 2006).

The recent state court cases challenging state education finance systems have been called "adequacy" cases because they are based on clauses in almost all state constitutions that, although utilizing differing terms, guarantee all students some basic level of education. The contemporary courts have, in essence, revived and given major political significance to the important provisions incorporated into state constitutions either as part of the 18th-century emphasis on the need for education to prepare new republican citizens or the mid-19th-century common school movement to promote equal educational opportunity.

Thus, the 1993 ruling of the Massachusetts Supreme Judicial Court in *McDuffy v. Secretary of Education* was grounded in the following provision of the Massachusetts Constitution, originally enacted in 1780:

> Wisdom and knowledge, as well as virtue, diffused generally among the body of the people, being necessary for the preservation of their rights and liberties; and as these depend on spreading the opportunities and advantages of education in the various parts of the country, and among the different orders of the people, it shall be the duty of the Legislators, and Magistrates, in all future periods of this Commonwealth, to cherish the interests of literature and the sciences, and all seminaries of them; especially the . . . public schools and grammar schools in the towns.

The Supreme Court of Ohio explicitly referred to the ideological origins in the common school movement of the constitutional language it relied on in its 1997 decision in *DeRolph v. State of Ohio* and expressed an awareness of the far-reaching democratic implications of that ideology:

> The delegates to the 1850–51 Constitutional Convention recognized that it was the state's duty to both present and future generations of Ohioans to establish a framework for a "full, complete and efficient system of public education." . . . Thus, throughout their discussions, the delegates stressed the importance of education and reaffirmed the policy that education shall be afforded to every child in the state regardless of race or economic standing. . . . Furthermore, the delegates were concerned that the education to be provided to our youth not be mediocre but be as perfect as could humanly be devised. . . . These debates reveal the delegates' strong belief that it is the state's obligation, through the General Assembly, to provide for the full education of all children within the state. (pp. 740–741)

The state defendants in many of these cases have argued that the education clauses in the state constitutions should be interpreted to guarantee students only a "minimal" level of education. Significantly, most of the state courts that have closely reviewed students' needs for education in contemporary society have called instead for school systems to provide substantially more than a minimum level of knowledge and skills. Their approach focuses on what is needed to ensure that all children have access to those educational opportunities that are necessary to gain the level of learning and skills that is now required to obtain a good job in our increasingly technologically complex society and to carry out their responsibilities as citizens effectively in our ever-more-complicated society (Rebell, 2002). Accordingly, many of the cases have specified that an adequate education must include, in addition to traditional reading and mathematical skills, knowledge of the physical sciences and "a fundamental knowledge of economic, social, and political systems, and of history and governmental processes; and academic and vocational skills." Some cases have held that it also includes "the ability to appreciate music, art, and literature, and the ability to share all of that with friends" (Rebell, 2007b, p. 1503).

One of the clearest rejections of a minimalist interpretation of a state constitution adequacy clause was the 2003 decision of the New York Court of Appeals, the state's highest court. Invalidating the Appellate Division's holding that the state constitution required an education that would provide students only 8th-grade-level skills, the court held that New York's schoolchildren are constitutionally entitled to the "opportunity for a *meaningful* high school education, one which prepares them to function productively as civic participants" (*Campaign for Fiscal Equity v. State of New York*, 2003, p. 332, emphasis added). In doing so, the court stressed that although in the 19th century, when the state's adequacy clause was adopted, a sound basic education may well have consisted of an 8th- or 9th-grade education, "the definition of a sound basic education must serve the future as well as the case now before us" (p. 349).

In focusing on the actual educational needs of students in the 21st century, some of the state courts have begun to recognize that some students who come to school disadvantaged by the burdens of severe poverty need a more comprehensive set of services and resources in order to have a *meaningful* educational opportunity. Thus, in ordering that additional resources, beyond the level currently enjoyed by students in affluent suburbs, be provided to students in the state's poorest urban districts, the New Jersey Supreme Court held:

> This record shows that the educational needs of students in poorer ur-
> ban districts vastly exceed those of others, especially those from richer
> districts. The difference is monumental, no matter how it is measured.
> Those needs go beyond educational needs; they include food, clothing
> and shelter, and extend to lack of close family and community ties
> and support, and lack of helpful role models. They include the needs
> that arise from a life led in an environment of violence, poverty, and
> despair. . . . The goal is to motivate them, to wipe out their disadvan-
> tages as much as a school district can, and to give them an educational
> opportunity that will enable them to use their innate ability. (*Abbott v.
> Burke*, 1990, p. 400)

At least two state courts have also held that students from backgrounds
of poverty must be given access to early childhood services in order to
receive the opportunity for a meaningful education. In October 2000,
trial court judge Howard Manning ruled in North Carolina's school
funding case that many disadvantaged children were unprepared for
school due to the absence of pre-kindergarten opportunities (*Hoke
County Board of Education v. State*, 2000). More recently, South Carolina state circuit court judge Thomas W. Cooper, Jr., held that poverty
directly causes lower student achievement and that the state constitution imposes an obligation on the state "to create an educational
system that overcomes . . . the effects of poverty" (*Abbeville County
School District v. State*, 2005, p. 157).

The widespread recognition by dozens of state courts throughout the country that ideological commitments to equal educational
opportunity must be accompanied by practical steps to provide the
resources necessary to render these opportunities meaningful attests
to the continuing vitality of the American egalitarian imperative.
Some of these judges are also beginning to understand the extraordinary burdens that have been placed on the schools by the society's
neglect of the needs of low-income and minority children in other social policy domains. This may be a precursor of a broader societal recognition of the impact of concentrated poverty on children's learning
and the need to consider this when determining the resources and
supports that should be provided to the schools that are educating
these children. In the next chapter, we will describe the enormous
impact of poverty on children and on schools before turning, in the
chapters that follow, to an analysis of what needs to be done to provide all children with meaningful educational opportunities that respond to these realities.

CHAPTER 2

Confronting Opportunity Gaps

Throughout its history, the United States has largely depended on the public school system to solve its problems of social and economic inequality. While other industrialized countries built comprehensive social welfare systems—subsidizing income, health care, pensions, and housing to create more equality among their citizens—the United States has relied on education as the prime means of improving the lives of the poor and disadvantaged (Wells, 2006). However, the cruel irony of the American education system is that low-income and minority children who come to school with the greatest educational deficits generally have the fewest resources and least expertise devoted to their needs—and therefore the least opportunity to improve their futures. Current federal education policy, though ostensibly designed to remedy this, does not sufficiently confront these inequities.

In this chapter, we examine the conditions of poverty and racial inequality in America today. We explore how these conditions create barriers to learning both in and out of school that profoundly influence students' learning opportunities and their achievement. Finally, we begin to examine the extent to which NCLB responds to these conditions. If NCLB is ultimately to be effective, it must be revised with an eye toward closing the opportunity gaps that are at the root of our nation's achievement gaps and thus creating a law that appropriately balances opportunity and accountability.

THE SCOPE OF POVERTY IN THE UNITED STATES TODAY

Though the United States is one of the richest nations on Earth, many Americans still struggle with poverty. In 2005, at least 37 million people, constituting 12.6% of our population, lived in poverty by official standards. Among Blacks and Latinos, the poverty rate was almost twice as high, amounting to 24.9% and 21.8%, respectively (Denavas-Walt, Proctor, & Lee, 2006, p. 13). The U.S. child poverty rate is the highest among affluent countries (Mishel, Bernstein, & Allegretto, 2005, cited in Berliner, 2005). The rate of childhood poverty in America is 21.9%, compared with less than 3% in Denmark and Finland, the countries with the lowest rates (UNICEF, 2005). Race also figures into the child poverty rate: in 2005, 14% of White children were living in poverty, as compared with 34% of Black children and 28% of Latino children (Child Trends DataBank, 2006b).

As shocking as these figures are, they probably minimize the number of children affected by poverty in America (Anyon, 2005; Douglas-Hall & Koball, 2006). The official poverty rate is calculated according to a formula from the 1960s that establishes the threshold below which families or individuals are considered to be lacking the resources to meet basic needs (Fisher, 1992). This formula does not reflect changes in policies and practices since the 1960s and resulting cost increases in areas such as child care and health care (UNICEF, 2005). As a result, some researchers estimate that families actually need an income of twice the federal poverty level to make ends meet (see, e.g., Berstein, Brocht, & Spade-Aguilar, 2000). If calculated at this level, two out of every five American children would be considered poor.

The United States also leads all other developed nations in the percentage of people who are "permanently" poor (Mishel, Bernstein, & Allegretto, 2005, cited in Berliner, 2005). This statistic is particularly significant because the longer a child lives in poverty, the more extreme its effects, especially if a child is poor during the early childhood years (Brooks-Gunn & Duncan, 1997). And long-term child poverty is increasing. The percentage of young children who spent 6 or more years during the past decade in poverty rose from 7% in 1977 to 11% in 1997. Black children are more likely to experience long-term poverty. One third of Black children were poor for at least 6 years of the previous decade in 1997, though less than 5% of other children experienced this extreme. In 1997, only 31% of Black children experienced no poverty at all during the past decade, compared with 75% of other children (Child Trends DataBank, 2006a).

Surprisingly, most poor families in this country are working families. More than half (56%) of American children living below the poverty threshold live in households where someone works full-time, year-round (U.S. Department of Labor, 2005). As Jean Anyon (2005) writes:

In 2000, at the height of a booming economy, almost a fifth of all men (19.5%) and almost a third of all women (33.1%) earned poverty level wages working full time, year round. . . . And in 1999, during the strong economy, almost half of people at work in the U.S. (41.3%) earned poverty zone (125% of the official poverty threshold needed to support a family) wages—in 1999 $21,299/year or less—working full time, year round. (pp. 18–19)

The median income of working-age households has fallen each year since 2000, though the U.S. economy has expanded during this same period (Bernstein & Gould, 2006). This trend is not likely to reverse itself naturally. The current value of the national wealth available per person is more than twice what it was in 1967, yet there are more children living in poverty today (Children's Defense Fund, 2005). This is because during the past several decades, much of the gain from a strong U.S. economy has gone to the people at the top of the income ladder, creating large and growing disparities in income and wages. The growing gap between "haves" and "have-nots" in America is illustrated by the fact that from 1973 to 2000, the average real income of the bottom 90% of American taxpayers declined by 7%, while the income of the top 1% rose by 148% (Boushey & Weller, 2005). Another reflection of these ominous trends is the fact that whereas in 1965 the average U.S. corporate CEO's income was 24 times the average wage, in 2005 it was 262 times the average wage (Mishel, Bernstein, & Allegretto, 2007).

A troubling, related trend is that the haves and have-nots are moving farther apart physically as well as economically (Anyon, 2005; Wells, Holme, & Duran, 2006).

Increasingly, poor and nonpoor families live in separate neighborhoods and go to separate schools. As poverty is concentrated in certain areas, its effects on communities and individuals are multiplied. As neighborhoods become dominated by joblessness, racial segregation, and single parentage, they become isolated from middle class society and the private economy. Individuals, particularly children, are deprived of local role models and connections to opportunity outside of the neighborhood. A distinct society emerges with expectations and patterns of behavior that contrast heavily with middle class norms. (Orfield, 2002, p. 18)

Concentrated poverty is most pronounced in urban and "urbanized" suburban areas populated almost entirely by Black and Latino families (Anyon, 2005).

THE ACADEMIC ACHIEVEMENT GAPS
OF CHILDREN LIVING IN POVERTY

The impact of poverty on children's learning is profound and multidimensional. Although other risk factors, such as being raised by a single parent, having parents with low educational attainment, or coming from a foreign-born, non-English-speaking family, can compound the risk of poverty, none is as predictive of poor academic performance as poverty (Allgood, 2006). Children who grow up in poverty are much more likely than other children to experience conditions, both in school and out of school, that make learning difficult and put them at risk for academic failure. Moreover, the longer a child is poor, the more extreme the poverty, the greater the concentration of poverty in a child's surroundings, and the younger the age of the child, the more serious the effects on the child's potential to succeed academically (Brooks-Gunn & Duncan, 1997).

Although research shows little difference in mental ability among very young children regardless of race or social class (Fryer & Levitt, 2006), achievement gaps for poor and minority children begin before they start school and widen throughout their school careers (Education Trust, 2003a, 2003b; Miller, 1995; Robelen, 2002). At the beginning of kindergarten, large achievement gaps can already be found between Black and Hispanic children and White children, and between low socioeconomic status (SES) children and middle and high SES children in both math and reading (Lee & Burkam, 2002). On the National Assessment of Educational Progress (NAEP), children who are eligible for free or reduced-price lunch perform significantly worse on average than children who are not eligible at both 4th and 8th grades, in reading and in math (Weiner, 2006). In 2007, only 17% of poor children demonstrated proficiency on the NAEP reading test in 4th grade, while 44% of non-poor children performed at or above the proficient level (National Center for Education Statistics, 2007c). On the 8th-grade math test, only 15% of students who were eligible for free or reduced-price lunch scored at or above the proficient level in 2007, but 42% of students who were not eligible demonstrated proficiency (National Center for Education Statistics, 2007b). Moreover, the greater the percentage of low-income children in a school, the further the average performance drops (National Center for Education Statistics, 2006a). High school students living in low-income families are four times more likely to drop out of school than their peers in non-poor families (Laird, DeBell, & Chapman, 2006).

Poverty is also a major contributor to racial achievement gaps. Black and Latino children are much more likely than White children to live in poverty or attend segregated schools in poor neighborhoods, where concentrated poverty compounds the barriers to learning experienced by students (Orfield & Lee, 2005; Ryan, 1999; Rumberger, 2007). Some 88% of high-minority schools (more than 90% minority) are also high-poverty schools (Orfield & Lee, 2005). Some 61% of students in the largest urban school districts come from low-income families, compared with 38% nationwide (Snipes, Williams, Horwitz, Soga, & Casserly, 2007). These socioeconomically and racially segregated urban districts house most of our "failing" public schools (Wells, Holmes, & Duran, 2006).

HOW POVERTY AFFECTS LEARNING

Attention was first drawn to the importance of out-of-school factors on children's academic achievement by the sociologist James Coleman and his colleagues in the 1960s. The government-commissioned "Coleman report" (1966) studied the effects of both school and family inputs on student achievement and concluded that family characteristics had an even greater influence on student achievement than school quality. In the decades since the Coleman report, many researchers have studied these family or out-of-school factors (see, e.g., Anyon, 2005; Barton, 2003; Brooks-Gunn & Duncan, 1997; Comer, 1997, 2004; Ferguson, 2005; Gordon, 1999, 2005; Leichter, 1975; Mercer, 1973; Rothstein, 2004; Varenne & McDermott, 1998; Wilkerson, 1979; Wolf, 1966) with the goal of reducing the educational disadvantages of children from poverty. Each argues that, although quality schooling is essential for closing achievement gaps, without the amelioration or elimination of these other effects of poverty, children from poor families will not be able to achieve their potential in school.

There are a number of "pathways" through which poverty exacts its toll on children's academic achievement (Allgood, 2006; Brooks-Gunn & Duncan, 1997; Rothstein, 2004). These can be roughly divided into the categories of health-related, home- and family-related, and community- and environment-related barriers to learning.

Health-Related Barriers to Learning

Poor children are more likely than other children to lack adequate health care and, as a result, to suffer from health-related barriers to learning. Without access to adequate health care, children from low-income households are less likely to receive routine medical check-ups and immunizations, and are more likely to suffer from serious diseases (Allgood, 2006; Rothstein, 2004). They miss more school as a result of illness than other children (Rothstein, 2004). They are more likely to have undetected vision impairments and hearing problems, as well as untreated cavities and toothaches, all of which can affect their performance in school (Rothstein, 2004). Poor children are more likely to have high blood-lead levels because of lead exposure, which is connected with lowered IQ scores (Brooks-Gunn & Duncan, 1997). They are more likely to have asthma (Barton, 2003; Brooks-Gunn & Duncan, 1997; Rothstein, 2004). Asthma is on the rise among all children, but poor children with asthma miss more school than other children with the disease (Allgood, 2006); children who do go to school are likely to be tired and inattentive as a result of interrupted sleep (Rothstein, 2004).

Poor families are more likely than other families to experience hunger or have inadequate access to a nutritionally sound diet. In 2002, 22% of families in poverty experienced "food insecurity"—the "lack of secure access to sufficient amounts of safe and nutritious food for normal development and an active and healthy life" (U.N. Food and Agriculture Organization, 2000)—and 13% of them experienced hunger (Barton, 2003). Hunger and malnutrition obviously affect children's school performance. Children who are hungry are less able to concentrate in school. Malnutrition in young children can impede brain development; in older children it can lead to illness and missed school (Allgood, 2006).

Home- and Family-Related Barriers to Learning

Children who are poor are more likely than other children to live in single-parent households (Lee & Burkam, 2002). They are more likely to have a larger number of siblings (Lee & Burkam, 2002). Their parents are more likely not to have received a high school diploma and are more likely to suffer from serious physical or mental health problems (Allgood, 2006). All of these factors negatively affect parents' ability to provide intellectual and academic support to their children. Each of these disparities is more pronounced in low-income African American and Latino families than in other families (Allgood, 2006; Lee & Burkam, 2002).

Children who are poor are less likely to be exposed to parenting practices that are associated with school readiness and achievement.

For example, low-income households are more likely to have lower-quality parent-child interactions, characterized by a smaller number of words spoken to children, fewer and less diverse exchanges, less complex interactions, and more punitive and directive statements (Brooks-Gunn & Duncan, 1997; Hart & Risley, 2003). In addition, the households of children who are poor have fewer of the material resources and at-home learning experiences that are positively associated with learning and readiness for school. They have fewer books in the home and are read to less frequently. They are less likely to have a computer and are likely to spend more time watching television (Ferguson, 2006; Lee & Burkam, 2002). They are less likely to have parents or other caring adults who are able to engage in what Lareau (2003) calls "concerted cultivation" (p. 2) and what Gordon (2005; Gordon & Bridglall, 2006) calls "affirmative development" of their children through "the demands, the routine provisions, the things that are done for fun, and even things that are forced under duress in the effort to ensure that optimal development and effective education are achieved" (p. 322).

Early childhood education programs have positive and lasting effects on children's academic performance (Barnett, 1995; Karoly, Greenwood, Everingham, Hoube, Kilburn, Rydell, Sanders, & Chiesa, 1998; Ramey & Ramey, 2000). Quality pre-K programs have been shown to improve children's cognitive and social development in the short term, and participation in model pre-K programs has been shown to reduce special education placement, improve high school completion, and reduce teen parenting rates, among other benefits (Belfield, 2005). However, children who are poor are still more likely than other children to lack access to high-quality early childhood programs (Kagan, 2006; Lee & Burkam, 2002). The same is true for one-on-one tutoring, before- and after-school programs, and summer programs, all of which have been shown to have benefits in raising achievement for low-income children (Allgood, 2006).

Poor families' lack of access to adequate housing affects children's academic achievement and contributes to the achievement gap. Low-income families are more likely to live in substandard housing or spend a larger share of their income on housing, leaving them fewer resources for other necessities (Allgood, 2006), such as food, health care, and child care. Children in substandard housing suffer disproportionately from asthma and lead poisoning, the effects of which have already been discussed. As a result of crowded living conditions, they often lack a quiet study space (Allgood, 2006).

Inadequate housing also contributes to frequent moves and a high school-mobility rate for children from low-income families. For example, a 1994 government report indicated that 30% of the poorest children had attended at least three different schools upon entering the 3rd grade (Rothstein, 2004). Students who move from school to school do not perform as well academically as students who move less; in addition, students who attend schools with higher rates of student mobility have lower achievement in general than students in schools with lower mobility rates (Rothstein, 2004).

Community/Neighborhood-Related Barriers to Learning

The neighborhoods in which poor children reside may be another "pathway" through which poverty depresses student achievement. Living in neighborhoods of concentrated poverty has been shown to have negative effects on student academic outcomes over and above family effects (Brooks-Gunn & Duncan, 1997). Unfortunately, housing policies and patterns leave low-income families few choices in where to live and where to send their children to school (Anyon, 2005). Poor Blacks are eight times as likely and poor Latinos six times as likely as poor Whites to live in high-poverty neighborhoods (Allgood, 2006).

Low-income neighborhoods often lack family supports and community resources that contribute in very important ways to children's ability to succeed in school. Scarce resources include quality child care, health facilities, community centers, cultural activities, positive role models, and parks and playgrounds. In short, low-income Black and Latino students are less likely to have access to what Coleman (1990) and others have called "social capital"—"the norms, the social networks, and the relationships between adults and children that are of value for the children's growing up" (p. 334) and achieving their full intellectual potential.

THE ADDED IMPACT OF SCHOOL RESOURCE GAPS

Despite the enormity of the deprivations suffered by children in poverty and the magnitude of their learning needs, in the United States, schools by and large not only fail to provide the high-quality resources children need to overcome the burdens of poverty, but they actually provide these children with fewer resources and lower-quality services than they provide to more advantaged children:

> Public education is brutally efficient at denying meaningful educational opportunities to children who are growing up in poverty. With relentless effectiveness, it shortchanges such children in everything from the qualifications of their teachers, to the quality of their school buildings, to the rigor of the daily assignments. (Weiner, 2006, p. 1)

The Education Trust (2006) has estimated that nationwide, on average, spending on children in high-poverty districts is $825 less per student than spending on students in low-poverty districts. The situation is even worse in particular states and districts. For example, in 1999–2000, the school district of Cuyahoga Heights, a wealthy Cleveland suburb, received $16,447 per student in state and local funds. Tri-Valley Local, a low-wealth rural school district in Ohio, received just $4,532 per student (*DeRolph v. Ohio*, 2000).

The discrepancies between what our schools provide to poor children and affluent children in dollar terms, as well as in the quality of educational services, have been documented extensively in the state court cases brought to challenge these inequities. In California, many high schools in low-income and minority communities do not offer the curriculum students must take just to *apply* to the state's public universities (*Williams v. California*, ¶ 280). Passing an examination in a laboratory science course is required for high school graduation in New York State, but 31 New York City high schools have no science labs (*Campaign for Fiscal Equity v. State*, 2003, p. 334, n. 4). In South Carolina, annual teacher turnover rates exceed 20% in eight poor, rural, mostly minority school districts (*Abbeville v. South Carolina*, 2005), and in those districts graduation rates fall between 33% and 57% (Hunter, 2003).

Although defendants in these cases often claimed that "money doesn't matter" in rectifying educational inadequacies, the courts in 30 of the state cases considered this question, often after hearing extensive testimony from the national experts on both sides of the issue. In 29 of the 30 cases, the courts held that money does matter and that additional resources are needed to provide meaningful educational opportunities to poor and minority children (Rebell, 2007b).

The decisions of the state courts that have analyzed the specific resources that poor and minority students need to obtain an adequate education have tended to agree that schools must provide the following education essentials:

- Effective teachers, principals, and other personnel
- Appropriate class sizes
- Adequate school facilities

- Rich and rigorous curricula
- A full platform of services, including guidance services, after-school, summer, and weekend programming and tutoring, and additional time on task for students from backgrounds of poverty
- Appropriate programs and services for English language learners and students with disabilities
- Instrumentalities of learning, including, but not limited to, up-to-date textbooks, libraries, laboratories, and computers
- A safe, orderly learning environment (Rebell & Wolff, 2006)

This list of education essentials in effect restates the elements of good schooling that students in affluent districts obtain as a matter of course. The extensive evidence set forth in the adequacy cases established both the extent to which poor and minority children are widely denied these basic educational resources and the remarkable progress that disadvantaged students have made when, in particular instances, high-quality resources were provided. For example, extensive research undertaken by Ron Ferguson of Harvard University has demonstrated that high-quality teaching has a profound effect on student learning. Ferguson's most extensive study used a massive data set involving 2 million children and 200,000 teachers in 90% of Texas's 1,000 school districts during the 1980s. He compared student achievement in schools with similar student demographics but with significant variations in the level of teacher qualification as measured by TECAT, a literacy skills test administered to every public school teacher in Texas. By high school, students in districts with the high-scoring teachers scored remarkably higher—1.7 standard deviations—than their peers with low-scoring, less-qualified teachers (Ferguson, 1998; see also *Campaign for Fiscal Equity v. State*, 2003). Ferguson's results are consistent with similar findings from studies of teacher effectiveness in Tennessee (Sanders & Rivers, 1996) and Boston (Haycock, 1998). Another major study of Texas teachers found that "having five years of good teachers in a row would overcome the average achievement deficit between low income kids and others from higher income families" (Rivkin, Hanushek, & Kain, 2000, p. 35).

One of the factors that most directly correlates with teacher quality is experience in the classroom. Stanford University professor Linda Darling-Hammond testified in *Campaign for Fiscal Equity v. State of New York* (1999) that "teachers do become more effective during their initial years of experience" and that "teachers with less than three years of experience tend to be less effective than teachers who have somewhere in the range of three to five years experience" (Wolff, 2001, p. 6). In a report submitted for *Williams v. State of California,* Darling-Hammond (2002) cites Goe (2002); Hanushek, Kain, and Rivkin (1999); and Kain and Singleton (1996) as evidence that "inexperienced teachers (those with less than two or three years of experience) are often found to be noticeably less effective than more senior teachers" (p. 30).

Overwhelmingly, poor and minority students are more likely to be taught by these less-experienced, less-qualified teachers. "As an example, in 2000, 28% of New York City teachers in the quartile of schools with the highest concentration of student-poverty were in their first two years of teaching, compared with 15% of teachers in the lowest-poverty group" (Loeb & Miller, 2006, p. 3). Similarly, 26% of non-White students had teachers who failed their general knowledge certification exam, compared with 16% of White students (Loeb & Miller, 2006, p. 5). An extreme example of the poor-quality teaching that is provided to low-income and minority students emerged from Arkansas litigation where the court found that Lake View, a poor rural school district, had one uncertified mathematics teacher covering all high school mathematics courses. The teacher was paid $10,000 a year as a substitute teacher, which he supplemented with $5,000 annually for school bus driving (*Lake View School District No. 25 v. Huckabee,* 2001).

Evidence in the cases also established that at-risk children are more likely to be taught by "out-of-field" teachers—in other words, teachers who do not possess specific qualifications (either certification or a major or minor) in the subject areas in which they teach. For example, the record in the *Hancock* litigation revealed that in Brockton, Massachusetts, in 2002, 50% of the middle school mathematics teachers were not appropriately certified in that field, and in Winchendon, Massachusetts, none of the 7th- and 8th-grade mathematics teachers were appropriately certified (*Hancock v. Driscoll,* 2005, p. 1166). These findings are consistent with national studies that indicate that, in secondary schools, 34% of classes in high-poverty schools and 29% in high-minority schools are taught by out-of-field teachers, compared with 19% in low-poverty schools and 21% in low-minority schools (Jerald, 2002, p. 4). The problem is much worse in middle schools, where over half of classes in high-poverty schools are taught by teachers who lack at least a college minor in the subject area that they teach (Jerald, 2002).

Trials in the adequacy cases also focused on the class size issue. The New Jersey Supreme Court noted, for example, that children in the poor urban districts "must also contend with gross overcrowding.

Some class sizes hover around forty" (*Abbott v. Burke*, 1998, p. 470). In Texas, one third of the school districts did not meet the state-mandated standards for class size, and "the great majority of these are low-wealth districts" (*Edgewood Independent School District v. Kirby*, 1989, p. 393). The evidence strongly affirmed the commonsense perception that smaller classes, which allow for more personalized instruction, are directly correlated with improved student achievement—especially for poor and minority students. The most widely documented study in this regard was the landmark Tennessee STAR study, which was initiated in the late 1980s and whose results have been extensively analyzed from the early 1990s until the present day. For 4 years in the 1980s, the state of Tennessee placed 6,500 students in different-size classes in 80 schools and 330 K–3 classrooms, and tracked their educational progress over time—thus creating large-scale control groups of similar groups of students that allowed for precise comparisons of the results of the main variable, differences in the students' class sizes. Jeremy Finn of the State University of New York at Buffalo and his colleagues concluded that several years' exposure to small classes showed lasting benefits that are statistically significant and educationally meaningful (Finn, Gerber, Achilles, & Boyd-Zacharias, 2001). Improvements in test scores remained significant through grade 8— fully 5 years after the small classes were disbanded. Few educational interventions have demonstrated this degree of longevity.

Further analysis of Tennessee STAR data by Princeton professors Alan Krueger and Diane Whitmore found especially pronounced educational benefits of small class sizes on African American children. While the academic achievement rose for all students who were in the smaller classes, Krueger and Whitmore (2001) found that standardized test score increases for Black children, which averaged 7–10 percentile points, were double the gains of the White children in those same classes. Because of this pronounced effect on the achievement of Black students, they concluded that "assigning *all* students to a class of 15 students as opposed to 22 students for a couple of years in grammar school would lower the black-white [standardized test score] gap by about 38%" (p. 16). The reason that small classes matter more for African American students, hypothesized Krueger and Whitmore (2001), is that they are more likely to attend schools with a range of educational deficiencies and, thus, greater numbers of "weak students" that require students to "move very slowly through the curriculum" (pp. 34–35). With fewer students, teachers can "effectively teach more material," an issue not faced in schools with less pervasive educational deficiencies (i.e., predominantly White or low-poverty schools) where teachers "can move quickly through the material regardless of class size" (pp. 34–35). White students attending predominantly Black schools, they found, enjoyed the same large benefits.

Evaluation of the impact of extra time on task for students with low achievement scores has also demonstrated substantial gains. Evidence in the New Jersey litigation established that "if you start kids in preschool, take them through summer . . . you will have them achieving at levels no one ever predicted" (*Abbott v. Burke*, 1990, p. 398, n. 29). The *Campaign for Fiscal Equity* litigation revealed that "pre-kindergarten programs, summer programs, and increased hours at school via after school and Saturday programs" positively affected student performance (*Campaign for Fiscal Equity v. State of New York*, 2001, p. 525). The evidence in this case particularly focused on Reading Recovery, an expensive but highly effective one-to-one tutoring program. Reading Recovery selects students from the lowest performing 20% of 1st graders. According to studies completed by researchers at New York University who testified at the trial between 1989 and 1996, 83% of all New York students who received the full Reading Recovery program of 60 or more lessons successfully developed self-sustaining capacities for reading. The *CFE* court found this program to be "extremely effective" (*Campaign for Fiscal Equity v. State of New York*, 2001, p. 526).

Teachers and administrators who work daily with students from poverty backgrounds have testified at length about their schools' and classrooms' lack of basic supplies, up-to-date textbooks, computers, well-stocked libraries, and other learning materials. Summarizing the testimony of one of these teachers, the Arkansas court wrote in *Lake View*, "In his geometry class he does not have compasses. Only one of four chalkboards is usable. His computer lacks hard- and software . . . and the printer does not work. Paper is in short supply and the duplicating machine, an addressograph, is generally overworked so that frequently documents, including examinations, have to be handwritten on the chalkboard" (*Lake View School District No. 25 v. Huckabee*, 2001, ¶ 24).

The impact of inadequate facilities was described in testimony in the case of *DeRolph v. State of Ohio* as follows: At the intermediate and high schools in Coal Grove, Ohio, there were no art or music rooms. The intermediate school had no science labs, and one shower room served both boys and girls. One of the high school's science labs had no running water or gas. In the town's elementary school, temperatures often exceeded 100 degrees at the beginning and end of the school year; if more than three teachers ran fans at the same time, however, the school's circuit breaker would fail (*DeRolph v. State of*

Ohio, 1994). In Mount Gilead, some students were being educated in former coalbins (*DeRolph v. State of Ohio*, 1997), and in Flushing, students as recently as the early 1990s had to use outhouses (*DeRolph v. State of Ohio*, 1994).

In Arizona, the perspective of the state court judges who heard testimony for weeks regarding the lack of basic tools of learning in schools that serve low-income and minority students was well summarized by the chief justice of the Arizona Supreme Court, who wrote:

> Logic and experience tell us that children have a better opportunity to learn biology and chemistry, and are more likely to do so, if provided with the laboratory equipment for experiments and demonstrations; that children have a better opportunity to learn English literature if given access to books; that children have a better opportunity to learn computer science if they can use computers, and so on through the entire state prescribed curriculum. . . . It seems apparent to me, however, that these are inarguable principles. If they are not, then we are wasting an abundance of our taxpayers' money in school districts that maintain libraries and buy textbooks, laboratory equipment and computers. (*Roosevelt Elementary School District No. 66 v. Bishop*, 1994, p. 822)

NCLB's FAILURE TO RESPOND TO STUDENTS' NEEDS

The preceding discussion has made clear that poor and minority students, whose readiness for learning is severely affected by conditions of poverty, are nevertheless more likely than their more affluent White peers to attend lower-quality schools—however school quality is measured—and to lack adequate educational resources to meet their learning needs. NCLB does not speak directly to this central issue. Of the six broad areas of school-based education essentials emphasized by the state courts, NCLB addresses only one, the need for effective teachers, and this is inadequately addressed. The Goals 2000: Educate America Act, a predecessor to NCLB, emphasized that to meet the national goal that "All children will start school ready to learn," all children should have access to high-quality preschools and "will receive the nutrition, physical activity experiences and health care needed to arrive at school with healthy minds and bodies" (Goals 2000, 1994, § 5812(1) (B) (iii)). However, NCLB contains no specific requirements for these critical out-of-school support services. The law has provided additional funding to states and school districts since 2002, but virtually all of these funds have been utilized for the development and administration of required tests, data collection, and data reporting systems, and increased administrative support devoted to compliance with the law's many provisions, rather than to increasing and improving services provided to students (Sunderman, 2006).

Not coincidentally, the one area in which NCLB has mandated specific resource inputs, that of teacher qualification, has been the one area that has shown some concrete success. Over the past 5 years, the number of uncertified teachers and minimally qualified teachers has, at least in some places, dropped substantially. For example, the number of uncertified teachers in California was cut in half by 2005, and the percentage of new hires in New York City who had failed the basic state certification examination on the first attempt was reduced from 16% to 6% (Loeb & Miller, 2006). California and New York have now totally eliminated emergency certificate hiring routes, but the number of new teachers certified through alternative certification mechanisms whose quality may be questionable has risen dramatically (Loeb & Miller, 2006).

Although the reduction in the numbers of uncertified and grossly unqualified teachers entering urban and rural school systems is significant, many students, and especially large numbers of low-income and minority students, still are not being taught by teachers who are really "highly qualified" and who are effective in meeting their learning needs. As we will discuss in Chapter 5, NCLB essentially equates its definition of *highly qualified teacher* with minimal state teacher certification or minimal evaluation requirements, and the law has no means of ensuring that teachers in our schools today are capable of providing students with a meaningful opportunity to learn the challenging content contained in most states' academic standards. Moreover, little progress has been made toward implementing the law's stated requirement that by 2006, low-income and minority students not be taught by inexperienced, unqualified, or out-of-field teachers at higher rates than other children (Loeb & Miller, 2006).

Overall, despite the lofty aims, purposes, and mandates of NCLB, actual progress toward improving the achievement of low-income and minority students in the United States and reducing achievement gaps has been minimal since 2002. Although a number of states have reported significant learning gains, as we will discuss in Chapter 7, it is difficult to credit many of these pronouncements because of the wide-ranging variations in the quality of their content and performance standards.

A more objective measure of absolute and relative progress is provided by the biennial scores reported by the National Assessment of Educational Progress (NAEP). The NAEP statistics for 2002–2007, the first 5 years that NCLB was in effect, show that nationwide, on average, in math, there was a five-point gain at grade 4 and a six-point gain at grade 8; reading scores increased by two points at grade 4 and decreased by one point at grade 8 (National Center for Education Statistics, 2007b, 2007c). The apparent trend of modest gains in the early grades being reduced as students advance through the middle and later grades is further substantiated by the fact that between 1992 and 2005, the percentage of students proficient in 12th-grade reading declined from 40% to 35% (Grigg, Donohue, & Dion, 2007).

The achievement gaps that NCLB seeks to eliminate also strongly persist. Looking at national performance averages at both the 4th- and 8th-grade levels as measured by the NAEP for 2005, the scores of White students are, on average, around the 60th percentile in all subjects, while Black students' scores are, on average, in the 30th percentile (Rothstein & Wilder, 2005; see also Weiner, 2006). The 2007 NAEP data show no significant reduction in this gap (National Center for education Statistics, 2007b, 2007c).

Even with very basic content standards and, in the case of many states, low cut scores defining proficiency on achievement tests, no state is on track to close the achievement gaps in the foreseeable future. If current trends continue, the percentage of all students that would be at the proficient level or above in math in 2014 would be 50% at grade 4 and 39% at grade 8, and the percentage that would be proficient in reading would be less than 33% (Linn, 2006). Moreover, based on current 4th-grade rates of progress, it will take until 2034 to eliminate the achievement gaps, and, if the more worrisome 8th-grade trends continue, it will take 200 years to achieve this goal (Kingsbury, Olson, Cronin, Hauser, & Houser, 2003).

The predominant "theory of action" that permeates the current version of NCLB is that "strong, external pressure on school systems, focused on student achievement, will produce a political dynamic that leads to school improvement" (Hess & Petrilli, 2006, p. 23). Although accountability pressures can affect the motivation of school personnel and influence their performance to some degree, the critical goals of the act—elimination of the achievement gaps and sustained, high-level academic achievement by virtually all students—cannot be achieved unless mechanisms are also put into place that recognize and overcome the severe opportunity gaps created by the conditions of poverty described in this chapter.

The next chapter will describe the evolution of the federal government's involvement in education and the factors that led to Congress's passage of NCLB, and will summarize the key provisions of the act.

Enactment of NCLB was a historic achievement that merged America's egalitarian imperative with the drive for educational excellence of the state standards-based reform movement. The political compromises that led to passage of the act ignored the need to ensure that schools and students were equipped with the essential tools they require to meet the act's ambitious goals. The chapters that follow thereafter will focus on remedying this critical defect and will propose specific revisions to the law that will provide workable mechanisms for ensuring that all students receive meaningful educational opportunities.

CHAPTER 3

NCLB and the
Changing Federal Role
in American Education

While the history of public schooling in the United States has been one of progress toward educational equity, the role of the federal government in the effort has, until recent times, been relatively minor. Consistent with the limited scope of government-sponsored education in the 18th century, the federal Constitution contains no mention of any specific role for the national government in public education. As systems of public education developed and expanded in the 19th and 20th centuries, the responsibility and rights for schooling came to be lodged largely with the states. This was in keeping with the Tenth Amendment to the U.S. Constitution, which provides that "The powers not delegated to the United States by the Constitution, are reserved to the States respectively, or to the people."

Beginning with the enactment of the Elementary and Secondary Education Act of 1965 (ESEA), and culminating in the passage of the NCLB (which technically was a reauthorization of the ESEA), Washington's involvement in educational policy has dramatically increased. Because of a broad national commitment to realize the equity vision of *Brown* a half century since that landmark decision, and the widely perceived importance of improving all of our schools in order to maintain the nation's global economic competitiveness, this extensive federal involvement in education is likely to continue.

The strong legacy of state and local control of education continues to complicate the implementation of NCLB. As we will discuss in further detail in the chapters that follow, part of the reason that NCLB is not achieving its objectives is that it has not struck the proper balance between federal and state power. Washington wields too much authority in certain areas and not enough in others. This chapter provides a context for understanding the political compromises that led to the current structure of NCLB and sets the stage for our later discussion of the changes that need to be made to create a more effective federal-state partnership that can provide meaningful educational opportunity to all of America's children.

EARLY FEDERAL INVOLVEMENT IN EDUCATION

Immediately after the Revolutionary War, the federal government's enormous land holdings gave it a powerful means for shaping the development of American educational policy. In fact, much of the initial funding for the establishment of schools in the late 18th and early 19th century came through federal largesse. The Northwest Ordinance of 1785, which governed the distribution of land in the new territories, mandated that one section of each township be devoted to the maintenance of public schools. Federal gifting of land—both through the ordinance and in subsequent additional gifts of land to the states—became especially important when industrialization and immigration prompted the beginning of the common school movement in the mid-1800s (Hirschland & Steinmo, 2003).

States and localities, lacking the capacity to take on the full financial responsibility for their rapidly expanding state school systems, were substantially aided by Congress's decision in 1837 to distribute back to the states surplus monies that had accumulated in the federal treasury. This money, coupled with $28 million in never-recalled "loans," gave states the financial means to develop their school systems (Hirschland & Steinmo, 2003). While the federal government largely financed the development and improvement of state school systems, its role was unofficial at this point and, thus, its assistance came without strings.

The last major grant of federal land, 30,000 acres to each state to support higher education, occurred right at the beginning of the Civil War. After the war, the federal government's educational initiatives focused on expanding access to education and aiding the newly freed slaves, a stance that generated strong resistance from the Southern states after they were readmitted to the Union during the Reconstruction era. In 1865, the national government established the Bureau of Refugees, Freedmen and Abandoned Land to aid the reconstruction of the South and improve the lives of the millions of freed slaves. Before its funding was terminated 5 years later, the bureau opened and staffed more than 2,500 schools and introduced more than 150,000 Black children to education (Hirschland & Steinmo, 2003).

In 1867, the federal government established a Department of Education, and a number of bills calling for a stronger federal role in funding and overseeing education were introduced into Congress. The most notable of these was the bitterly contested "Hoar Bill" of 1870, which would have established a federal system of educational oversight that could "compel by national authority the establishment of a thorough and efficient system of public instruction throughout the whole country [that] is not to supersede, but to stimulate, compel, and supplement action by the State" (Lee, 1949, p. 42). Federal aid for the states' provision of general education would have been distributed in proportion to the rate of illiteracy in each state under this proposal (Dawson, 1938).

After the Southern states were readmitted to the Union, the Department of Education was downgraded to a bureau housed in the Department of the Interior, with a greatly reduced budget, and the Hoar Bill was defeated. (Its language calling for "a thorough and efficient system of public instruction" did, however, inspire the drafters of many state constitutions, who included this potent language in the education provisions that were written into their state constitutions.)

By the late 19th century, strong opposition had developed to involvement of the federal government in educational affairs. The basis for this opposition is often summarized in terms of the "three Rs: race, religion, and regulation." Bills to provide federal aid to education repeatedly failed because of a threat that federal aid would be coupled with demands for racial justice or assistance to schools for African American children, that it would provide aid to parochial schools, and/or that it would undermine local control of schools (Kaestle, 2001; McGuinn, 2006).

THE MODERN ERA

The continuing limited involvement of the federal government in education during the first half of the 20th century was exemplified by the fact that although Franklin D. Roosevelt's "New Deal" included federal construction projects, agricultural subsidies, welfare grants in aid, and Social Security, it did not encompass any major efforts to improve public schooling (Kaestle, 2001). The New Deal experience, together with the country's massive mobilization for World War II, did, however, acculturate the population to greater federal involvement in social and economic affairs, and, in the postwar era, the federal government's association with educational funding and educational policy issues slowly began to grow.

The first major federal foray into the education arena was the GI Bill, which offered millions of veterans the means to attend college or receive vocational or technical training. "This program transformed the federal government's role in education and, in the process, transformed American society by expanding opportunities for higher learning to hundreds of thousands of veterans and their families" (Cross, 2004, p. 3). The military buildup during the Korean War then led to passage of the Impact Aid Act, which made permanent the federal government's provision, initiated during World War II, of general aid to school districts that bore the impact of military bases and federal employees (Cross, 2004).

The return of millions of GIs and the postwar baby boom era also led to an explosion in school enrollments during the 1950s and to pressure for federal aid for school construction. The major school construction bill, the Cooper Act, which would have provided $500 million in federal construction aid, came up for a vote in 1956, shortly after the Supreme Court's decision in *Brown*. Northern civil rights advocates, led by Representative Adam Clayton Powell (D-N.Y.), attached to the bill an amendment that would require each state to certify that its schools were desegregated before they would be eligible to receive federal funds. The presence of the Powell amendment ignited strong Southern opposition, and the bill was then defeated (Cross, 2004).

The Soviet Union's launch of the world's first orbiting satellite, *Sputnik*, in 1957 precipitated widespread apprehension that America was falling behind in the development of science and technology. These national security concerns led Congress the next year to enact the National Defense of Education Act of 1958 (NDEA), which provided states with about $1 billion in categorical aid for summer institutes devoted to teacher professional development in math, science, and foreign language instruction; science labs; and other specified purposes. A major reason that this bill passed was that the Powell amendment grafted onto it was limited to students receiving aid to attend college, and did not apply to the bill's major public school and state institutional components (Cross, 2004).

Following numerous failed attempts to pass bills that would have provided general aid to schools, the NDEA established the political precedent of targeting aid for specific categorical purposes, which proved to have a better chance of succeeding in Congress (McGuinn, 2006; Kaestle, 2001). Nevertheless, even with categorical aid, there was strong local resistance to what was viewed as federal government intrusion. Thus, though categorical aid had a specific intent, government officials trod lightly in their oversight, and there was little accountability for how the funds were actually spent (Kaestle, 2001; McGuinn, 2006).

Although the NDEA may have been an important breakthrough for advocates of federal aid to education, it still did not soften the political ground for general aid. During his short presidency, John F. Kennedy (1961) pushed for general aid for education for the purposes of creating an "educational system that will permit the maximum development of the talents of every American boy and girl," but he was not successful. In the wake of Kennedy's assassination, however, President Lyndon Johnson was able to capitalize upon public goodwill and a large democratic congressional majority (after the 1964 election) to promote a federal education agenda as a part of his "war on poverty." Building on his own experience as a child whose schooling opportunities allowed him to rise out of poverty and his sometime career as a schoolteacher (Cross, 2004), Johnson highlighted the role of education in his overall domestic program when he stated, "the answer to all our national problems comes down to a single word: education" (Tyack & Cuban, 1995, p. 2).

Johnson's Elementary and Secondary Education Act (ESEA) of 1965 was the most comprehensive federal education legislation in U.S. history (until its 2001 reauthorization as the No Child Left Behind Act) and substantially strengthened the role of the federal government as guarantor of equal educational opportunity. But even with strong majorities of his party in both houses of Congress, Johnson was able to steer the ESEA through Congress only because of his deft handling of the "three Rs."

The usual opposition of the powerful Southern committee chairs to the Powell amendment was finessed in this instance by the passage the year before of Title VI of the 1964 Civil Rights Act. Title VI, which authorized the total cutoff of federal aid to states that operated funded programs in a discriminatory manner, in effect established a permanent Powell amendment, and removed this issue as a consideration in the passage of future legislation.

To deal with the strong conflicting pressures from Catholic groups that sought aid for parochial schools and from the National Education Association (NEA) and other liberal groups that were opposed to it, the ESEA was structured to provide services to eligible children through supplemental services that would be provided directly to the child, and not to the private school (Cross, 2004; McGuinn, 2006). In this way, through its focus on poverty, ESEA was able to reconcile the traditional differences between public school and private school advocates, "for while only public agencies would receive funds, poor children in non-public schools would be eligible to share in its benefits" (Ravitch, 1983, p. 148).

Opposition based on local control concerns was overcome by funding formulas that maximized the number of eligible districts (about 95% of districts received some Title I funds) and placed only very limited constraints on how the money could actually be spent (DeBray, 2006; McGuinn, 2006). These political compromises allowed the ESEA to pass both the House and Senate with large majorities, but, at the same time, they also blunted its potential as a redistributive policy meant to address the needs of educationally deprived children and inhibited the development of strong evaluation and accountability requirements.

With the passage of ESEA, federal spending on education increased tenfold between 1958 and 1968, rising from $375 million, or a 3% share of all school funding, to $4.2 billion, or a 10% share (McGuinn, 2006). It became clear with the law's implementation, however, that the original intent to target these funds toward students with the greatest educational needs had been subverted. Audits by the U.S. Office of Education (USOE) found that 30% of children participating in Title I–funded activities in 1968 did not meet the criteria for educational disadvantage, and millions of eligible students were left unserved (Murphy, 1991). The following year, the NAACP Legal Defense Fund and the Washington Research Project highlighted these abuses of Title I funds, which, in some cases, included buying swimming pools and new band uniforms, but the Office of Education had limited capacity to respond (DeBray, 2006; McDonnell, 2005). Even with its implementation difficulties, however, the ESEA was 1) symbolically powerful as a legislative effort to provide equal protection to the students most often neglected by their schools, 2) financially powerful in granting large amounts of fairly flexible aid to schools, and 3) politically powerful in involving the federal government in a major effort to promote educational equity throughout the land.

As the federal government took on a stronger role in education policies, the role of state governments also grew. When the ESEA was enacted, most state education departments were weak and without the institutional capacity to take on the new regulatory duties that the law thrust upon them. Title V of the act sought to remedy this problem by providing funding to build administrative capacity in the state education departments (Manna, 2006). As a result, ironically, state education departments came to be dependent on federal funding.

The growth of the federal and state roles in education resulted in major shifts in education spending patterns. As a percentage of total education spending, federal funds reached a high of 16% in 1985. As the federal share increased, so did the states' vis-à-vis the local school districts; the states' share of total educational spending rose from 41% in 1960 to 55% in 1985 (McGuinn, 2006). While the change in spending patterns reflected the changing power arrangements, it also resulted from attempts by many local districts to reduce their financial support for programs for educationally disadvantaged children. The USOE found evidence early on that Title I monies were being used in lieu of state and local funds. This led Congress to enact a "supplement, not supplant" provision, requiring that Title I services be offered in *addition* to whatever eligible students would have received in its absence (McDonnell, 2005).

STANDARDS REFORM AND GOALS 2000

By 1980, the lack of solid evidence that the massive amounts of Title I spending had made any real difference in student achievement (McLaughlin, 1975) led to growing discontent over the federal role in education among Republicans, and even some Democrats. This frustration was exacerbated by President Carter's promotion of the USOE to Cabinet-level status in 1979, which many opponents viewed as a political prize for the NEA (Cross, 2004). The landslide election of President Ronald Reagan and the Republican capture of the Senate in 1980 led to a major reconsideration of the purposes and structure of ESEA.

Although Reagan did not make good on his threat to abolish the recently established Department of Education, he did consolidate education programs and dramatically cut expenditures as part of his overall vision of creating a smaller federal government and devolving responsibilities to states and localities. In 1981, Congress renamed Title I "Chapter 1," cut appropriations by about 20%, and combined much of its funding into block grants to the states; the law's focus on funding supplemental services for educationally disadvantaged children was, however, retained (Cross, 2004; McDonnell, 2005). It took about a decade for the number of children served by Title I to reach pre-1980 levels again (Jennings, 2000).

In 1983, the National Commission on Excellence in Education released its blockbuster report, *A Nation at Risk,* which famously concluded that "a rising tide of mediocrity" was threatening the nation's ability to compete in the global economy. The report put education reform at the top of the national agenda and placed a new emphasis on bolstering academic standards and academic requirements, improving teacher competency, and raising student achievement. The new emphasis on achievement and results was integrated into ESEA's 1988 reauthorization. Chapter 1 was revised to require states to specify academic achievement goals for eligible students, to identify those schools that were not meeting the specified outcomes, and to develop improvement plans for underperforming schools (McGuinn, 2006). Another significant change allowed more schools to use Chapter 1 funds for schoolwide projects, in place of the pull-out services that had predominated in the past (Jennings, 2000).

When President George H. W. Bush took office in 1989, pledging to be an "education president," he pushed for even greater emphasis on outcomes such as higher achievement test scores. After his first proposal for education legislation became bogged down in Congress, Bush called upon the nation's governors, together with the CEOs of major American corporations, to attend a seminal education summit in Charlottesville, Virginia, symbolically on the grounds that housed "Mr. Jefferson's University, the University of Virginia" (Cross, 2004).

The Charlottesville summit was a defining moment for future federal education policy. Governors with strong education agendas in their own states, such as Bill Clinton, Richard Riley, and Lamar Alexander, used this opportunity to guide the federal agenda. The outcome of the summit was a basic agreement that a small working group, which included Governor Clinton, would write national education goals based on the topics discussed at the summit. Following their recommendations, Bush announced the following six education goals for the year 2000 in his 1990 State of the Union address:

1. All children in America will start school ready to learn;
2. The high school graduation rate will increase to at least 90%;
3. Students in grades 4, 8, and 12 will be competent in English, mathematics, science, foreign languages, civics and government, economics, arts, history, and geography;
4. Every school will be free of drugs, violence, firearms, and alcohol, and will offer a disciplined learning environment;
5. U.S. students will be the first in the world in mathematics and science achievement; and
6. Every adult will be literate and will possess the knowledge and skills necessary to compete in a global economy. (McGuinn, 2006, pp. 61–62)

Each goal had associated objectives, many of which specified the inputs necessary to achieve the output goals, but these received much less attention than the goals themselves (Cross, 2004). After announcing these highly ambitious goals—which were also adopted by the National Governors Association—Bush created the National Education Goals Panel in July 1990 to monitor and report on progress (Cross, 2004; McGuinn, 2006).

Although Goals 2000 emerged from a bipartisan consensus, there were strong disagreements between the parties on what exactly the goals meant and how they should be implemented. Democrats tended to see the national goals as a means for highlighting the need for increased federal spending, while Republicans favored strong accountability measures (but with limited federal control) to change the behavior of administrators and teachers (McGuinn, 2006). "Many became convinced that the vague national goals would have to be supplemented by more specific national standards and tests in order to push states forward in their reform efforts and to provide a yardstick against which such efforts could be measured" (p. 62).

Bush tried to enact a moderate bill, called "America 2000," to implement the national goals, but his attempt foundered in the face of opposition from Democrats who argued that the bill lacked sufficient funding and from conservative Republicans who opposed national tests and increased federal involvement (DeBray, 2006). The bill did, however, provide the blueprint for reform legislation, and, in addition, it prompted Secretary of Education Lamar Alexander to use discretionary funds to provide grants to professional organizations to develop subject-matter standards. Although the standards were entirely voluntary, many states and local districts adopted them or used them to guide the development of their own standards (Cross, 2004).

The Charlottesville summit and the resulting Goals 2000 did, therefore, help establish the standards-based reform movement that was embraced by most of the states in the mid-1990s. Standards-based reform is built around substantive content standards in English, mathematics, social studies, and other major subject areas. Ideally, these content standards are set at sufficiently high cognitive levels to meet the competitive standards of the global economy, and they are premised on the assumption that virtually all students can meet these high expectations, if given sufficient opportunities and resources. Once content standards have been established, every other aspect of the education system—including teacher training, teacher certification, curriculum frameworks, textbooks and other instructional materials, and student assessments—should be revamped to conform to these standards in order to create a coherent system that will result in significant improvements in achievement for all students (Fuhrman, 1993; Rothman, 1995). Although the quality varied, by 1994, 42 states had developed or were in the process of developing content standards, and 30 were developing performance standards (DeBray, 2006).

President Bill Clinton came into office in 1993 after serving as a strong education governor in Arkansas and being a key player in codifying the national education goals adopted by President Bush and the National Governors Association. In early 1994, he decided to revive Bush's America 2000 plan in a separate bill, now known as the Goals 2000: Educate America Act, prior to the reauthorization of ESEA, so that it could serve as a blueprint to focus all federal education programs on national standards (McGuinn, 2006). The original proposal called for states to submit their standards to the U.S. Department of Education for approval before receiving Goals 2000 funding. It also called for the creation of an Opportunity to Learn Commission that would recommend the levels of funding necessary to achieve academic improvements (McGuinn, 2006). Both Republicans and Democrats, however, feared that these provisions would result in limited flexibility and expensive mandates (Rothman, 1993). As a result, the final bill was watered down to include only voluntary general national standards and a modest amount of funding for states to develop their own standards.

Perhaps the most controversial aspect of the law, even in its heavily compromised final version, was the inclusion of modified provisions for "opportunity to learn standards" (OTLs). The act called for voluntary national school delivery standards to be developed by a National Education and Standards Improvement Council (NESIC) that states could choose to adopt. Alternatively, states could develop their own OTLs in conjunction with their own content and student performance standards. The statute defined the opportunity to learn concept as "the criteria for, and the basis of, assessing the sufficiency or quality of the resources, practices, and conditions necessary at each level of the education system. . . . to provide all students with the opportunity to learn the material in voluntary national content standards or State content standards" (Goals 2000, 1994 , § 3.a (7)).

Clinton renewed his efforts to promote national standards-based reform in connection with the 1994 reauthorization of the ESEA (which returned to the original term of Title I for the main section dealing with funding and programs for economically disadvantaged students). Based on the school improvement strategy outlined in the Goals 2000 bill, the president now sought to use the leverage of Title I's hefty funding to ensure that disadvantaged students in Title I schools made substantial progress toward meeting the challenging content standards and performance assessments that states were applying to all other children in the state (McGuinn, 2006). The new reauthorization proposal, known as the Goals 2000: Improving America's Schools Act (IASA), moved away from the ESEA's traditional focus on input equity and stressed accountability for results. It required states to develop content and performance standards for *all* children and to align achievement tests with these standards. At the same time, the IASA aimed to target Title I money to the neediest students more effectively by requiring districts to rank schools and provide funds to those with a 75% or higher poverty rate first (Cross, 2004; DeBray, 2006). These changes reduced the number of low-poverty schools (under 35% poor students) receiving Title I funds from 49% in 1993 to 36% in 1999. Over the same time period, the number of high-poverty schools (75% or more poor students) receiving Title I funds increased from 79% to 95% (DeBray, 2006).

The final version of the IASA included a number of important accountability innovations. In exchange for Title I grants, states were required to develop school improvement plans based on high content and performance standards. Assessments aligned with the content standards had to be administered at some time between grades 3 and 5 and again between grades 6 and 9 and grades 10 and 12. States were required to establish benchmarks for "adequate yearly progress" that Title I students would need to make toward meeting the standards. Performance on the assessments would be disaggregated by race, gender, disability, limited-English proficiency status, migrant status, and economic status. Schools identified as needing improvement would be required to undertake specific improvement activities and would be subject to corrective action if sufficient improvement did not occur within 2 years.

Shortly after the IASA was signed into law, Republicans took control of both the House and the Senate in the 1994 midterm elections, beginning 2 years of partisan battles over the appropriate federal role in education. The 104th Congress was committed to change and quickly introduced its Contract with America, which called for massive tax cuts and the elimination of numerous government programs and agencies; the Department of Education was a prime target for these cutbacks. Republicans succeeded in passing several amendments to Goals 2000, among the most significant of which were the repeal of federal authority to establish opportunity-to-learn standards and the dismantling of the National Education Standards and Improvement Council. Although the Republican Congress succeeded in weakening aspects of Goals 2000, Clinton and the Senate Democrats managed to maintain the core provisions and funding for the IASA with strong support from the business community and the National Governors Association (Cross, 2004; McGuinn, 2006). After Clinton's victory in the 1996 presidential election, Republican leaders modified their approach from fighting a federal role in education to participating in the conversation about how to make education more effective. The ESEA was next scheduled for reauthorization in 1999, but with the 2000 presidential election looming, the act was not reauthorized on schedule for the first time in its almost 35-year history, setting the stage for the most recent reauthorization: NCLB.

POLITICS, COMPROMISES, AND THE EMERGENCE OF NCLB

In 2000, for the first time in U.S. history, education issues dominated a presidential election, with voters ranking education as their most important priority. Both the Republican candidate, George W. Bush, and the Democratic candidate, Al Gore, campaigned on platforms that included a strong federal role in education and emphasized raising student achievement through high standards and accountability. Traditionally, education had been a core issue for the Democrats, but because of his experience with a standards-based reform program as governor of Texas and his political judgment that Republicans needed to speak to domestic issues on which they had traditionally been at a disadvantage, Bush convinced his party to adopt a comprehensive centrist federal education plan that put Gore on the defensive (McGuinn, 2006). Bush eked out a narrow electoral victory, but Democrats gained seats (and leverage) in Congress. Determined to enact an ESEA reauthorization bill that would be strong on standards and accountability, Bush signaled to the Democratic leadership that he was willing to work with them to enact a bipartisan bill.

Congressional leaders were given the lead role in drafting the bill based on a 30-page legislative brief entitled "No Child Left Behind," which Bush submitted to Congress in January 2001. The key elements of Bush's proposal were based on the accountability system that had been used in Texas. These included increasing accountability through annual assessments, focusing federal funds on programs and practices with demonstrated effectiveness, giving states and school districts increased flexibility in exchange for results, and "empowering" parents through information and choice (Bush, 2001a).

One of the Bush blueprint's key components provided that students in schools demonstrating consistent low performance would be entitled to use the schools' Title I funds to transfer to higher-performing public or private schools, essentially a voucher program funded with Title I monies. Traditional Democratic constituencies, such as teachers' unions, education groups, and most civil rights organizations, had been adamantly opposed to vouchers for the preceding 2 decades, even as conservative groups lobbied for them. In a sign of his willingness to make significant concessions to get a strong bill enacted, the president signaled early on that vouchers would be off the table as a sign of "realism and goodwill" (McGuinn, 2006). Conservative Republicans' attempts to add voucher amendments to the House bill failed, but resulted in Democrats' begrudging acceptance of a supplemental educational services provision that allowed Title I dollars to be used for tutorial services provided by both nonprofit and for-profit entities, during nonschool hours when a school failed to demonstrate improvement after 3 years (DeBray, 2006; McGuinn, 2006).

The addition of annual testing requirements also was a thorny issue to resolve. Bush's blueprint proposed annual reading and math assessments for every student in grades 3–8. Virtually all states had made progress in developing content standards and assessments in the 1990s, but only 15 states had a system that precisely fit those specifications (DeBray, 2006). Many Republicans objected to imposing this heavy testing regime on the states; many Democrats opposed the strong reliance on testing altogether. Some Republicans were also concerned about a provision that required states to administer the National Assessment of Educational Progress (NAEP) to corroborate state achievement results. This smacked of national testing, an issue on which they had vigorously fought President Clinton. To assuage Republicans' fears, Bush emphasized another key component of his plan: flexibility. States had the freedom to select and design their own assessments, with the only requirement being that achievement levels be comparable from year to year. The final version of the bill also limited the NAEP testing to every other year. Ultimately, the desire to support the president's education agenda won out over most Republicans' uneasiness with testing (Cross, 2004; McGuinn, 2006).

One of the Democrats' major concerns was the level of funding. The president's original proposal included only a 3% increase in

ESEA funding. Ted Kennedy, chairman of the Senate committee with jurisdiction over education, and George Miller, the ranking Democrat on the House committee, made it clear that they would not use their influence to encourage other Democrats to support the bill unless Republicans agreed to major funding increases well above that level. As Miller put it, "Reform without adequate funding is cruelty" (DeBray, 2006, p. 113). The final bill provided for a 20% increase in ESEA authorized funding (Riddle, 2006b; McGuinn, 2006), including a $5 billion increase in Title I funding for the next fiscal year (DeBray, 2006).

Accountability was the other major stumbling block. Although lawmakers from both sides agreed that there should be sanctions for continuously low-performing schools, many Democrats opposed the act's demanding adequate yearly progress (AYP) requirements. Apprehension grew when a report from the Congressional Research Service indicated that the vast majority of schools in three major states would be labeled as "failing" under the proposed AYP definition—a politically unacceptable outcome. After months of negotiations, Congress settled on modifications to the AYP formula meant to allay these concerns (Commission on No Child Left Behind, 2007; DeBray, 2006).

Despite the resolve of President Bush and the leadership in both parties to enact a bill, both conservative groups (e.g., the Fordham Foundation, the Heritage Foundation, and Excellence for Parents, Children, and Teachers [EXPECT]) and establishment educational organizations (e.g., the American Association of School Administrators, the National School Boards Association, and the National Conference of State Legislators) began to express their unease with the proposed legislation. Among the concerns that began to surface were that the states might lower their proficiency standards to avoid sanctions and that achieving NCLB's goal of 100% proficiency in 12 years might prove impossible (DeBray, 2006; Cross, 2004). Nevertheless, there was still strong public support for accountability and testing and continued endorsement from the Governors Association and the major business organizations. Moreover, the final conference negotiations took place in the aftermath of the September 11, 2001, terrorist attacks and the leadership of both parties wanted to pass a bipartisan education bill that could "reassure a jittery public by providing a symbol of a unified and functioning government" (McGuinn, 2006, p. 176). Consequently, the compromise bill that emerged from the conference committee was approved by overwhelming majorities in both houses of Congress in December 2001.

SUMMARY OF NCLB's STRUCTURE AND MAJOR PROVISIONS

The version of NCLB ultimately passed by both the House and Senate represented a bipartisan compromise that encompassed a convergence of two historical themes: Title I's commitment to providing resources for the purpose of promoting equal educational opportunity and the standards movement's emphasis on high expectations for all and accountability for results. NCLB established the ambitious and heretofore unheard-of goal that all students reach proficiency in reading and math by the 2013–2014 school year. President Bush described NCLB's acceptance of this goal as an "exercise in hope," explaining, "When we raise academic standards, children raise their academic sights. When children are regularly tested, teachers know where and how to improve. When scores are known to parents, parents are empowered to push for change. When accountability for our schools is real, the results for our children are real" (Bush, 2001b).

Many of the key elements of NCLB—challenging content standards and performance assessments, periodic testing, AYP benchmarks, disaggregation of data, and corrective action for failing schools—had already been incorporated into the ESEA through the Improving America's Schools Act of 1994. But because enforcement of the IASA was largely ineffectual, states were at varying levels of compliance when NCLB took effect in 2002. The key differences between IASA and NCLB are the following:

- The mandatory nature of the 12-year proficiency target
- Calibration of AYP indicators to that mandated target
- Heavier sanctions for schools and school districts that do not make adequate progress toward meeting the 100% proficiency standard
- Indications that the federal government would use a heavier hand in enforcing the new law

A very brief review of the main elements of NCLB highlights the more demanding nature of its accountability requirements and of the consequences for success or failure.

Content Standards

NCLB requires each state to complete its development of "challenging" academic content standards in reading/language arts, math, and science. These standards must specify what students should know and be able to do at each grade level; the high school standards should describe what will be expected of students by the time they graduate. States are expected to hold *all* elementary and high school students accountable to these high standards of learning. Decisions about the actual substance of these standards, however, are left to individual states.

Achievement Standards

In order to determine to what extent students are meeting the learning expectations put forth in the content standards, states also must develop academic achievement standards (called "performance standards" in the IASA) representing varying levels of proficiency. At a minimum, states must define three achievement levels: basic, proficient, and advanced. Decisions about the assessment cut scores that separate one level of proficiency from another are also left to the states.

Testing

NCLB requires schools to administer "high-quality" reading and math assessments annually in grades 3–8 and once in high school by the 2004–2005 school year. By the 2007–2008 school year, schools must also administer science assessments at least once in grades 3–5, 6–9, and 10–12. Because the results of these tests are used to make accountability determinations about how well students are mastering the material delineated by the state at the levels specified in the achievement standards, the assessments are expected to reflect the depth and breadth of the state's content standards. Assessments should be valid and reliable for the purposes for which they will be used, and should be consistent with recognized professional and technical standards. A sample of fourth and eighth graders in each state must participate in the National Assessment of Educational Progress (NAEP) every other year to provide a comparison point for the results on the states' own tests.

All children are subject to NCLB's testing requirements, including special education students and students with limited English proficiency (LEP) (also referred to as English language learners, or ELLs). The testing requirements for special education and LEP students have been modified in response to concerns about these students' special needs. In 2003, the Department of Education announced that up to 1% of all students or 10% of special education students (those with the most severe cognitive disabilities) could be exempt from the regular testing requirements. As of 2005, an additional 2% of students with severe learning disabilities could take tests specifically geared toward their abilities. In 2004, the Department of Education allowed LEP students who have been in the United States for less than 1 year to be exempt from the reading assessment, although they must take math assessments in their native language and an English language proficiency exam.

Disaggregation of Test Scores

In order to assess the extent to which different populations of students are achieving proficiency on the learning goals, states must report disaggregated test score data for four different subgroups. These subgroups include all racial/ethnic groups present in the school, economically disadvantaged students, special education students, and LEP students. With the exception of those students excluded due to cognitive disabilities, severe learning disabilities, or having been in the country for less than 1 year, at least 95% of students in each subgroup must take the exam. This requirement is waived if a subgroup is so small that the reporting of its results would yield statistically unreliable information or would reveal identifiable information about the student. Depending on the size of the school, subgroups— as small as five to as large as 100—do not need to be reported. (Test score data must also be disaggregated by gender and migrant status, but these subgroups do not contribute to the evaluation of schools and districts under NCLB's accountability system.)

Adequate Yearly Progress

Under NCLB, schools and districts must demonstrate that they are making adequate yearly progress (AYP), overall and for each subgroup, toward the state-designated performance goals and toward proficiency for all by 2014. If any one subgroup does not meet its improvement target (or if less than 95% of the students within that subgroup take the test), the school does not make AYP. There is also a "safe harbor" provision that allows a school to make AYP if it reduces the percentage of students who are not proficient by at least 10% from the previous year. This applies to the school as a whole, as well as to each subgroup.

Each state makes two determinations that affect the calculation of AYP for schools and districts within the state. The first is the cut score at which a student is deemed "proficient." The second is the rate at which a state expects students to make progress toward the 2014 universal proficiency goal. While the Department of Education requires movement toward the 100% proficiency target, the improvement does not have to be consistent. Some states, therefore, have "back-loaded" student performance goals, requiring only minimal growth in the percentage of students deemed proficient in the first few years of implementation, but necessitating dramatic gains between 2010 and 2014 (Hess, 2006; Linn, 2003).

Consequences

Embedded in NCLB are consequences for schools that do not meet AYP. These consequences apply to all Title I schools, but states can choose whether to apply the various interventions and sanctions to schools that do not receive any Title I funds. The consequences required by NCLB vary in their severity based on the number of years a school has missed its AYP goals. After 2 consecutive years of not meeting AYP, a school is designated "in need of improvement." Students attending a school in need of improvement must be given the option to transfer to another school within the district, and the school itself must submit a school improvement plan that includes certain specified elements, such as increased professional development and greater parental involvement. If the school fails to make AYP for a third consecutive year, it is required to use its Title I funds to provide students with the opportunity to access "supplemental educational services" in the form of tutoring or other academic support. In the fourth consecutive year of not making AYP, the school must implement "corrective action," such as replacing certain staff, adopting a new curriculum, or extending the school day. Finally, in the fifth year of insufficient progress, the school would be identified for restructuring and be required to develop a new governance structure, such as reopening as a charter school, replacing a majority of the staff, hiring a private management company to run the school, or being taken over by the state.

Input Components

In addition to the components of NCLB's accountability system, which focus on outcomes, NCLB makes two provisions that relate to inputs: "highly qualified" teachers and "scientifically based" research.

Highly Qualified Teachers. The highly qualified teacher provision of NCLB is meant to address the differential in teaching quality between advantaged and disadvantaged schools and districts. This component of the law required states to ensure that all students be taught by "highly qualified teachers" by the 2005–2006 school year, a deadline that has since been extended. The precise definition of *highly qualified* is left to the states, although NCLB does set some basic parameters. To be considered highly qualified, all teachers must be certified by the state. Teachers must also demonstrate subject-matter competency. At the elementary level, this constitutes earning at least a bachelor's degree and passing a test in basic elementary subject areas. At the middle and high school levels, teachers must pass a state academic test in the subject area in which they teach or have an academic major or graduate degree relevant to each subject they teach. Veteran teachers can also demonstrate subject mastery by meeting a state-designated "high objective uniform state standard of evaluation" (HOUSSE). A state's HOUSSE standards might consider a veteran teacher's professional development, performance evaluation, or classroom experience in lieu of a subject-matter test or academic coursework.

Scientifically Based Research. NCLB also includes a provision designed to improve the quality of educational programs and practices by limiting federal funding to those that rely on *scientifically based research*, defined in the law as "research that involves the application of rigorous, systematic, and objective procedures to obtain reliable and valid knowledge relevant to education activities and programs" (NCLB, 2001, § 7801 [37]). This component of NCLB is notable for its implications for instructional methods and curricular materials, areas of education that have historically been far outside the bounds of federal intervention. The most far-reaching effect of NCLB's insistence on scientifically based research has been its application to the Reading First Program, where a number of established programs, and especially many that are not phonics-based, have been deemed ineligible for federal funding (Pressley, 2005).

Funding

The final version of NCLB provided for an authorization level that through year to year increases would raise Title I spending by 2007 by almost $16 billion above its actual appropriation level in 2001 (Riddle, 2006b). Although in the early years, approximately 75% of the authorized increase was actually appropriated, by 2007, actual Title I appropriations totaled only 51% of the authorized amount for that year. In fact, since 2004, Title I funding has remained flat at approximately $12.8 billion; this still represents approximately a $4 billion (or 45%) increase in spending over the 2001 level (Riddle, 2006b).

Title I funds are allocated to states and school districts on the basis of funding allocation formulas. Two of those formulas, targeted assistance grants and education finance incentive grants, were amended by NCLB to increase the proportion of funds channeled to high-poverty districts. Under these two formulas, only school districts with at least 5% disadvantaged children are eligible for grants (Fagan & Kober, 2004). The targeted grant formula is calculated so that the amount of the grant per disadvantaged student increases as the concentration of poverty in the district increases. Education finance incentive grants increase the amount of funds available to school districts in states where per pupil expenditures are equitable. All increases in Title I appropriations above the 2001 baseline of $8.76 billion must be allocated through these two formulas (Fagan & Kober, 2004). Thus, school districts that have been eligible for Title I funds in the past may no longer be eligible under the more targeted formulas, resulting in reduced funding for them, even as NCLB demands improved school performance (Center on Education Policy, 2006).

NCLB substantially increased the federal role in overseeing progress toward definitive results and raised ESEA appropriations. However, no attempt was made to correlate the amount of federal funding (or the amount of current state funding) with the level of resources that would actually be required to meet NCLB's outcome expectations. Further, with the exception of specific requirements for "highly qualified" teachers, and the abstract emphasis on "scientifically based research," NCLB does not focus on how to ensure that schools, and especially the many schools designated as needing improvement under the act, have the capacity to provide meaningful educational opportunity for their students. The next chapter will propose an approach for dealing with this critical shortcoming.

CHAPTER 4

Meaningful Educational Opportunity: A Vital and Viable Mission for NCLB

The previous chapters have made clear that the roots of America's achievement gaps are significant opportunity gaps endured by millions of low-income and minority students. NCLB is falling far short of achieving its ambitious goals because it mainly concentrates on accountability for results but largely neglects the resources and supports that students need to achieve those results.

The drafters of the law were not unmindful of the importance of providing meaningful opportunities for students. The law begins with a clear statement of two primary purposes: 1) to ensure that all children have a "fair, equal and significant opportunity to obtain a high quality education" and 2) to ensure that all children reach, at a minimum, "proficiency on challenging State academic achievement standards" by the 2013–2014 school year (NCLB, 2001, § 6301). Although the drafters recognized initially the importance of both of these objectives, the law's actual provisions largely ignore the first goal—opportunity—and skew heavily toward carrying out the second goal—accountability.

In the compromises that led to the law's enactment, heavy emphasis was put on the mandate that all children must be proficient in challenging state standards by 2014, and on achieving adequate yearly progress toward that goal. Extensive sanctions are set forth for schools and districts that fail to achieve AYP targets for any or all of the subgroups covered by the law, but little is said about the actual capacity of the schools to reach these goals. Our commonsense position is that to overcome achievement gaps we need to restore vital balance to the act: The nation needs to close its opportunity gaps in order to attain its achievement goals.

Over the past few years, NCLB has, in effect, tried to achieve universal proficiency without giving proper emphasis and attention to this critical corresponding requirement to provide all students with the tools they need to reach this goal. Mandates and motivation will not result in significant reductions in the achievement gaps, let alone in full proficiency, if meaningful educational opportunities are not first provided, especially to children living in poverty. To bring new effectiveness, feasibility, and credibility to NCLB, it is critical to flesh out the law's now-neglected requirement that all children be provided with a "fair, equal and significant opportunity to obtain a high quality education." Specifically, we recommend that, to rectify the imbalance in its implementation of the two major purpose clauses of the act, Congress should revise the NCLB to set aside, at least until the next reauthorization date, its timetable for achieving high proficiency levels and require instead that by 2014 the states provide *meaningful educational opportunity* for all their public school children.

It is important to note that NCLB requires opportunities that are not only "fair" and "equal," but that also are "significant." Although the predecessor statutes had called for "fair" and "equal" opportunities, the inclusion of the word *significant* was an innovation that was added to the NCLB in the last phase of the congressional negotiations. *Significant* is a synonym for *meaningful* (*American Heritage Dictionary*, 1997). Given the basic equivalence of these terms, we prefer to use the latter. Many state legislatures and state courts have given substance to the term *meaningful educational opportunity* by using it in connection with requirements for concrete resources, programs, and practices that will provide tangible benefits for children.

As discussed in Chapter 1, the courts, the Congress, and the state legislatures have made their greatest strides toward implementing equal educational opportunity when they have defined exactly what such an opportunity entails in particular contexts. The Supreme Court was most effective in implementing equal educational opportunity when it adopted as a clear goal the dismantling of *de jure* segregation in Southern schools and insisted on immediate, concrete desegregation plans (*Green v. County School Board*, 1968). Similarly, equal educational opportunity for English language learners got its greatest boost when the Supreme Court insisted that educational services provided to them be "meaningful" (*Lau v. Nichols*, 1974), and Congress, the lower federal courts, and the U.S. Department of Education then articulated in very precise terms the types of services that would meet that requirement. The long history of neglect of children with disabilities ended when Congress specified in clear terms the types of special education and related services that would be provided to meet the individual needs of each of these children through the IDEA and its predecessor statute.

In recent years, the most significant progress in specifying the concrete educational opportunities students require and to which they are entitled has been made in the state court litigations that have challenged the constitutionality of state systems for financing public education. The focus of these litigations for the past 2 decades has been on gaining basic quality educational services for all children. Despite the vagueness of the overarching term *education adequacy* that has come to describe these cases, they have been able to equalize education financing substantially in many states and to promote educational reforms that have raised student achievement significantly because they focus on providing the specific resources that are needed for a decent education. The New York Court of Appeals understood this point when it specifically held in *Campaign for Fiscal Equity v. State of New York* (2003) that the state constitution requires that each child be provided the opportunity for a "meaningful" high school education that included certain "essential" resources such as qualified teachers, small class sizes, and books and other "instrumentalities of learning," and that children must be taught the specific skills that will prepare them to function productively as civic participants capable of voting and serving on juries.

To implement NCLB effectively and to realize the *Brown* vision, then, what is needed at this point is to identify the key elements of meaningful educational opportunity that have been substantiated by educational research and articulated in legal and legislative terms by the courts, Congress, and state legislatures in the past, and to shape them into statutory concepts that can give substance, direction, and coherence to the act. In this chapter, we draw on these resources to define *meaningful educational opportunity* and to develop a statutory framework that encompasses the concept. In the chapters that follow, we will discuss in more detail the essential resources, adequate funding, challenging standards, and mechanisms for building capacity in low-performing schools that are truly needed to provide all students with a meaningful educational opportunity.

DEFINING *MEANINGFUL EDUCATIONAL OPPORTUNITY*

Recognition of the need to delineate and ensure requisite resources and opportunities for all children is not new. Historically, most state educational finance schemes included as the starting point for their allocation formulae "foundation" levels that purported to guarantee schools sufficient funds to provide all of their students with a basic education. Few states, however, actually carried through on that abstract commitment, a failing that the state court education adequacy litigations have sought to rectify. In the 1980s, partially in reaction to *A Nation at Risk* and other reports that claimed that America was losing its competitive edge because of the mediocrity of our schools, states began to press for greater "excellence" in education. They attempted to do this by beefing up teacher certification and curriculum requirements and by adopting stricter requirements for high school diplomas (Rebell, 2002). Although there was little argument against improving the quality of our nation's schools, concerns arose within the civil rights community that "excellence" might be pursued at the expense of "equity," and that this new emphasis on making the nation economically competitive might displace the national commitment to implementing *Brown*'s equal educational opportunity mandate. Many worried that raising the bar for success would leave those who were already struggling even further behind.

This issue was brought to a head by a legal challenge lodged against Florida's newly strengthened graduation requirements by a class of minority students. These plaintiffs claimed that in order to graduate from high school, they were being required to pass a literacy examination that tested them on material they had never been taught in their schools. The U.S. Court of Appeals for the Fifth Circuit held that as a matter of constitutional due process of law, the students did have a right to be tested only on material that they actually had been taught (*Debra P. v. Turlington*, 1981). The Court specifically held that "the test was probably a good test of what the students should know but not necessarily of what they had an *opportunity to learn*" (p. 405, n. 11, emphasis added).

As we explained in Chapter 3, President George H. W. Bush, and all 50 governors, meeting at the 1989 National Education Summit in Charlottesville, Virginia, sought to provide coherence and sustainability to the excellence movement by emphasizing the need for specific outcomes toward which the educational improvements should aim. They also stressed the importance of preparing *all* of the nation's children to meet these educational outcomes. The drive for excellence was now combined with a commitment to equity and transformed into a comprehensive reform centered on the development of challenging academic content standards that all students would be expected to master and around which teacher training, curriculum development, and student assessments would be oriented.

LEARNING FROM "OPPORTUNITY TO LEARN"

The original proponents of standards-based reform also assumed that a commitment to provide the resources and supports necessary to give all students an opportunity to learn the new challenging standards would be an integral part of the standards-based reforms. Requirements for students to meet challenging new outcome standards were, therefore, balanced with "school delivery" or "opportunity to learn" standards designed to ensure that each school has the capacity to bring its students to high levels of achievement (O'Day & Smith, 1993). A federal task force, established to propose mechanisms for implementing the "Goals 2000" that emerged from the national summit, explained why "opportunity to learn" (OTL) standards should be considered a necessary part of any standards-based reform approach:

> If not accompanied by measures to ensure equal opportunity to learn, national content and performance standards could help widen the achievement gap between the advantaged and the disadvantaged in our society. If national content and performance standards and assessments are not accompanied by clear school delivery standards and policy measures designed to afford all students an equal opportunity to learn, the concerns about diminished equity could easily be realized. Standards and assessments must be accompanied by policies that provide access for all students to high quality resources, including appropriate instructional materials and well-prepared teachers. (National Council on Education Standards and Testing, 1992, quoted in Darling-Hammond, 1993, p. 38)

The Clinton administration's original Goals 2000 legislative proposal included provisions for national opportunity to learn standards that would be developed by a National Education and Standards Council (NESIC). This proposal met substantial opposition. Critics, including legislators and governors, were concerned that federal oversight of states' efforts to provide opportunities to learn would limit state flexibility and impose excessive costs. As noted in Chapter 3, the concept was included as part of the Goals 2000 legislation enacted in 1994, but in a watered-down form that omitted any federal compulsion and instead called for "voluntary" national school delivery standards that states could choose to adopt or state opportunity to learn standards that states could voluntarily develop in conjunction with their own content and student performance standards.

Even this minimal, voluntary form of opportunity to learn standards engendered strong opposition. In addition to fears that the voluntary standards might someday become mandatory (McDonnell, 1995), controversy developed over the meaning of the vaguely defined opportunity to learn concept and whether enough was known about which resources and which practices and conditions were necessary to provide meaningful opportunities, especially to children from disadvantaged backgrounds (McDonnell, 1995; Porter, 1995). Questions were also raised about the capacity of state education departments and school districts to implement these standards (Elmore & Fuhrman, 1995). Whether or not feasible opportunity to learn standards could have been developed and implemented through the NESIC mechanism remains unknown, since the opportunity to learn requirements were promptly revoked by Congress after the Republicans took control later in 1994 and these requirements never took effect (McGuinn, 2006).

Since Congress rejected the opportunity to learn standards in the mid-1990s, there has been no systematic effort to develop national policies to provide young Americans with the meaningful educational opportunities necessary for real progress toward closing achievement gaps. States have felt no federal pressure or incentive to deliver any particular level of resources or school quality, and the enormous inequities between schools in affluent communities and schools in low-income communities have persisted. NCLB's lack of emphasis on necessary resources and learning opportunities for students has, as the NCEST Task Force predicted, significantly limited the ability of disadvantaged students to meet the challenging new state standards and has perpetuated the achievement gaps. It is time, therefore, to revive the discussion about resources and opportunities for students to learn and to rectify the perilous imbalance between accountability and opportunity in the current NCLB design.

A focus on meaningful educational opportunity in 2007 need not and should not, however, revive the contentious debate over the opportunity to learn standards of the 1990s. The question of what resources and opportunities students would need to meet challenging state standards was an abstraction in 1993. Now, 15 years later, these needs have become concrete realities: the national experience with NCLB over the past 5 years has demonstrated the importance of facing this issue, and advances in research, the emergence of sophisticated cost study methodologies, and the vast experience of the state courts in grappling with this issue in 30 fiscal equity and education adequacy cases around the country now provide an experience base for defining and providing the resources and opportunities that children actually need.

THE COMPONENTS OF
MEANINGFUL EDUCATIONAL OPPORTUNITY

State by state, courts in adequacy cases are specifying the necessary components of a meaningful educational opportunity and are identifying the resources necessary to provide it. It is time that federal education policy apply similar concepts and rights to *all* students on a national basis. Meaningful educational opportunity as the concept has been developed in the state courts includes the opportunity to be taught in accordance with a challenging set of academic standards that reflect the knowledge and skills that students need to function productively in the 21st century and to be provided with the essential resources that are required to develop the necessary knowledge and skills. It also requires policymakers to ensure adequate funding so that these essentials are available to all students and to ensure a strong system of accountability to make certain that these dollars translate into demonstrable improvements in student learning. We will deal with the funding and accountability issues in Chapters 6 and 8. Here we will discuss in detail the broad-based knowledge and skills that students need to learn and the essential resources that must be in place to give them a reasonable chance to do so.

Necessary Knowledge and Skills

A meaningful educational opportunity must be defined in relation to the full range of knowledge and skills that America's students need to function successfully as citizens and workers in the 21st century. The original Goals 2000 had made clear that if American schools were to meet the global challenge, students would need to be competent not only in reading, math, and science, but also in foreign languages, civics and government, economics, arts, history, and geography (McGuinn, 2006). NCLB, however, puts forth a very limited definition of schooling outcomes; the law requires each state to adopt "challenging academic content standards and challenging student academic achievement standards" (NCLB, 2001, § 6311(b) (1)), but the subject areas covered by the testing requirements are limited to mathematics, reading or language arts, and science.

NCLB's demanding AYP requirements and the sanctions that are tied to them, however, apply only to test results in mathematics and reading. (Students must now be tested in science, but those results are not counted for AYP purposes.) This narrow focus on a very few subject areas has begun to restrict the time and attention that schools are giving to subjects other than math and reading, particularly in schools serving low-income and minority students. (We will discuss this problem in further detail in Chapter 7.) Thus, even if students attain proficiency in the few core areas emphasized by NCLB, it is far from clear that they will, in fact, be receiving a meaningful educational opportunity or that the full scope of the achievement gaps between advantaged and disadvantaged students will have been addressed.

Defining the broad range of skills that students need to function effectively has, however, been a major concern of the state courts that have considered constitutional challenges to state education finance systems in recent years. In order to determine whether students are receiving a "sound basic education," a "thorough and efficient education," or a "high-quality" education, as required by clauses in the various state constitutions, the courts have had to define these terms, and, in doing so, the starting point for their analyses has often been a thorough consideration of the basic purposes of a public education.

The state courts that have focused in depth on these issues have, in fact, arrived at a general consensus regarding the goals and expected outcome of public education. This state court consensus holds that a basic quality education is one that provides students with the essential skills they need to function productively as civic participants in a democratic society and to compete effectively in the 21st-century global economy (Rebell & Wolff, 2006). The types of knowledge and skills that students need to be effective citizens and workers, as articulated in the state court adequacy cases, are:

- Sufficient ability to read, write, and speak the English language and sufficient knowledge of fundamental mathematics and physical science to enable them to function in a complex and rapidly changing society
- Sufficient fundamental knowledge of social studies—that is, geography, history, and basic economic and political systems— to enable them to make informed choices with regard to issues that affect them personally or affect their communities, states, and nation
- Sufficient intellectual tools to evaluate complex issues and sufficient social and communication skills to work well with others and communicate ideas to a group
- Sufficient academic and vocational skills to enable them to compete on an equal basis with others in further formal education or gainful employment in contemporary society (Rebell & Wolff, 2006)

These court findings are largely consistent with the types of educational outcomes that American schools have historically been expected to generate. Rothstein, Wilder, and Jacobsen (2007) recently identified the historic goals of education in America and confirmed their continuing significance by polling representative groups of educators and the general public on their current expectations of the skills and knowledge that an educated person needs for the 21st century. Based on their historical analysis and polling data, Rothstein and colleagues assert that schooling must continue to ensure successful outcomes in *all* of the following categories:

- Basic academic skills in core subjects
- Critical thinking and problem solving
- Social skills and work ethic
- Citizenship and community responsibility
- Physical health
- Emotional health
- The arts and literature
- Preparation for skilled work (Rothstein et al., 2007)

To serve our students and our country fully, the national goals and expectations expressed in federal education policy should similarly be grounded in the context of real 21st-century needs and identified in these broad terms. Proficiency must be defined in accordance with this full range of knowledge and skills; resources need to be provided in amounts that will allow students successfully to meet expectations in all of these areas; and states and schools should be held accountable for this range of expectations, rather than just for core reading and math skills.

Comprehensive Educational Essentials

The state courts have also considered in detail the specific resources that students need for a meaningful opportunity to obtain a basic quality education. As we listed in Chapter 2, the state court consensus identifies the following school-based resources as essential for acquiring the basic knowledge and skills described in the previous section:

- Effective teachers, principals, and other personnel
- Appropriate class sizes
- Adequate school facilities
- Rich and rigorous curricula

- A full platform of services, including guidance services, after-school, summer, and weekend programming, tutoring, and additional time on task for students from backgrounds of poverty
- Appropriate programs and services for English language learners and students with disabilities
- Instrumentalities of learning, including, but not limited to, up-to-date textbooks, libraries, laboratories, and computers
- A safe, orderly learning environment (Rebell & Wolff, 2006)

This list of constitutional education essentials is, of course, based on the services students need during the years and the times they are in school; constitutional requirements relate only to student needs during their compulsory schooling years, typically from ages 6 to 16. To reach our national goal of improving proficiency for all children and closing the achievement gaps, however, we must broaden our conception of educational essentials. Depending on their circumstances, children will require different levels and types of resources, programs, and services in order to make their educational opportunity meaningful. As we have pointed out, children who come from poverty, who are English language learners, and/or have disabilities have additional requirements both in and out of school.

As Chapter 2 describes, for some children, health, home, and family- and community/neighborhood-related factors create substantial barriers to learning. Further, as psychologist Edmund W. Gordon (2005, Gordon & Bridglall, 2006), among others, has emphasized, students who lack access to other institutions, such as libraries, museums, faith-based institutions, media outlets, offices, factories, and farms, miss out-of-school learning experiences that are also vital for learning. The state defendants in many of the education adequacy cases agreed that, because of these factors, students from backgrounds of concentrated poverty cannot achieve at the challenging levels required by the state's academic standards. However, they used these truths not to announce that they, therefore, would make intensive efforts to deal with these problems. Rather, they argued that because state constitutional clauses do not cover out-of-school needs, states should be exempted from providing adequate *school-based* resources that the constitutional clauses do cover (Schrag, 2003).

NCLB is not subject to such constraints, and, accordingly, in order to achieve its stated proficiency and achievement gap reduction aims, the act must focus on providing not only basic in-school resources, but also an important complement of out-of-school services, experiences, and opportunities. Specifically, we believe that, in order to provide a meaningful educational opportunity to at-risk children from communities of concentrated poverty, students must be provided, as needed, with specific out-of-school educational essentials, including:

- High-quality early childhood education
- Necessary levels of nutrition and physical activity
- Physical and mental health care
- Home, family, and community support for student academic achievement
- Access to arts, cultural, employment, community service, civic, and other critical nonacademic experiences

Congress has already accepted the basic concept that, in order to benefit from educational opportunities, certain children need special supports and services geared to their individual needs. In the Individuals with Disabilities Education Act, Congress has set forth an extensive—and expensive—panoply of procedural and substantive rights that require school districts to assess the full range of physical, psychological, and emotional issues that may be impeding a child's readiness to learn, and to provide whatever special education and related services the child may require in order to benefit from education. Approximately 13% of the nation's public school students are students with disabilities who are covered by these provisions (Hochschild & Scovronick, 2003), and school districts throughout the country expend billions of dollars each year to meet the needs of these children.

Logic and fairness would dictate that children with educational disadvantages stemming from poverty or English language learner status should similarly be entitled to have the schools prepare an individual education plan (IEP) for them, as it presently does for every child with a disability, that would diagnose their learning difficulties and then prescribe the specific educational supports and related services that are needed to deal with them. We do not make such a recommendation, however, because we believe that extending the IDEA's rigorous regulatory structure to these larger student cohorts would be unreasonable and unworkable.

Nevertheless, the logic that has impelled Congress to take affirmative steps to overcome the impediments to meaningful educational opportunities for millions of students with disabilities should apply equally to the analogous needs of millions of students from backgrounds of concentrated poverty. Accordingly, NCLB should be revised to require states to demonstrate in their plans that adequate and appropriate resources and opportunities in all of the above-stated in-school and out-of-school resource areas are being provided to these students. This approach would allow the states broad discretion to devise methods for identifying the most significant issues and the most cost-effective ways of meeting them. The provision of these services will also necessarily involve a variety of collaborative arrangements with community and governmental agencies, and, clearly, in this area broad discretion to devise and experiment with effective ways to meet children's needs is necessary.

Over the past few decades, numerous initiatives have been implemented to provide out-of-school educational essentials and to coordinate them with in-school services. In Portland, Oregon, for instance, the Schools Uniting Neighborhoods (SUN) initiative joins a range of libraries, neighborhood health clinics, community organizations, and area churches and businesses in an extensive collaboration with more than 50 schools in six districts to develop community schools that extend the school day and serve as "community hubs" in their neighborhoods (Blank, 2004). A major goal is to provide enrichment and recreational opportunities that will connect the curriculum of the in-school and after-school activities for the students. Programs are also provided for parents and other adults in the community. Initial evaluations have indicated a range of positive results, including improved academic performance in reading and math at both the elementary and middle school levels (Iverson, 2005), and improvement in attendance, classroom behavior, homework completion, and class participation (Nave, Woo, Kruger, & Yap, 2006). Similarly, the Harlem Children's Zone (HCZ) project seeks to enhance the quality of life for children and families in one of New York City's neighborhoods that is most devastated by poverty, unemployment, and a paucity of public resources. HCZ runs 15 community centers that provide a comprehensive range of education, health, nutrition, parent education, and early childhood support services to more than 12,500 children and adults, including more than 8,600 at-risk children in a 60-block area in central Harlem.

The need now is to understand how the best of coordinated, comprehensive approaches like these can be made to work in a cost-effective manner to ensure the systematic delivery to public school students of the resources that are most vital for meaningful educational opportunity. This approach to educational policy and practice recognizes the complex relationship between education, class, and poverty, and, while not attempting the total elimination of poverty or the righting of all social and political wrongs, does not ignore their profound effects on children's ability to learn.

REVISING NCLB TO PROMOTE REFORM

As noted in Chapter 3, one of the important predecessors of NCLB was the Goals 2000 legislation, which codified the understandings reached by President George H. W. Bush and the governors who attended the National Education Summit in Charlottesville in 1989. The first of these goals was that "All children in America will start school ready to learn." The bipartisan drafting committee that produced the original version of Goals 2000 had agreed that school readiness had to be the number-one goal and that this goal could not be achieved without a national commitment to provide specific school readiness inputs, such as "all children will have access to high-quality and developmentally appropriate preschool programs that help prepare children for school" (Goals 2000, 1994, § 5812(1) (B) (i)) and that

> children will receive the nutrition, physical activity experiences and health care needed to arrive at school with healthy minds and bodies, and to maintain the mental alertness necessary to be prepared to learn, and the number of low-birth weight babies will be significantly reduced through enhanced prenatal health systems. (Goals, 2000, 1994, § 5812(1) (B) (iii))

The statute that reauthorized Title I later that year, known as the Improving America's Schools Act, reiterated the importance of addressing the need to provide the range of resources required for school readiness, stressed the need for "a fair and equal opportunity [for a] high-quality education for all individuals," and also noted that developments since 1988 had shown, among other things, that "equitable and sufficient resources, particularly as such resources relate to the quality of the teaching force, have an integral relationship to high school achievement" (Improving America's Schools Act, 1994, §1001).

With the exception of its requirement for "highly qualified" teachers, however, NCLB did not further develop these concepts. Instead, the statute put its major emphasis on the accountability and sanction provisions. This reorientation is reflected in the fact that the opening purposes clause of the law, which in previous versions had exclusively stressed "fair and equal opportunity," now added as a second—and, arguably, dominant provision—the emphasis on measurable achievement of proficiency.

The legislative history of the purposes clause further indicates that the original Senate version had included a list of programs and strategies that would have expanded on the opportunity-oriented specifications of purposes of Goals 2000 and the IASA. Specifically, these included items such as:

> (2) providing children an enriched and accelerated educational program, including the use of schoolwide programs or additional services that increase the amount and quality of instructional time. . . .
> (3) promoting schoolwide reform and ensuring access of children . . . to effective instructional strategies and challenging academic content. . . .
> (5) coordinating services under all parts of this title with each other, with other educational services, and to the extent feasible, with other agencies providing services to youth, children, and families;
> (6) affording parents substantial and meaningful opportunities to participate in the education of their children. (U.S. House of Representatives, 2001, p. 691, n. 10)

This delineation was omitted from the final version of NCLB, although, at the same time, the term significant modifying "opportunity to obtain a high quality education" was added to the overall statement of purpose. Presumably, addition of this term was an affirmation of a continuing congressional understanding of the importance of "significant" or "meaningful" opportunities if all children were to meet high standards, but, unfortunately, this statement of purpose was not accompanied by specific references to mechanisms that would promote or ensure that such opportunities actually are provided.

That omission must be corrected. To do so, Congress should revise the NCLB purposes clause so that it again articulates the need for the coordinated provision of a range of in-school and out-of-school services for students from communities of concentrated poverty and gives substantive content to the concept of "significant" or "meaningful" opportunity. More important, specific "meaningful educational opportunity" requirements should be added to the law, covering the eight categories of in-school educational essentials and the five categories of out-of-school educational essentials discussed in this chapter.

Education adequacy cases in more than half of the states have made clear that the constitutional right to a basic quality education requires the states to provide essential educational resources to every American child. Federal education policy must ensure that these educational essentials are in place for all children nationwide, if we are to eliminate achievement gaps and meet NCLB's ambitious proficiency goals. The requirement that the states provide all students with core educational essentials should, however, be done in a way that does not lead to federal micromanagement of the states' implementation of this requirement. Given the complexity of school-based programs and practices, extensive top-down regulation is not likely to be effective (Elmore, 2006).

NCLB should, therefore, require the states to ensure that every local school district provide sufficient resources in each of the basic categories of essential resources to all of its students. Currently, NCLB specifically requires states to ensure only one specific resource category, namely "highly qualified" teachers. We would extend that input mandate to include all of the essential areas. The statute should define the category in general terms like *highly effective teachers* (a term we would substitute for *highly qualified teachers* for the reasons set forth in Chapter 5), *additional time on task*, and *adequate facilities*. The determination of which specific services will be provided in these areas and the manner in which they will be put into place should, however, be left to the discretion of the individual states. The states should be responsible for determining specifically who are "effective" teachers, what programs would meet requirements for "additional time on task," specific definitions of "adequate" facilities, and so on. The U.S. Department of Education should support research on such practices and should disseminate and recommend exemplary practices developed by successful states.

This general federal requirement would place opportunity needs at the top of the policy agenda and induce each state to engage professional organizations, school boards, community groups, and the public at large in important debates and ongoing research and evaluation about the level and combination of services that are needed to provide a meaningful educational opportunity (Elmore & Fuhrman, 1995). Each state would, in essence, develop the basket of goods, services, and practices that is most consistent with its particular needs, local culture, and perspectives. The aim should be to "encourage practices that focus more on effectiveness than compliance . . . [and to] identify the areas in which schools . . . might create ongoing processes for inquiry, self-evaluation, learning, consultation and problem-solving" (Darling-Hammond, 1993, p. 41).

As with the essential school-based resources, a general federal requirement for coordinated out-of-school resources for students from communities of concentrated poverty would allow for extensive state and local discretion in determining which out-of-school and community-based resources are most critical for meeting students' educational needs, which methods for providing these resources would best promote productive interagency coordination, and which approaches

would be most cost-effective (Schuck & Zeckhauser, 2006). The antici-
pated public dialogue on the specific components of a "meaningful educational opportunity" and how they can best be provided by schools
in collaboration with other agencies would be particularly useful in
this critical, newly developing area. Extensive state-based consideration of these issues may also motivate policymakers to implement
other social and economic policies that might mitigate the effects of
poverty on children in areas such as housing, health insurance, and
income maintenance.

The resource requirements we recommend would, like the opportunity to learn standards proposed in the 1990s, ensure that states
provide all students with the tools they need to meet high standards.
However, they would do so in a way that would maximize the policymaking discretion of the states and avoid much of the political controversy that accompanied the OTL proposals. In the first place, the types
of resource needs we have delineated emerged from the "laboratory of
the states" (*New State Ice Co. v. Liebmann*, 1932, p. 311) and represent
a consensus of what state courts, based on evidence of local needs, determined to be essential elements of a basic quality education. Second,
our recommendation is that NCLB require each state to provide the
basic *categories* of resources that emerged from the consensus of state
court decisions, while leaving the determination of the precise types
and levels of resources to the discretion of states and localities.

The opportunity to learn standards that were the subject of political controversy in the 1990s were, as defined in the Goals 2000 legislation, "the criteria for, and the basis of, assessing the sufficiency or
quality of the *resources, practices, and conditions* necessary at each level
of the education system . . . to provide all students with the opportunity to learn the material in voluntary national content standards
or State content standards" (Goals 2000, 1994, § 5802 (7), emphasis
added). At the time, the major concerns about federal intervention
centered on the "practices and conditions" about which there was
little understanding and certainly no national consensus. We are not
recommending that the federal government develop a menu of pre-
ferred educational practices and mandate them for the states. Effective
practices and conditions, although of critical importance to meaningful educational opportunity, by their nature are context-specific, and
they should be developed by the states and local school districts. What
the federal authorities can do effectively is to provide comparative information on resource allocations and effective practices developed in
successful states and models or "visions" of "practices and conditions"
recommended by researchers for the states to consider (Porter, 1993).

The development and dissemination of cost study methodologies through the education adequacy litigations provide an example of the way the different states can experiment with new means of responding to a problem, develop a variety of mechanisms for dealing with it, and then offer their colleagues a range of models that they may decide to adopt or modify. The notion of developing formal methods for determining the amount of money that is needed to provide all students with a basic quality education originated with remedial orders in the Ohio and Wyoming litigations in the mid-1990s. The two core methodologies devised in those cases inspired the development of additional methodologies, and cost studies based on this range of methodologies have now been undertaken in more than 35 states, in most instances without a court order (Rebell, 2007a). These cost studies will undoubtedly continue to be a major mechanism that many states will use to respond to a federal statutory requirement for ensuring meaningful educational opportunities in the designated essential categories, and further improvement and refinement of the techniques now in existence will undoubtedly be made. But states will also develop other approaches to resource identification and allocation issues, and will continue to experiment with a variety of instructional practices and organizational reforms. This laboratory of the states, and not fixed methods and specific practices developed by a federal review board, would determine the way that meaningful opportunities for learning would be guaranteed for all children.

Federal oversight of this process should have two main dimensions. First, the current requirement that all students must be proficient by 2014 should be revised to charge the states with the responsibility to provide the full range of meaningful educational essentials, as each state defines these concepts, by 2014. Each state should then be required to revise its state plan to describe how this responsibility will be met. The U.S. Department of Education, in reviewing the state plans, should ensure that substantive steps are being taken to provide all students with significant opportunities in each of the comprehensive education essential areas, in accordance with their needs. This should essentially be a process review, but a probing process review that will ensure that action is being taken in good faith to meet children's needs; in other words, the department should not, in most cases, have authority to second-guess the mechanisms that the state has chosen to use or the amounts it chooses to spend in each category.

States would be also be required to demonstrate that they have put into place reasonable methods and data systems for assessing their resource allocation schemes and major program initiatives on state, district, and school levels. Interdistrict and interschool variations in the availability of resources should also be tracked (Elmore & Fuhrman, 1995). Each state should further be required to show that its state education department itself has the capacity to oversee an effective process for ensuring the availability of comprehensive educational essentials for all students (Elmore & Fuhrman, 1995).

Second, the states should also be required to include in their annual report cards descriptions of the steps being taken to provide each of the educational essentials, including the equity of the distribution of these essentials, as well as disaggregated data on the progress that students in the state are making toward greater proficiency. Currently, NCLB requires that each state issue an annual report card that sets forth detailed information on the state's adequate yearly progress and on the professional qualifications of its teachers (NCLB, 2001, § 1111 (h) (1) (C)). The act also states that the annual report card may, on an optional basis, include information such as average class size in each grade, the incidence of school violence and drug abuse, the extent and type of parental involvement in the school, the percentage of students completing advanced placement courses, and a "clear and concise description of the state's accountability system, including a description of the criteria by which the State evaluates school performance. . . ." (NCLB, 2001, § 1111 (h) (1) (D)). Our proposal would expand these reporting categories by requiring information in all the categories of essential resources and would also make those requirements mandatory.

The department should issue an annual report of its own that provides comparative data from the state plans and state report cards on methods that the various states are using and the progress they are achieving. These reports, together with the state's AYP information, will allow parents, civic and business leaders, and the interested public in each state to evaluate the opportunities that the state is providing and the annual progress it is achieving, and to compare their state's efforts and achievements with those of other states. (As we will discuss in Chapter 7, the AYP indicators would be calibrated in terms of challenging but realistic annual growth targets and not in terms of an unattainable full proficiency by 2014 mandate.) With that information, concerned citizens in states that are not making adequate progress will be able to press their policymakers and elected officials to improve their efforts and to consider adopting policies and practices that have proved successful in other states.

If a state's educational outcomes are unsatisfactory for an extended period of time, it may, however, be appropriate for the Department of

Education to require that state to adopt one of the model approaches that have been utilized by successful states. Probably the appropriate time for the department to invoke this ultimate authority would be at the time of the next reauthorization of the law (likely to be in or about 2014). Although we have argued throughout this chapter that maximum discretion be given to the states to develop the means for meeting their obligation to provide meaningful educational opportunities for all their students, ultimately, if some states prove unwilling or unable to accomplish this task, federal intervention will be unavoidable if the students' interests and the national interests are to be upheld.

Even this highly limited invocation of federal coercive authority, undertaken only after the states have been afforded a maximum opportunity to pursue their own paths to compliance, raises serious issues of federal versus state power, and some will see it as inconsistent with important traditions of local control. These concerns must be taken seriously, even though the imperatives of equity, democracy, and the nation's economic competitiveness ultimately override them. We will discuss these federalism issues in more detail in Chapter 9.

CHAPTER 5

Providing Effective
Teachers for All Students

Over the past 2 decades, experience with standards-based reform and education adequacy litigations has produced a clearer understanding of the essential resources needed to provide all students with a meaningful educational opportunity. Specifically, as discussed in Chapters 2 and 4, a virtual consensus emerged from the adequacy litigations of the core school-based resources needed to ensure student success. In addition, research amassed over the same period indicates that educationally disadvantaged children from communities of concentrated poverty also need, at a minimum, a constellation of out-of-school resources. The education adequacy litigations have revealed, however, that, in state after state, many students—especially low-income and minority students—have been denied access to essential in-school and out-of-school educational resources on a massive scale.

TEACHING: A PRIME EXAMPLE OF THE RESOURCES
NEEDED FOR MEANINGFUL EDUCATIONAL OPPORTUNITY

We have argued that NCLB should be revised to require that the states make all of the essential elements of a meaningful educational opportunity available to all students, in accordance with their educational needs. As we emphasized in the previous chapter, in the main, the detailed mechanisms for implementing this requirement should be left to the states, with limited federal oversight. This approach should, we expect, create a laboratory of the states, promoting creative dialogue among educators, policymakers, parents, and researchers within each state on how best and most efficiently to provide the resources and services needed in each essential area. These separate efforts to identify best practices may lead in some or many of these areas to common understandings regarding the core methods and costs for providing a meaningful education that most or all of the states will adopt. Or it may lead to a range of successful alternate practices.

To illustrate the types of issues that states will need to confront in each of the essential areas of meaningful educational opportunity, we present in this chapter a detailed analysis of the problems and possibilities involved in providing the first—and, arguably, the most important—of the resource categories, namely "effective," and not merely "minimally qualified," teachers. Teacher quality is the sole resource area that presently is mandated by NCLB. We will examine the problems posed by the current "highly qualified" teacher requirement. We will then advocate modifying that requirement to substitute a more substantive concept of "highly effective" teacher, which we would leave to each of the states to define fully.

NCLB's CURRENT "HIGHLY QUALIFIED TEACHER" MANDATE

Research shows what parents and students already know, that the most essential resource that a school can provide to any student is a truly effective teacher. NCLB acknowledges this and it therefore includes a teacher quality requirement as its sole resource input mandate. In doing so, the act purports to set a new bar for America's teaching force. The law requires states to ensure that every teacher who teaches a core subject is "highly qualified." A "highly qualified" teacher, under NCLB, is one who has obtained a bachelor's degree, acquired state certification, and demonstrated competence in the subject matter he or she teaches (NCLB, 2001, § 7801(23)). To prove subject-matter competence, elementary school teachers must pass a "rigorous" state test of elementary curriculum and teaching skills (NCLB, 2001, § 7801(23)). Middle and high school teachers must either pass a "rigorous" state subject test or complete a college major (or graduate degree or "advanced certification or credentialing") in the subject he or she teaches (NCLB, 2001, § 7801(23)).

Neither the act nor the regulations issued to implement it, however, specify what it means for a certification test to be "rigorous," nor do they provide any meaningful guidance on the standards that should be used in certifying teachers. Rather, the law leaves it to each state to develop its own criteria for what it means to satisfy NCLB's "highly qualified" teacher requirements. State tests for initial teacher certification historically have been far from "rigorous." The Education Trust (1999), after analyzing teacher certification tests in the 43 states that have such tests and the District of Columbia concluded,

"Unfortunately, existing mechanisms are not even close to adequate for assuring teacher quality" (p. 2). The Trust found the standards for the tests to be so minimal that they were "effective in excluding only the weakest of the weak" (p. 2).

Although the Education Trust's researchers focused their study on the highest-level tests available, they found that most of the tests contained primarily high-school–level material and that the exams rarely used challenging formats, such as essay questions and complex multiple-choice questions. Thus, the tests could not measure whether teachers had acquired the kind of deep subject-matter knowledge necessary to teach students to "high levels of understanding" *(*p. 4). Moreover, the report noted, states that administer subject-matter tests set their own passing scores. Thus, in states that established low passing scores, subject-matter tests could not even guarantee that teachers possessed the level of subject-matter knowledge required of their students. Moreover, early on, the Department of Education informed the states that they would not be required to submit these tests for review and approval by the department (Loeb & Miller, 2006).

In enacting NCLB, Congress recognized that teachers cannot prepare students to meet state proficiency standards if they do not understand the content students are expected to learn. It therefore required that veteran teachers be evaluated using criteria that are "aligned with challenging state academic content and student academic achievement standards and developed in consultation with core content specialists" (NCLB, 2001,§ 7801(23)). Nevertheless, the Department of Education's regulations for certifying veteran teachers as "highly qualified" speak only in terms of demonstrating "competency in each academic subject area in which the teacher teaches" (NCLB Regulation, 2007, § 200.56). The department's regulations do not require states to demonstrate that either new or veteran teachers understand the content that their students are expected to learn, let alone have the depth of knowledge necessary to teach students to high levels. Furthermore, although 44 states have reported taking steps to align state standards for teachers with state content standards for students, the department's failure to review these claims means that the extent of the alignment between teacher and student standards remains unclear (U.S. Department of Education, 2006a).

While veteran and new teachers alike can prove subject-matter competency by majoring in a subject area or by taking a content exam, veteran teachers have an additional option. They can demonstrate subject-matter proficiency by meeting a set of requirements developed by their state for this purpose, which NCLB calls the High

Objective Uniform Standard of Evaluation. As with the certification of new teachers, the Department of Education has taken a hands-off approach to the HOUSSE method of certifying veteran teachers as "highly qualified" by allowing states to set their own HOUSSE standards (Loeb & Miller, 2006).

Nearly all of the states have taken advantage of this flexibility. The most common type of HOUSSE plan requires veteran teachers to acquire a set number of points to be considered highly qualified. In most instances, the activities for which points are awarded bear only a weak relationship to a teacher's subject-matter knowledge. Such activities include volunteering on school committees, participating in educational travel, and mentoring other teachers (National Council on Teacher Quality, 2004). As the National Council on Teacher Quality (2004) has observed, the HOUSSE plans in most states "are little more than an elaborate restatement of the status quo" (p. 2). Recognizing the inadequacy of the HOUSSE procedures, the Department of Education has recently called for the phasing out of the HOUSSE method of deeming veteran teachers "highly qualified," indicating that the department would limit the use of the procedures to a few types of teachers, such as high school teachers teaching multiple subjects in rural school districts, certain categories of special education teachers, and visiting teachers from other countries (Spellings, 2006).

In implementing the teacher quality provisions of No Child Left Behind, the Department of Education has focused almost entirely on teachers' content knowledge while paying scant attention to teachers' ability to transmit knowledge to students. Former Secretary of Education Rod Paige went so far as to dismiss the value of pedagogical training and skills. Ignoring contrary research, the former secretary, in his first annual report on teacher quality, stated that the only "teacher attributes that relate directly to improved student achievement are high verbal ability and solid content knowledge" (U.S. Department of Education, 2002, p. 39). Because, in Paige's view, certification requirements that are unrelated to verbal ability and content knowledge pose unnecessary hurdles to candidates seeking entry into the teaching field, the secretary encouraged states to eliminate student teaching requirements (p. 40). Although the department has more recently acknowledged the importance of pedagogical training (U.S. Department of Education, 2005), it has failed to hold states accountable for ensuring that teachers are capable of teaching students. The department has interpreted NCLB as permitting middle school and high school teachers to be labeled "highly qualified" if they have simply majored in the subject they teach. These teachers are not required to demonstrate that they are able to translate their academic knowledge into effective instruction for the easiest-to-educate students, let alone for the subgroups targeted by NCLB.

Since the passage of NCLB, the Department of Education has encouraged states to expand preparation programs for alternate-route teachers as a means of increasing their numbers of "highly qualified" teachers. Alternate-route teachers enter the field by participating in a shortened training program, lasting from a few weeks to 2 years, and by meeting their state's certification requirements for alternate-route teachers. In the first few years following the passage of NCLB, the department took a similar approach to alternative and traditional certification. For both routes, education coursework and student teaching, according to the department's leaders, were considered to be of trivial value. Although recently the department has recognized that successful alternate-route programs should provide "extensive pedagogical training in instruction" and "practice in lesson planning and teaching," it nevertheless permits states to count graduates of shortcut programs as "highly qualified" teachers (U.S. Department of Education, 2005, p. 10). Moreover, the department does not even require alternative certification candidates to complete their programs in order to be considered "highly qualified." According to the department's regulations, so long as candidates are enrolled in an alternate-route program and are making progress toward meeting their state's certification requirements, they can teach in schools without certification for up to 3 years under the "highly qualified" label (NCLB Regulation, 2007, § 200.56).

In August 2007, a California advocacy group filed suit against the U.S. Department of Education, charging that these regulations violate NCLB's teacher quality provisions that require "highly qualified teachers" to have full state certification or licensure, in addition to a bachelor's degree and subject-matter knowledge (Public Advocates, 2007). According to the plaintiffs in this case, *Renee v. Spellings*, a large proportion of teachers with alternative certification are found in schools that are low-performing and enroll higher concentrations of students of color. Before NCLB, hard-to-staff schools coped with teacher shortages by hiring uncertified teachers or teachers with emergency credentials. Since NCLB requires schools to employ only "highly qualified" teachers in core subjects, hard-to-staff schools now recruit a disproportionate number of alternate-route teachers who, as indicated above, are designated as "highly qualified" by the Department of Education even though they have not yet met the same minimum entry requirements as other teachers (Southeast Center for Teaching Quality, 2004).

Although alternative-route credentials require less preservice training than traditional certification, alternative routes generally require holders to demonstrate more skills and subject-matter competency before entering the classroom than did the emergency or temporary permits regulations that many school districts used in the past to fill their hard-to-staff classrooms. Evidence from New York City suggests that teachers entering through the new routes have stronger academic backgrounds than the temporary-license teachers they replaced. In 2003, only 6% of newly hired teachers from these new routes failed the state teacher certification general knowledge test on their first attempt, compared with 16% of newly hired traditional-route teachers and 33% of temporarily licensed teachers (Loeb & Miller, 2006). However, researchers at the Southeast Center for Teaching Quality (2004) found that most alternatively certified teachers in hard-to-staff schools are only nominally more qualified than their uncertified predecessors. Furthermore, graduates of short-cut alternative certification programs, like their uncertified predecessors, quit at substantially higher rates than other teachers (Darling-Hammond & Youngs, 2002; Darling-Hammond & Sykes, 2003; Raymond, Fletcher, & Luque, 2001).

Teachers in high-poverty, low-performing schools still are dramatically less qualified, on average, than teachers in other schools. For example, in 2000, 28% of New York City teachers in the quartile of schools with the highest concentration of student poverty were in their first 2 years of teaching, compared with 15% of teachers in the lowest-poverty group. Similarly, 26% of non-White students had teachers who had failed their general knowledge certification exam initially, compared with 16% of White students (Loeb & Miller, 2006). Recognizing the connection between teacher quality and the achievement gap, Congress included the elimination of inequalities in access to qualified teachers as a central element in its strategy to close the achievement gaps under NCLB. Specifically, Congress directed states to ensure that minority and low-income students are not taught at higher rates than other children by inexperienced, unqualified, or out-of-field teachers (NCLB, 2001, § 6311 (8) (c)). Yet, in the early years of NCLB, the Department of Education largely neglected to enforce this provision of the law.

In mid-2004, the department began to send monitoring teams to each state to assess their progress in meeting the "highly qualified" teacher requirements of NCLB. The department first signaled its intention to enforce the teacher-quality equity provisions of NCLB in February 2005, when it included teacher-quality equity as an element in the monitoring reports of the last 38 states visited (Loeb & Miller, 2006). The department, however, was satisfied if the states simply demonstrated that they had policies or programs to address teacher-quality equity. In 2006, the department, for the first time, instructed all states to submit plans on the strategies they are implementing to meet NCLB's teacher-quality equity requirements (Loeb & Miller, 2006).

Because states were unaccountable for their compliance with NCLB's teacher-quality equity requirements until 2006, most states have not even developed the data systems necessary to compare the rates at which minority, low-income, and other students are taught by second-rate teachers. Consequently, merely *three* states—Tennessee, Ohio, and Nevada—reported data on all four dimensions of equity required under NCLB:

1. Whether minority students are more likely than other students to be taught by inexperienced teachers
2. Whether the same is true of low-income students
3. Whether minority students are more likely than other students to be taught by unqualified and/or out-of-field teachers
4. Whether the same is true of low-income students (Education Trust, 2006)

Moreover, only two states—Ohio and Nevada—developed rigorous plans to remedy the inequitable distribution of teachers in their schools.

What, then, has been accomplished by NCLB's mandate that all teachers in core subject areas be "highly qualified"? On the one hand, there has apparently been a significant increase in the number of certified teachers—many of whom entered teaching through alternative certification routes—at least in some hard-to-staff inner-city and rural schools (Loeb & Miller, 2006). On the other hand, it is not clear that these new teachers, many of whom have been deemed "highly qualified" through alternate-route mechanisms that have lesser requirements than the already minimal state certification norms, have substantially improved the overall quality or effectiveness of the teacher corps. For example, based on more than 160 interviews in four southeastern states and 24 high-need schools, the Southeast Center for Teaching Quality (2004) found that teachers and principals observed no improvement in the quality of teachers in their schools after the passage of NCLB.

The general conclusion that can be drawn at this point is that even if NCLB has increased the number of state-certified teachers in hard-to-staff schools, the law has not ensured that children are being taught by teachers who are really *highly* qualified to meet their needs. By using hyperbole that conveys the misleading impression that *minimally* qualified teachers are *highly* qualified, NCLB creates misinformation. The law thus actually impedes public understanding of how many teachers in any school or school system really are highly qualified and how many truly highly qualified teachers are currently serving in schools with large numbers of poor and minority students who have the greatest need for their services.

ATTRACTING, DEVELOPING, AND RETAINING TRULY EFFECTIVE TEACHERS

In order to provide all children with a meaningful educational opportunity and to enable them to meet challenging proficiency standards, maximum efforts must be made to attract, develop, and retain teachers who truly are effective, especially in the schools attended predominantly by low-income and minority students, which historically have been hard to staff. Such efforts are complicated—and potentially hindered—by the obfuscation that NCLB currently creates regarding teacher qualifications. As we have said, the current labeling makes it difficult to know how many teachers are truly highly qualified and effective when all of those who are minimally qualified are given the same designation. Moreover, continued public support and investment in quality teaching could be jeopardized if virtually all teachers in our schools are (inaccurately) labeled "highly qualified" and student achievement does not substantially improve.

If states are to provide teachers who are truly highly qualified to all of their students, their certification requirements should be demanding. They should distinguish between initial entry-level requirements and advanced effective teaching classifications that are based on appropriate examinations and/or evaluation and rating systems that consider strong learning gains for students, regular classroom observations and feedback conducted by multiple sources, and that utilize validated evaluation rubrics. The schools of education that the states accredit should be required to emphasize curricula that are fully aligned with the state content standards, to inculcate in their students teaching skills relevant to an increasingly diverse student population, and to motivate students to prepare themselves to teach the subjects—such

as math, science, and special education—and the schooling levels—
such as middle schools—that now have the greatest shortages and the
greatest needs (Levine, 2006; T. Rogers, personal communication, July
23, 2007).

Although there is widespread agreement in the literature that effective teachers make a huge difference in student achievement
(Hanushek, Kain & Rivkin, 2005; Darling-Hammond & Sykes, 2003;
McCaffrey, Lockwood, Koretz, & Hamilton, 2003), there is little evidence that one can predict in advance from certification status or academic degrees which individuals will prove to be effective (Goldhaber,
2004; Loeb & Miller, 2006). States, therefore, should focus not only on
hiring teachers with strong basic credentials, but also on working with
local districts to promote effective induction, mentoring, and professional development programs that will develop a maximum number
of teachers who are truly effective on the job, particularly in improving the performance of at-risk low-income and minority students. The
teacher professional development activities that promote this type of
teaching encompass more than the usual one-time workshop; instead,
high-quality professional development is sustained, coherent, collaborative, and integrated into the structure of the school (Porter, Garet,
Desimone, Yoon, & Birman, 2000; Smylie, Allensworth, Greenberg,
Harris, & Luppescu, 2001; WestEd, 2000).

Although a seemingly simple way to effectuate these important
improvements in teacher training and support would be to amend
NCLB to include federal mandates covering these needs, we do not
recommend such heavy-handed federal regulation for the reasons we
discussed in the previous chapter. Instead, we believe that the states
should be required to provide relevant information on the rigor of
their certification requirements, the accreditation standards for their
schools of education, and their induction, mentoring, and professional development practices in their annual report cards to the
public and in the state plans they submit to the U.S. Department of
Education. Both the department and the interested public would then
be in a position to assess the steps being taken by each state to improve and equitably distribute their teaching corps with the progress
they have made over time in student learning outcomes. They would
also have the basic information they need to compare the state's efforts and achievements in this regard with the accomplishments of
other states.

To aid this process, NCLB must be amended to induce states to
describe the qualifications of their teaching corps accurately and to
eliminate its current exaggerated and misleading "highly qualified"

teacher designation. In doing so, a distinction also should be made between teachers who have met minimum qualification requirements and teachers who have demonstrated effectiveness in improving student performance. Specifically, we propose that NCLB be revised to distinguish among three categories of teachers: "provisionally qualified teachers," "qualified teachers," and "highly effective teachers":

- "Provisionally qualified teachers" should be defined as teachers in training who meet the state's alternative certification requirements.
- "Qualified teachers" should be defined as those who have a college degree with a major in a field directly related to the subject area in which they are teaching, and who meet the state's entry-level certification requirements.
- "Highly effective teachers" should be defined as teachers who have deep subject-matter knowledge, a thorough understanding of state academic content standards and proficiency requirements, and a demonstrated ability to impart effectively the knowledge and skills required by state standards to students from diverse backgrounds and with diverse needs. (Interstate New Teacher Assessment and Support Consortium [INTASC], 1992)

NCLB's current requirements for equitable distribution of "highly qualified" teachers should be applied to all of these categories; this means that low-income and minority students should not be disproportionately assigned to teachers who are inexperienced or less than highly effective.

By emphasizing the importance of "effective" teachers and distinguishing effectiveness from minimal qualifications, NCLB would promote the dissemination of more accurate and useful information to parents, state policymakers, and the general public about the true competency level of the teachers in each state. These revisions would also raise expectations regarding the types of teachers that states need to attract and retain in order to provide their students with a meaningful educational opportunity.

Within the parameters set forth above, the states should be required to articulate in their state plans the methods they will use to develop effective teachers and to identify those who qualify for this designation. The annual report card should list the number of such highly effective teachers in each school district and in the state as a whole, as well as specific information about the equitable distribution of such teachers. The availability of accurate data and the public interest in these data should motivate the states to maximize their numbers of effective teachers and their equitable distribution among schools throughout the state. The U.S. Department of Education's annual report should publish a compendium of the states' effective teacher definitions and evaluative mechanisms and should highlight those that best serve NCLB's purposes. As noted in Chapter 4, states that continue to show poor performance over time and whose numbers of effective teachers and/or definitions of effective teachers vary substantially from the effective teacher practices of successful states may ultimately be required to adopt practices in line with the model states.

If candor is to prevail, we must acknowledge that, even in the best of circumstances, not every child will have a "highly effective" teacher. Even if many more talented people are attracted to the profession, if teacher preparation is dramatically improved, and if effective induction, mentoring, and professional development practices are in place, some teachers, and especially those who are inexperienced, will simply be less effective than others. Although by definition all students cannot have "the best," policymakers and education officials can (consistent with the "adequacy" concept that has been developed by the state courts) establish a high floor of expectations for professional qualifications and professional functioning so that all students are, in fact, taught by "qualified" teachers and many are even better served by "highly effective" teachers. Equity distribution requirements should insist that students with the greatest needs are served by at least a proportional share of these highly effective teachers.

Attracting, developing, and retaining many more highly effective teachers is a plausible expectation for a system that is designed to promote meaningful educational opportunity. Cost analyses (to be discussed in more detail in the next chapter) will highlight the pay scales and incentives that are needed to attract more talented people into the teaching profession. Although we expect that some increase in current pay scales will be required, we doubt that these would be of the magnitude recommended by some of the recent studies (National Center on Education and the Economy, 2007; The Teaching Commission, 2004). In most areas, present salaries attract a sufficient number of new candidates to the teaching profession. Present teacher shortages and teaching quality shortfalls result from the fact that nationally one third of all teachers leave the profession and nearly half—46%—leave teaching within 5 years (Ingersoll, 2003). In hard-to-staff, high-poverty schools, the proportion of teachers who quit is 50% higher than among their suburban counterparts (Ingersoll, 2001). Since it is not possible generally to predict in advance which individuals who meet basic qualifications will prove to be highly effective on the job, the major efforts in improving the caliber of the teaching force should be focused on professional development to establish and maintain teacher effectiveness, and on initiatives aimed at retaining those teachers who do prove to be effective.

The two go hand in hand. Teachers who at the beginning of their careers participate in high-quality induction programs, which include mentoring, are substantially less likely to leave teaching, because such programs improve their instructional skills and reinforce their sense of efficacy (Darling-Hammond & Sykes, 2003). School districts, such as those in Toledo, Ohio, and Rochester, New York, have reduced new teacher attrition rates by over two thirds by matching teachers with expert mentors during their first year (Berry, 2004). Furthermore, a 2000 National Center for Education Statistics study reported that teachers who did not receive induction support left teaching at a rate almost 70% higher than that of teachers who were provided with such support (Henke, Chen, & Geis, 2000). Despite the strong correlation between strong induction programs and teacher retention, in 2007, only 21 states had policies that encouraged the use of mentoring programs (Education Commission of the States, 2007).

There is no consensus on what other steps need to be taken to retain more teachers, and especially those who have proven effective on the job. Although increased pay obviously is a factor, economists differ in their analyses of how much of an incentive salary increases provide. In one interesting study, researchers at the RAND Corporation found that for every $1,000 increase in new teacher salaries, teacher attrition rates decrease by about 3%. Moreover, they observed that the impact of the same pay raise on attrition rates was more than twice as large in high-need districts (Kirby, Berends, & Naftel, 1999). There is also some evidence that some types of merit pay programs and bonuses for teachers willing to make long-term commitments to teach in hard-to-staff schools, aid in the retention of highly effective teachers (Clotfelter, Glennie, Ladd, & Vigdor, 2006; Milanowski, 2003; Odden, Kellor, Heneman, & Milanowski, 1999; Price, 2002).

Working conditions and opportunities for collaboration and exercise of professional judgment also play a large role in the decision of many teachers to leave their jobs or to abandon teaching (Berry, Hoke, & Hirsch, 2004; Ingersoll, 2001; Johnson & Birkeland, 2003; Louis, Marks, & Kruse, 1996). Working conditions are likely to be even more important than salaries in determining the current distribution of teachers across schools, given the great variation in working conditions among schools (Loeb & Miller, 2006). Large class sizes, poor leadership, inadequate facilities, lack of instructional materials, and other factors that constitute poor working conditions are, of course, most pervasive in high-poverty schools. It is not surprising, therefore, that although a quarter of all exiting teachers report dissatisfaction with teaching as their reason for quitting, teachers leaving high-poverty schools are more than twice as likely as teachers leaving affluent schools to cite this as their reason for quitting (Darling-Hammond & Sykes, 2003). A federal requirement that states provide the essential elements of a meaningful educational opportunity in every school would dramatically improve working conditions for teachers, especially in hard-to-staff schools, and should thereby also improve the states' ability to retain more of their effective teachers and to ensure proportionate distribution of such teachers to schools that are presently hard to staff.

To create the conditions necessary to ensure that all students are taught by qualified teachers and that many are taught by highly effective teachers, states will also need to deal with the political challenges of revising their statutes or collective bargaining agreements to eliminate practices that undermine effective teaching, the retention of the best teachers, and the equitable distribution of teaching quality. Seniority systems that favor veterans, whatever their present level of commitment and performance, and allow them to transfer and "bump" highly effective teachers with less seniority are a prime case in point. Many current tenure systems would also likely need to be modified to ensure veteran teachers reasonable job security but only so long as they maintain their instructional effectiveness. Given the power and influence of teacher unions, these changes obviously may not easily be accomplished.

In an education system oriented toward meaningful educational opportunity, however, reconsideration of teacher tenure could occur in a very different manner. If the aspects of meaningful educational opportunity that would be highly attractive to teachers (such as pay raises, improved working conditions, class size reductions, clinical supports to deal with students' physical and mental health needs, and enhanced professional development and professional support) are implemented through collective bargaining processes that also call upon teachers to reconsider aspects of the tenure system and other practices that impede effective teaching, a host of new possibilities for partnership and progress will emerge. To meet the teacher effectiveness expectations of the NCLB provisions that we recommend, states might implement meaningful educational opportunity through contracts with school districts that would guarantee school districts additional funding and benefits in exchange for district-level planning for meaningful educational opportunity reforms, including new collective bargaining agreements to accomplish this end (T. Rogers, personal communication, July 23, 2007).

Just as we must understand that it is unrealistic and counterproductive to mandate 100% student proficiency by 2014, it is similarly impossible and unreasonable to mandate 100% "highly effective" teachers in the near future. But by setting aside rhetoric and hyperbole, articulating clear expectations on what can and must be done, and establishing a workable division of labor between the federal government and the states, we can substantially increase the number of highly effective teachers in all of our nation's schools.

Because of the importance of quality teaching and the failure of NCLB provisions to secure it, we have discussed in depth what is needed to ensure that all students have qualified teachers and to maximize teaching effectiveness. Although quality teaching is a *sine qua non* of meaningful educational opportunity, this resource alone is not enough to ensure it, especially for at-risk students. Along with quality teaching, students must be provided with the full range of school-based and out-of-school resources discussed in Chapter 4. While this short volume does not provide the space to detail them, similar policies should be adopted to require states to develop effective practices for providing the other essential school-based and out-of-school resources that are vital to the academic achievement of English language learners, students from communities of concentrated poverty, and other at-risk groups.

CHAPTER 6

Securing
Adequate Funding

Although NCLB imposes a host of mandates on the states and local school districts, and provides some additional funding, the law grossly neglects the need to ensure that *adequate* levels of funding are in place to allow students a meaningful opportunity to make solid academic progress, much less the unprecedented results that are being mandated. In the preceding chapters, we have argued that a meaningful educational opportunity is not only a right to which all American children are entitled but an imperative if our nation is to succeed in maintaining the vigor of our democracy and the competitiveness of our economy. We have also delineated the necessary elements of a meaningful educational opportunity. Revising NCLB to ensure the funding necessary to provide these essential elements is critical if the law is to achieve its goals.

MONEY MATTERS

In a nation committed to providing equal educational opportunities to all children and to eliminating achievement gaps, one would expect that the greatest amount of resources would be allotted to those with the greatest needs. Unfortunately, in the United States today, that is clearly not the case. Affluent school districts that serve children who attend high-quality preschools and come to school ready to learn continue to have more resources and better teachers, while poorer districts that serve children who did not have access to preschool and have greater educational needs consistently have fewer resources with which to meet those needs.

As noted in Chapter 2, the Education Trust (2006) has estimated that nationwide, on average, spending on children in high-poverty school districts is $825 less per student than spending on students in low-poverty districts, or over $20,000 per year for each class of 25 students. In certain states, the situation is even worse: in New York, the funding gap between students in rich and low-income districts is $2,319; in Illinois, it is $1,924; and in Minnesota, it is $1,349. Even starker inequities are revealed by specific district-to-district comparisons. For example, in New York, per capita spending on students in New York City, where 81% of the students come from backgrounds of poverty, is $12,896, compared with $23,344 in Manhasset, where only 4.4% are from poor backgrounds (New York State Department of Education, 2005).

The cause of these dramatic inequities is that, in almost every state, public school funding is based largely on local funding and local property taxes. The American system of local control and local funding of public schools originated in an agricultural economy at a time when wealth was relatively evenly distributed and land provided the tangible and predominant basis for taxation (Cubberley, 1934). Given the current large differences in property wealth between urban, rural, and suburban areas, however, the traditional property tax system has become anachronistic. Other developed countries either equalize funding across the board or have systems that effectively compensate for any disparities in local funding (Slavin, 1999).

As we have pointed out, these inequities in state education finance systems have been challenged in many state courts, and decisions in these cases have had a substantial impact in reducing patterns of inequity in many states (Evans, Murray, & Schwab, 1999; Hickrod, Hines, Anthony, & Dively, 1992). However, recent state court cases show a shift in emphasis from equity (equalizing funding) to adequacy (ensuring a sufficient level of funding for all schools). This shift highlights the fact that, in many states, in addition to inequities in the distribution of funds among school districts, the average level of spending is not high enough to provide reasonable opportunities for students—especially for students from backgrounds of poverty, English language learners, and students with disabilities—to meet state academic standards. Thus, as a result of the adequacy litigations, state funding for public schools in Kansas will increase by $755.6 million, or 26%, from 2004–2005 to 2008–2009 (Hunter, 2006). In New York City, funding is slated to rise by $5.2 billion, or about 30%, from 2006–2007 to 2010–2011 (Hunter, 2007). Similarly, in Arkansas, the adequacy litigation led to state funding reform and the unprecedented state commitment to school facilities of $846 million, with additional bonding authorized, and to operating aid increases of over $400 million in the 2003–2005 biennium, over 17% (*Lake View School District No. 25 v. Huckabee*, 2001). Although state defendants in many of these litigations argued that "money doesn't matter" to school quality and student achievement, 29 out of 30 state courts that have considered that proposition have rejected it, as have most of the economists and policy analysts who have considered the issue (Rebell, 2007b). Indeed, even Eric Hanushek, the economist whose work is most often cited to support the "money doesn't matter" proposition and who has testified for the state defendants in more than a dozen of the adequacy litigations, has himself agreed with the commonsense logic that "money spent wisely, logically and with accountability would be very useful indeed" (*Montoy v. State*, 2003).

There can be little doubt, then, that adequate funding is a *sine qua non* for broad-based and sustained academic progress, and that effectively used money will make a difference. These truths validate NCLB's implicit covenant that additional funding should be tied to demonstrable results. The current problem is that NCLB is demanding accountability and better results, but without ensuring the level of funding that is necessary to achieve these results.

DETERMINING COSTS OBJECTIVELY

At the state level, the amount of money needed to provide all students with a meaningful opportunity for a basic quality education has generally been determined through the use of "costing-out" or "adequacy" studies—objective analyses of education costs undertaken by education finance specialists or economists. Only a handful of such studies were attempted prior to 1990, but since that time, adequacy studies have been conducted in more than 35 states, and their use appears to be accelerating. Some of these studies were directly ordered by the courts, and others have been undertaken by state legislatures or governors, or sponsored by advocates, school board associations, unions, or foundations (Rebell 2007a).

The impact of the cost studies has been powerful in changing education finance practices to make them more rational and more transparent. An increasing number of state legislatures have directly relied on these studies in formulating their education funding decisions, and courts have repeatedly cited their findings as evidence of constitutional violations or as a basis for structuring remedial decrees. The studies make use of several different technical methodologies, and aspects of these methodologies have begun to generate controversy and criticism (Guthrie, 2007; Hanushek, 2006). It is important to note, however, that these studies openly and professionally analyze the needs of children and calculate costs based on these analyses. This is a vast improvement over the usual past practice of determining educational allocations through purely political negotiations (and often through backroom political deals), without regard for children's actual needs (Duncombe, 2006; Rebell 2007a).

One of the most dramatic examples of the traditional political deal-making approach to educational funding came to light during the trial of the New York adequacy case. Although the state's school finance system consisted of a complex set of approximately 50 separate formulas and funding streams that ostensibly accounted for the educational needs of the state's children in a variety of specific priority areas, in reality, the formulas proved meaningless. They were manipulated to yield exact percentage allocations for each region of the state, as determined each year by "three men in a room": the governor and the two legislative leaders (*Campaign for Fiscal Equity v. State*, 2001, p. 533). For most of the years preceding the trial in that case, New York City's "share" of any annual increase in state education funding was precisely 38.86%. Each year, the legislative staff was directed to work the formulas backward in their computer programs "until the politically negotiated 'share' for the City schools and other districts is hit in the calculations" (*Campaign for Fiscal Equity v. State*, p. 533). The failure of these annual political deals to "align funding with need" was the critical deficiency "that [ran] afoul of [the New York State Constitution]," the Court held (*Campaign for Fiscal Equity v. State,* 2003).

NCLB's FUNDING SHORTFALLS

NCLB virtually ignores the funding equity and adequacy problems that have been highlighted by the state court litigations and quantified by the numerous cost studies that have been undertaken in recent years. Although NCLB funding issues have created heated political battles in Washington over the past few years, what the politicians have been debating is the gap between the authorization and appropriation levels in the law. As we noted in Chapter 3, between 2001 and 2007, federal funding for Title I increased by over $4 billion, or approximately 45% (Riddle, 2006b). However, these appropriations fell far short of the $16 billion authorization increase by 2007 that Congress had established in the law.

The Bush administration points out that authorizations are often aspirational targets and that actual appropriations frequently fall short of authorized levels, as exemplified by the IDEA, which for decades has been funded at a level that is less than half of the authorized amount. Democratic congressional leaders argue that the bipartisan endorsement of the NCLB legislation was based on an explicit commitment to provide full funding at the agreed-upon, authorized levels. From the perspective of meaningful educational opportunity, this entire authorization/appropriation dispute in Washington is a sideshow. Even the authorized level of federal funding for NCLB does not begin to approach the additional funding needed to meet the goals and demands of the law. Overall spending on education in the United States exceeds $500 billion (National Conference of State Legislators [NCSL], 2005); in this context, the current dispute over an additional $12 billion in Title I aid pales in significance.

The current level of NCLB funding does not even cover the costs of its own requirements. In a recent sample of 300 school districts nationwide, 80% reported that they had to absorb extra costs, beyond the federal aid they were receiving to carry out NCLB requirements, and two thirds of state education departments reported that they had insufficient funds to assist schools in need of improvement, as NCLB requires (Jennings, 2007). Two federal lawsuits brought by the National Education Association and a number of school districts (*Pontiac School District v. Spellings*, 2005) and the state of Connecticut (*Connecticut v. Spellings*, 2006) have challenged the administration's failure to fund the act fully and to reimburse the states for the full costs of administration and testing. The district courts have rejected both of these claims, which are currently on appeal. Even if the full, authorized levels were appropriated, the amounts in question might cover the extra costs to the states of conducting the extensive testing program required by NCLB, extra state administrative costs, and program costs for Reading First and other particular programs, but they would not approach the levels of funding needed to provide the range of educational essentials that are required to overcome our nation's opportunity and achievement gaps.

The real funding issue for NCLB is how the federal government can most effectively ensure that all schools have sufficient funding to provide the effective teaching, appropriate class size, extra time on task, health services, and other fundamental in-school *and* out-of-school resources required to afford all children a meaningful educational opportunity and to ensure that state education departments have the resources they need to assist low-performing local school districts and schools in improving their instructional capacity. To accomplish this, a combination of increased federal grants, improved incentives, *and* mandates for the states to increase funding will likely be necessary.

On average, the costing-out studies conducted in the various states have indicated that increases on the order of 20–30% are necessary to provide adequate in-school resources for all students to have an opportunity for a basic quality education (Mathis, 2004). But most of these studies have not taken into account the higher costs of NCLB proficiency mandates. A few states have attempted to conduct preliminary studies of the costs of meeting NCLB's AYP requirements over the next few years (as contrasted with the costs of complying with the law's testing and administrative requirements). In Ohio, for example, a study projected that the costs of the additional school-based programs required for K–3 students to meet the state's 75% AYP proficiency requirements by 2010 would be $1.5 billion (Driscoll & Fleeter, 2003). A Texas study indicated that, for all districts in the state to make AYP at the 55% proficiency level required in 2005–2006, the state would need to increase its annual education spending by $1.65 billion; to reach the 70% proficiency level required in future years, the cost would be $4.7 billion (Imazeki & Reschovsky, 2006).

These studies indicate that if Congress were to continue to mandate full proficiency by 2014, and the states seriously attempted to comply, the costs of compliance would substantially exceed the 20–30% general range of cost increases in the general state studies. The Ohio and Texas estimates were based on interim year AYP proficiency goals of 70–75% and did not attempt to calculate the additional amounts that would be required to reach the 100% proficiency. Most economists believe that efforts to meet this goal would entail prohibitive levels of expenditures, especially in the costs of bringing the last—and most difficult—10–15% of underachieving students to proficiency levels. To avoid grappling with the momentous implications of costing out 100% proficiency, the studies to date have either arbitrarily based their calculations on 80% or 90% compliance targets, or, as in Ohio and Texas, have focused on interim year AYP goals that are substantially below the 100% level (Rebell, 2007a).

The real price tag of meeting the 100% proficiency by 2014 mandate may partially explain why Congress has avoided directly confronting the critical cost issues involved with NCLB. This, of course, is another strong reason for revising NCLB to eliminate the unrealistic

100% proficiency requirement. If all children are to obtain a meaningful educational opportunity, and NCLB is to achieve its stated goals, challenging but reasonable expectations for improvements in student achievement must be established and the resources necessary for students to reach these levels must be provided. As long as students attend schools that lack adequate funding to provide essential educational resources, NCLB cannot succeed.

PROVIDING ADEQUATE FUNDING FOR MEANINGFUL EDUCATIONAL OPPORTUNITY

We believe that the federal government should be responsible for identifying the true costs of compliance with NCLB and determining a fair allocation of funding responsibility between the federal government and the states. Given the important national interests that are at stake and the significant federal mandates that are being imposed on the states, the federal government clearly should increase its overall share of educational spending, especially for those states that simply lack adequate resources to meet their students' needs (Liu, 2006). Nevertheless, federal funding need not cover the full increase in costs associated with its mandates; it is appropriate to expect the states to continue to bear most of the costs of public education and to provide adequate resources in order to allow all of their students a meaningful opportunity to meet their own state standards and graduation requirements.

Once realistic estimates of the magnitude of the costs involved in providing all students with meaningful educational opportunities are available, serious discussions about the magnitude of necessary increases and the appropriate federal/state shares can be undertaken. NCLB should require states to include in their state plans information on present and projected funding levels that will enable local school districts to provide the essential resources in all of the categories described in Chapter 4. The plans should also describe the states' efforts to ensure equity in funding and to enable districts with large numbers of low-income and minority students to provide adequate levels of essential resources and services to these students. The annual report cards should document the extent to which these goals are being met. Although state funding systems could continue to be based on a combination of state and local funding sources, states should be held responsible for ensuring that school districts with low tax bases and high needs receive sufficient state aid to meet the basic requirements for providing all of their students with a meaningful educational opportunity. For similar reasons, federal aid to the states should, at a minimum, ensure that states that lack sufficient resources to ensure the availability of essential resources and services to all of their students receive sufficient federal assistance to meet these obligations.

In order to identify the actual costs of providing all students with a meaningful educational opportunity, Congress should, as the NCLB Task Force of the National Conference of State Legislatures (2005) recommended, undertake "a comprehensive study on the costs to states and local districts of 1) complying with the administrative processes of NCLB; and 2) achieving the proficiency goals of NCLB and/or closing the achievement gap" (p. 43). The comprehensive federal cost study would provide critical information for Congress's discussions about appropriate future federal funding levels and for informing the states of the range of costs they need to consider in developing their plans for providing meaningful educational opportunities. These studies should be more than a compilation or repetition of current state-based cost studies; rather, they should induce fiscal policy analysts to advance the state of the art in two ways.

First, comprehensive cost analyses should consider the costs not only of essential school-based resources, but also the costs of the most important out-of-school support services that students from backgrounds of concentrated poverty need to succeed on a sustained basis. Although these comprehensive studies will undoubtedly call for overall spending that exceeds present levels, the actual needs may be more moderate and more manageable than projections based on current practices and policies might imply. For example, major costs that school districts and human services agencies currently bear to compensate adolescents for the absence of adequate resources during their critical early formative years may be unnecessary if the range of necessary services is in fact provided during the early years. In addition, better coordination of the services and funding for child welfare that are already being provided by an array of governmental and private agencies can also result in both significant cost savings and more effective support programs (Kirst, 1993). (A pilot study that seeks to identify the range of in-school and out-of-school services that are most essential to provide meaningful educational opportunities to students from birth through high school and to determine which are most cost-effective is currently being undertaken for the Campaign for Educational Equity by Richard Rothstein and his colleagues.)

Second, the comprehensive cost studies should focus not only on present practices, but also on best practices that can overcome achievement gaps in a cost-effective manner. Most current cost studies defer to the judgments of distinguished educators or researchers, look to the results of districts that currently have successful outcomes, or conduct complex computer projections of levels of funding that will be needed to bring all low-performing students up to proficiency levels. In doing so, each of these different methodologies bases its analyses and conclusions on present practices, present program designs, and present standards for teacher qualifications (Rebell, 2007a). Little attention has been paid in the past to cost study methods that might suggest improvements in efficiency and accountability while still estimating costs that would effectively meet students' educational needs.

Some current studies do propose creative new mechanisms for advancing practice in a cost-effective manner. For example, the New York Adequacy Study proposes class sizes of 14 for elementary school students from backgrounds of concentrated poverty, but minimizes the cost impact of these dramatic reductions in class size by calling for a comprehensive inclusion approach that assumes that virtually all special education students attend these classes, thereby eliminating the many expensive self-contained special education classes that are now pervasive throughout the New York City school system (American Institutes for Research, 2004).

One promising technique for achieving multiple ends is the Quality Education Model (QEM) that has been used for a number of years in Oregon. A QEM is a mechanism for determining both the amount of money and the effective educational practices that will lead to high student performance under a state's learning standards. In Oregon, a Quality Education Commission consisting of state board of education officials, business leaders, superintendents, principals, and teacher representatives was established by the governor and the legislature in 1999. The commission developed a detailed set of educational prototypes and cost analyses and has regularly updated the model and issued reports on a range of cost analysis and best-practice recommendations based on its model (Oregon Quality Education Commission, 2004; Rebell 2007a).

A variation of a QEM approach was recently undertaken in California, where a team of researchers at Stanford University oversaw an extensive project called "Getting Down to Facts," which involved 22 studies at the state, district, and school levels (Loeb, Bryk, & Hanushek, 2007). It addressed a series of interrelated questions on sufficient funding levels in relation to the state's education goals, ways in which resources could be used more effectively to improve student outcomes, and structural changes needed in the state's education finance system. The study was undertaken with the bipartisan support of the governor and the legislature, and included a variety of public engagement processes (Loeb et al., 2007; Rebell, 2007a). The QEM and "Getting Down to Facts" methodologies show great promise for meeting the challenges of identifying the actual costs of efficiently providing all students with a meaningful educational opportunity and, to this end, need to be evaluated, adapted, and extended for the purposes of a comprehensive NCLB cost study. This process will necessarily complement and advance the national dialogue that should identify the specific resources, policies, and practices that are needed to define and implement the concept of meaningful educational opportunity discussed in Chapters 4 and 5.

To accomplish a comprehensive study based on cost-effective best practices, the federal government should solicit proposals and challenge educators, fiscal policy analysts, and economists to develop the innovative techniques needed. Requests for proposals (RFPs) for large-scale studies of this type would focus efforts nationwide on examining and answering the key questions of precisely what resources, policies, and practices are needed to provide all students with meaningful educational opportunities and how these can be implemented in a cost-effective manner. The studies presumably would be based on a representative sample of states and would consider a range of acceptable policies and practices. The government should fund several of these major studies in order to promote maximum consideration of these critical topics and to encourage development of diverse approaches and methodologies for meeting them (Rebell, 2007a). In the past, the government's General Accounting Office (GAO) has estimated education costs of school facilities nationwide and the costs of testing under NCLB based on a seven-state sample (U.S. General Accounting Office, 1995, 2003). The GAO should update these studies, and allow them to be used as a starting point for the more extensive comprehensive studies that we recommend.

The RFPs should specifically call for intensive attention to the needs of English language learners and students with disabilities, groups of students that receive inadequate attention in the present state-based adequacy studies. They should also require analyses of the additional funding that state education departments need not only to administer required tests, but to oversee and assist efforts at capacity-building to ensure that all schools and school districts are capable of providing meaningful educational opportunities. Since NCLB, state education departments have been required to do more, but often with a staff that has been substantially reduced. Michigan's state education department, for example, has lost three quarters of its employees over the past decade, and the New York State Education Department office with prime responsibility for monitoring Title I and low-performing schools was reduced from a staff of more than 90 professionals in 1991 to fewer than 30 professionals in 2004. The result of this severe lack of capacity at the state level is that no state is able to provide adequate intervention services to all or even most of the schools and school districts that need its assistance (Rebell & Wolff, 2006; Sack, 2005).

The end product of these studies will not be definitive analyses that will tell each state or the federal government precisely what amount they need to spend. Rather, the result will be realistic information on costs for policymakers and the public—and solid information on cost effectiveness and best practices for states and localities. These studies will provide a database that will allow for planning and projections to determine the range of resources and services that children need to have a meaningful educational opportunity and directly relate these needs to the states' funding obligations.

With the information provided by these studies, Congress can make informed judgments about how much additional federal funding will be necessary and appropriate to assist states not just with the testing and administration required by the law, but in helping states and localities to build the instructional capacity to meet objectives in a cost-effective manner. This information will also provide the basis for Congress to develop incentives and mandates to ensure that the states match federal resources with the level of state financial effort that is necessary to provide all students with a meaningful educational opportunity.

Moreover, the level of increased funding that is likely to result from these comprehensive studies and the actions that Congress and the states take on the basis of the evidence they present will, over time, be more than compensated for by the benefits that will flow from improved productivity, economic growth, and reductions in other social costs that society now bears. Extensive analysis of the broad range of social costs of inadequate education presented at the 2005 Symposium of the Campaign for Educational Equity at Teachers College concluded that the impact on the American economy in terms of lost income, lost taxes, extra health costs, and increased crime amounts to over $250 billion per year (Belfield & Levin, 2007).

For example, only about half of the nation's high school dropouts now maintain regular employment, compared with 69% of high school graduates, and 74% of college graduates. Those dropouts who are employed earned only 37 cents for each dollar earned by a high school graduate (compared with 64 cents for every dollar earned by a high school graduate in 1965). Lower earnings among dropouts alone could be costing the United States as much as $158 billion in lost earnings and $36 billion in lost state and federal income taxes for each class of 18-year-olds (Rouse, 2005). Increasing the educational attainment of that cohort by only 1 year could recoup almost half of those losses (Rouse, 2005).

Moreover, if one third of all Americans without a high school education went on to get more than a high school education, the savings in regard to welfare programs would range from $3.8 billion to $6.7 billion for Temporary Assistance for Needy Families (TANF), $3.7 billion for food stamps, and $400 million for housing assistance (Waldfogel, Garfinkel, & Kelly, 2005). Similarly, the total lifetime health-related losses for the 600,000 dropouts in 2004 add up to at least $57.9 billion, or nearly $100,000 per student. Just 1 additional year in educational attainment for those 600,000 dropouts could reduce U.S. health costs by $41.8 billion (Muennig, 2005). Increasing the high school completion rate by only 1% for all men ages 20 to 60 could also save the United States up to $1.4 billion each year in the costs of crime; raising the average number of years of schooling by just 1 year reduces murder and assault by almost 30%, motor vehicle theft by 20%, arson by 13%, and burglary and larceny by about 6% (Moretti, 2005).

In addition to the quantifiable financial costs in the areas described above, chronic educational inequities threaten the viability of the nation's civic and political life. For instance, 39% of those with less than a 9th-grade education voted in 2004 versus 56% of those with a high school degree/GED, 78% of those with a bachelor's degree, and 84% of those with advanced degrees (Junn, 2005). These correlations between education and civic participation also have racial and ethnic implications: For example, in 2004, only 28% of Latinos and 56% of Blacks voted, compared with 66% of Whites.

Current educational spending in the United States is third highest in the world for elementary school and fourth highest for high schools, but at the bottom of the scale among affluent nations for preschool services (OECD, 2004). Especially since America emphasizes schooling as its prime antipoverty social program (Anyon & Greene, 2007; Wells, 2006), increased financial effort to narrow achievement gaps and meet the nation's stated educational objectives is appropriate and necessary.

In an increasingly "flat" world, providing an inadequate education to our students will progressively threaten the United States' economic viability in the competitive global marketplace (Friedman, 2005). Perhaps intuitively recognizing the economic and social costs that the nation bears for educational inadequacy, Americans have repeatedly indicated that they are willing to accept higher costs for public education. State and national polls have revealed a consistent willingness of overwhelming majorities (59–75%) to pay higher taxes for education, especially if there is a reasonable expectation that the money will be spent well (see, e.g., *Americans Willing to Pay for Improving Schools*, 1999; *Phi Delta Kappan*, 2006). Including in future cost studies coordinated analyses of cost-efficient best practices, rectifying the imbalance between achievement and opportunity in NCLB, and undertaking the frank and realistic steps that are needed to provide children with a meaningful educational opportunity will enhance the credibility of the act and promote public support for funding increases that are determined to be necessary.

CHAPTER 7

Ensuring Quality Standards, Assessments, and Progress Requirements

The political pact that led to the enactment of NCLB was based on the theory that if schools were given a major increase in their Title I funding, they could reasonably be held accountable for consistent progress toward full proficiency on challenging state content standards as measured by valid and reliable annual tests. But, as the previous two chapters have demonstrated, the statute in its current form does not afford schools and school districts adequate funds or adequate means for accomplishing the goals set for them. Of equal concern, as this chapter will discuss, is that the system for setting and assessing student proficiency standards is badly flawed: Most state content standards have not been shown to be "challenging," and many state assessment systems are not valid in accordance with professional and technical standards. Moreover, the current requirements for measuring progress toward proficiency impose technically impossible demands that increasingly are undermining the effectiveness and credibility of the act. Fair and valid measurement of student progress is vital for educational equity. All of these deficiencies must be rectified if NCLB is to help ensure that all of our students are provided with a meaningful educational opportunity.

CHALLENGING STATE STANDARDS

Challenging state standards that provide American students with the knowledge and skills they need to succeed in life in the 21st century are critical to efforts to secure our national welfare, both economically and socially. Setting uniform high standards and raising expectations

This chapter was written by Michael A. Rebell and Elisabeth K. Thurston.

for all students have also been important strategies in many state and local efforts to advance educational equity. NCLB seeks to expand on these efforts. The act requires every state to adopt "challenging academic content standards in academic subjects that (1) specify what children are expected to know and be able to do; (2) contain coherent and rigorous content; and (3) encourage the teaching of advanced skills" (NCLB, 2001, § 1111(b)). However, at the same time that the statute proclaims these important expectations, it explicitly states that the states "shall not be required to submit such standards to the Secretary" (§ 1111(b)), thereby precluding the Department of Education from reviewing the standards adopted by each state to ensure that they are indeed "challenging."

This inconsistency results from a collision between conflicting policies, on the one hand, the national education goals articulated by the National Education Summits (and endorsed by Presidents George H. W. Bush and Bill Clinton) and, on the other, the traditional prerogative under our federal system of states and local districts to set education policy. Robert Schwartz (2006) summarizes how this tension played out in the initial Goals 2000 context:

> At the outset of the standards movement the hope was that we could forge enough of a political consensus around national standards so that, even if they were voluntary, virtually all states would use them as guideposts in the development of their own standards. In fact this is what happened in mathematics where, at least until the outbreak of the math wars in California, virtually all states adopted nearly *in toto* the standards developed by the National Council of Teachers of Mathematics. Unfortunately, the well-intentioned efforts on the part of the Bush I administration to encourage the development of similar standards in English and history backfired, leading to an environment for the next decade in which it was nearly impossible for elected officials to utter the words "national" and "standards" in the same sentence. Consequently, the Clinton and Bush II administrations had to resort to much more indirect strategies to address the challenge of bringing some measure of national quality control to the standards and assessment development work of states. (p. 7)

Although President Clinton's original proposal for his America 2000 bill would have required states to submit their standards to the Department of Education for approval before receiving funds, the final version of the 1994 act called only for "voluntary" national standards to be developed by a National Education Standards and Improvement Council (NESIC), and to which states could voluntarily bring their standards and tests for review and comment (McGuinn, 2006). At the time, governors such as Roy Romer (CO) and John Engler (MI) spoke in favor of an external review process by which they could verify their own state education officials' claims that the standards under development were, in fact, "world class" (Schwartz, 2006).

Following the Republican takeover of Congress in 1995, the more conservative Republican majority repealed the provisions for voluntary national standards even before President Clinton had nominated a slate of individuals for the NESIC board. Despite hardening opposition to standards from some members of Congress, continuing support from moderate Republicans and the business community allowed the Clinton administration to again address the issue of the quality and comparability of state standards at the beginning of Clinton's second term. Then the president proposed the development of voluntary national tests in reading in grade 4 and math in grade 8 (DeBray, 2006). As Schwartz (2006) explains,

> The unstated premise behind this proposal was that, even though these exams were to be voluntary and have no stakes attached, parents would be motivated to take action if the information they received about their child's achievement from the national test was wildly at variance with what they were told from the state test. Under the most optimistic scenario the voluntary national tests would acquire sufficient political salience to motivate states to use them as benchmarks against which to align their own standards and tests. Again, however, a Republican-controlled Congress opposed the Clinton proposal as an undue expansion of the federal role, and the program died for lack of Congressional authorization. (p. 8)

In light of this history, when NCLB was enacted in 2001, Congress was reluctant to revive the political battles regarding national standards and instead adopted the seemingly contradictory language that requires "rigorous" and challenging state standards, but precludes the Department of Education or any other federal authority from reviewing the standards or ensuring their rigor. Consistent with the statutory prohibition against federal review of the state standards, the Department of Education's protocols for peer review of state standards and assessments emphasize process factors (formal adoption of standards, inclusion of education stakeholders in their development, and so on) and omit any directions for the reviewers to analyze the quality of the state's standards (U.S. Department of Education, 2005). With the great federal pressure to demonstrate high levels of student achievement and progress toward 100% proficiency in 2014 and the high stakes for failure, the predictable result of this feeble enforcement approach is that states have a "perverse incentive" to adopt less challenging standards (Ryan, 2004).

Analyses of State Content Standards

Given the lack of any federal oversight and NCLB's perverse incentives to keep standards low, it is not surprising that, by and large, NCLB has not inspired states to adopt truly challenging content standards or to strengthen weak pre-NCLB standards. Beginning in the mid-1990s, organizations such as the Fordham Foundation and the American Federation of Teachers (AFT) have published assessments of the quality of state content standards. The Fordham Foundation, which focuses on the appropriateness of the content explicated by the standards, has tended to levy somewhat harsher critiques than the AFT, which emphasizes specificity and alignment between standards and assessments. Despite these differences, both organizations have exposed numerous problems with state content standards, as well as wide variation between the states.

An initial Fordham Foundation evaluation of the quality of content standards in multiple subjects (English, math, science, history, and geography) reported a nationwide average of D+, with only three states earning average marks in the B range (Finn, Petrilli, & Vanourek, 1998). Similar results followed in the Fordham Foundation's 2000 analysis, which found only slight improvements, up to an average C– level (Finn & Petrilli, 2000). The AFT, focusing on the four subject areas of English, math, science, and social studies, found only 17 states with standards that were "clear, specific, and well-grounded in content" for all four subjects in 1997 (Gandal, 1997, p. 15). The AFT later disaggregated its results by elementary, middle, and high school standards in each of the four subject areas. Using this approach, the AFT (2001) reported that only six states met the requirements for high-quality standards in all subjects at all grade levels, but 30 states met the criteria for being clear, specific, and well-grounded at least 75% of the time.

Since the implementation of NCLB, some 37 states have revised or replaced their content standards, but the national average, as calculated by the Fordham Foundation, remains at the same C– level as it was prior to NCLB (Finn, Julian, & Petrilli, 2006). This report was based on expert reviews of the specificity and grade-level suitability of the knowledge and skills represented in the standards. Overall, Fordham found that content standards were vague and emphasized skills rather than knowledge. Their bottom line is that only three states deserve an A for the quality of their standards—California, Indiana, and Massachusetts; six more deserve some form of B; the rest—more than half—get Ds and Fs. Some states, such as Utah, Nebraska, and New Hampshire, actually got worse overall post-NCLB (Finn, Julian, & Petrilli, 2006). Rather than focusing on the grade appropriateness of the content standards, the AFT's 2006 report emphasized alignment between each state's content standards and assessments. In its 2006 report, the AFT looked for states that, in its judgment, had both strong content standards and tests that were well aligned with those standards. The AFT credits only 11 states with meeting those criteria.

Achieve, a bipartisan organization established by the governors and corporate leaders after the national education summits, has undertaken benchmarking studies for 14 states that voluntarily asked the organization to assess their standards against "world-class" criteria. Its overall conclusions were that most of the state standards more effectively covered basic skills than analytic skills and that only one of the 14 states had "world-class" balance and range (Schwartz, 2006, p. 5). The Achieve findings pinpoint one of the major problems with the standards that have been adopted in many of the states: They tend to focus on breadth of content, rather than on the depth of higher-order thinking skills that are necessary to function productively in the 21st century.

NAEP and Comparability

In an effort to provide some level of comparability and quality control over state achievement and content standards, NCLB requires states to participate in the National Assessment of Educational Progress (NAEP), a federally administered test whose results are often referred to as the "nation's report card." NAEP assessments in reading and math must be administered biennially to a representative sample of the student population in each state in grades 4 and 8 (NCLB, 2001). Although NAEP cannot be directly aligned with the specific standards in each of the 50 states, its frameworks were developed with attention to state curriculum frameworks and with feedback from state education officials. In addition, Popham (2004) has observed that in the case of reading and math, "there is substantial overlap with respect to what's to be learned by children in those two subject areas. Some differences will occasionally be encountered from state to state, but in reading and mathematics, educators in different states usually want kids to learn pretty much the same sorts of things" (p. 17). Thus, at least in theory, student progress toward state proficiency should coincide with similar progress toward proficiency as demonstrated according to NAEP. This has not been the case. Although nearly three quarters of all states and school districts report that overall achievement is rising and achievement gaps are decreasing on state tests (Jennings, 2006), a comprehensive comparison of national and state reading and math outcomes by the Harvard Civil Rights Project demonstrated that achievement has remained virtually flat on NAEP and reductions in achievement gaps have not been sustained (Lee, 2006).

A study by Policy Analysis for California Education (PACE) that compared national and state testing results from 2002 to 2006 had similar findings. PACE reported that in the vast majority of states, the disparity between the percentage of students proficient on state assessments and the percentage of students proficient on NAEP has remained the same or widened since the implementation of NCLB. PACE attributes this to NCLB sanctions creating an incentive to set a low bar for proficiency (Fuller, Gesicki, Kang, & Wright, 2006). In an extreme example from 2003, 87% of students in Mississippi were judged to be proficient in reading on the state assessment, but only 18% of the state's students demonstrated proficiency on NAEP; similarly, 86% of students in Texas were considered proficient in reading based on the state test, while only 27% met NAEP proficiency levels (Commission on NCLB, 2007). In states known to have demanding content standards, the discrepancies between state scores and NAEP scores are starkly reduced: In Massachusetts, 56% of students demonstrate proficiency on the state test and 40% perform at proficient levels on NAEP.

NCLB's "perverse incentives" have also led some states to lower their effective proficiency levels in order to avoid sanctions for failing to meet AYP requirements geared to 100% proficiency by 2014. For example, when developing its state accountability system in 1999, Louisiana had matched its proficiency goals to the NAEP levels; it aimed to educate all students to the basic level by 2009 and to the proficient level by 2019. Knowing that it could not meet NAEP proficiency levels by 2014, Louisiana now uses its "basic" rather than "proficient" level when reporting student achievement for AYP purposes (Hoff, 2002). Pennsylvania and Colorado use similar approaches in reporting NCLB proficiency levels (Hoff, 2002; Kingsbury et al., 2003).

For NCLB to be effective and to have integrity—and for proficiency, by whatever date, to have reliable, substantive content—the federal government must take a more proactive role to ensure that all state academic content standards are, in fact, challenging. It is both inequitable and inconsistent with the national purpose of preparing all of our children to be capable of citizenship and to compete in the global economy for children in Mississippi and Texas to be educated at substantially lower levels than children in Massachusetts. Congress has failed to confront this glaring problem since the mid-1990s in order to avoid a repetition of the political battles that raged over the issue of national standards at that time. But, as one recent report on this subject put it, "the times are a changing. Business leaders' concerns about economic competitiveness . . . indicate that national standards and tests may no longer be politically taboo" (Finn et al., 2006, p. 14).

Ensuring Quality Standards

The Aspen Institute's commission on No Child Left Behind (2007), a bipartisan body headed by two former governors, has called for the development of voluntary model national content and performance standards and tests in reading or language arts, mathematics, and science, based on NAEP frameworks. It recommends that a distinguished national panel be commissioned to create the standards and tests for grades 4, 8, and 12, based on NAEP frameworks. The Aspen commission further recommends that once these model standards and tests are created, states be given a choice of 1) adopting the national model standards and tests as their own; 2) building their own assessment instruments based on the national model standards; or 3) keeping their existing standards or tests (or revamping them in response to the national model standards and tests). States choosing the second or third option would have their standards and tests analyzed and compared with the national model. The U.S. secretary of education would then periodically issue reports comparing the quality of all state standards to the national model and tests using a common metric.

This proposal provides a sensible approach for balancing the clear need for national criteria to ensure that all state standards are challenging and rigorous while retaining sufficient local control of education. Like our proposal to encourage states to develop the criteria for providing the essential resources and services needed to provide all students with a meaningful educational opportunity, the Aspen approach allows states to develop and shape their content standards to meet local needs and values, but, at the same time, provides federal guidance on quality standards and a mechanism for informing the public in clear terms when particular state standards fail to conform to federal expectations for challenging content. Presumably, business leaders, parents, advocacy groups, and the public at large in states that are identified in the secretary's report as having deficient standards will be motivated to pressure their policymakers to raise their standards to acceptable levels.

The commission also sensibly emphasizes the importance of having NCLB test all students at the 12th-grade level, instead of only in the earlier grades, to "help ensure continuous student growth through high school and create a useful measure of a school's effectiveness in preparing students for work and college" (Commission on No Child Left Behind, 2007, p. 136). Since 12th grade is the culminating point for the citizenship and employment knowledge and skills that students need to succeed in the 21st century, assessment at that stage is critical to meeting the act's goals.

We suggest two major qualifications to this proposal, however. First, we believe that the model standards to be adopted by the national panel must extend beyond the core subjects of English language arts, math, and science. There is increasing evidence that NCLB's focus on these three core subjects is taking time and attention away from the teaching of other important subjects, especially in schools that serve low-income and minority students (Von Zastrow & Janc, 2004). As James Popham (2004) notes, "Content not assessed on a high-stakes test is content cast aside" (p. 65.) For example, data from a federal survey from the 2003–2004 school year showed that instructional time in history in grades 1–4 dropped by about 30 minutes per day from the early 1990s (Cavanagh, 2007). A recent in-depth case study analysis of the impact of exit exams on two urban school districts found that the emphasis on test exam preparation limited the availability of time to study longer pieces of literature, to go into topics in depth, or to take electives (Zabala & Minnici, 2007).

The state court adequacy cases have given considerable attention to the purposes of public education, and, as discussed in Chapter 4, a basic consensus has emerged from these cases regarding the types of broad knowledge and skills that students need to be prepared for competitive employment and to function productively in a democratic society. We recommend, therefore, that NCLB adopt this state court adequacy consensus in order to provide a solid floor of educational quality for the proficiency requirements of NCLB and to guard against a narrow interpretation of the educational opportunities that schools need to provide. The National Assessment Governing Board (NAGB), the federal body that sets policy for NAEP, advocates expanding NCLB requirements for state-based NAEP testing to include—in addition to mathematics, English language arts, and science—history, geography, civics, foreign language, the arts, and economics, in that priority order, to the extent that resources are available (NAGB, 2006). We believe that the necessary resources *must* be made available to develop national model standards and NAEP testing related to them in all of these important subject areas.

The national panel should also incorporate in its model standards the valuable insights on aligning high school graduation standards with the specific levels of knowledge and skills needed for college and for work currently being developed by the American Diploma Project (2007). This will help ensure that state standards and state exit examinations properly emphasize the higher-order cognitive skills that students need to succeed in college and in the world of work.

The panel should include at least some of these skills in their 4th-grade and 8th-grade model tests. Although an emphasis on reading and math skills in the early grades may be a necessary prerequisite for advanced learning, NCLB must rectify the current imbalance in subject-matter emphases and between basic skills and advanced conceptual thinking by highlighting the importance of students' gaining deep knowledge and skills in a broad range of subject areas by the time they graduate from high school (National Center on Education and the Economy, 2007). Some states, such as Kentucky, already include assessments in a broad range of subject areas in their accountability systems (Linn, 2006); NCLB should require all states to do the same.

We realize that the recommendation to increase the number of mandatory tests under NCLB may be problematic for those who are critical of the current tests. Tests that are addressed to a broad range of subject areas and that seek to evaluate higher-order conceptual skills must, by their very nature, be more formative that the standardized tests that tend to be used for elementary school reading and mathematics assessments. Teaching to such tests would promote student learning rather than constrain it. Moreover, removing the perverse incentives created by the unattainable 2014 full proficiency mandate, and utilizing reasonable AYP criteria, should reduce much of the test anxiety and apprehension that now exists. In any event, if we accept the fact that outcome measures are the core of the accountability system for standards-based reform and for NCLB, a substantial amount of testing is unavoidable. Better efforts can be made, however, to ensure that the right things are being tested and that the tests themselves are both technically valid and coordinated with the learning process to the maximum extent possible.

The Aspen proposal is also vague on what authority the secretary of education will have to require states that have declined to adopt the national standards and are using lesser state standards to either adopt the national standards or upgrade their own. We believe that states that are using low-grade standards or setting unreasonably low proficiency requirements should promptly be required to adopt the national benchmark standards or bring their own standards up to a satisfactory level of quality. Although we proposed in Chapter 4 that any ultimate federal enforcement action regarding the level of essential educational resources be deferred to give the states sufficient time to respond to these broad new requirements, because the validity of all of the states' adequate yearly progress assessments depends on the integrity of their standards and proficiency levels, enforcement of requirements for challenging standards should promptly be put into effect as soon as the federal benchmark standards have been developed and the evaluation of state standards in relation to them has been completed.

VALID STUDENT ASSESSMENTS

In order to measure the annual performance of each state and local educational agency and each school, NCLB requires states to implement a system of "high quality, yearly academic assessments . . . that are aligned with the State's challenging academic content and student achievement standards . . . and are used for purposes for which such assessments are valid and reliable, [consistent] with relevant, nationally recognized professional and technical standards" (NCLB, 2001, § 1111 (b) (3) (C)). However, the Department of Education has not effectively enforced these requirements, even though there is evidence that most state tests used to measure progress under NCLB are neither aligned with state content standards nor valid in accordance with applicable professional standards.

Alignment with Content Standards

The basic purpose of the annual assessments in reading, math, and science required under NCLB is to determine the extent to which students are developing the skills and learning the subject matter encompassed by each state's content standards. To carry out this purpose, the domains covered by these tests obviously must closely reflect the skills and knowledge set forth in the standards. However, according to analyses conducted by the Fordham Foundation, the AFT, and Achieve, few states seem to have substantially aligned their tests with their standards in this manner (AFT, 2006; Cross, Rebarber, & Torres, 2004; Rothman, 2004). Analyzing both the degree to which individual test items reflected a state's grade-level content standards and/or whether the test as a whole demonstrated the same depth and breadth of content coverage as the standards, the Fordham Foundation determined that only five of the 50 states demonstrated strong alignment between their standards and their tests (Cross, Rebarber, & Torres, 2004). As was mentioned earlier, the AFT's 2006 analysis indicated that the standards and tests in only 11 states were fully aligned.

Achieve reported an improvement in alignment between content standards and assessments since the early days of standards-based reform, but cautioned that, in many cases, this alignment was superficial or imbalanced in terms of the standards assessed (i.e., particular standards are overemphasized in the test items, while other standards might not be represented at all) (Rothman, 2004). The Achieve studies found that state tests tended to measure the least cognitively complex concepts in the standards, and, in many cases, they measured student mastery of content that was several years below the grade level being assessed (Rothman, 2004).

Test Validity

Test validity refers to the "degree to which evidence and theory support the interpretations of test scores entailed by proposed uses of tests" (American Educational Research Association, American Psychological Association, & National Council on Measurement in Education, 1999, p. 9). In essence, a test is not "valid" in and of itself; rather, its validity depends on whether the inferences that can be drawn from the evidence developed about the content of the test and the test takers' performance on the test reasonably relate to the purposes for which the test is being used. For example, a test of teacher competency that assesses minimum competency skills may be valid for purposes of initial certification, but would not be valid for determining eligibility for tenure of an experienced teacher.

Since the purpose of the requirements for annual testing in reading, math, and science in the NCLB is to determine the progress each school, school district, and state is making toward attaining 100% proficiency by 2014, for state assessments to be valid for this purpose, they must provide an accurate picture of how much instructional progress is really taking place in relation to the state's proficiency standards (Popham, 2004). Given the apparent lack of alignment of many state tests with state content standards, a serious question arises as to whether many of these tests are, in fact, valid for the extensive purposes for which they are being used. The Department of Education's peer review team process does require documentation of test validation, although the extent to which the peer review team probes beyond process to determine the substantiality of the validation evidence that has been accumulated is not clear (Davis & Buckendahl, 2007). In any event, based on these reviews, in July 2006, the Department of Education notified 37 states that their funding was in jeopardy because of deficiencies in their testing programs (Commission on No Child Left Behind, 2007). Some of these issues have apparently been resolved, but, to date, the assessment systems of only 20 of the 50 states have received full approval from the U.S. Department of Education (2007b).

An additional significant validation issue is raised by states' cut scores. Cut scores indicate the percentage of questions that must be answered correctly to reach varying levels of achievement ("basic," "proficient," and "advanced"). They are generally determined through a process by which a panel of "judges" (individuals with expertise in the subject matter) review all of the test items and estimate the percentage of students at each proficiency level that could correctly answer that question. Their pooled judgments are then presented to the state board of education or other policymakers for a final decision about precisely where the cut score for determining proficiency should be. Policymakers often lower the score determined by the panel by one or two standard deviations, or even more (Rotherham, 2006). Theoretically, these downward adjustments are made to account for margins of error, but these decisions are also often made with an eye toward the numbers of students who are likely to receive acceptable scores at different cut score levels (Rotherham, 2006).

The available evidence suggests that manipulation of cut scores to inflate the number of students designated as "proficient" is rampant (Achieve, 2002; Lee, 2006; Fuller et al., 2006). The Northwest Evaluation Association, a nonprofit organization specializing in assessment, and the Thomas B. Fordham Institute concluded in a recent report that of 19 states studied from 2002–2006, reading and/or math tests became significantly easier in eight states and harder in four states (Cronin, Dahlin, Adkins, & Kingsbury, 2007). In another study comparing student achievement levels on state tests used for NCLB compliance with performance on their own norm-referenced tests, the Northwest Evaluation Association found that students who attained the proficient level for reading in the 8th grade in Wyoming were at the 74th percentile, while those in neighboring Colorado who attained proficiency were at the 12th percentile (Kingsbury et al., 2003).

The National Center for Education Statistics (NCES) found comparable results in its June 2007 report, *Mapping 2005 State Proficiency Standards onto the NAEP Scales*. NCES calculated a NAEP equivalent for each state's proficiency cut score. To meet the state's math proficiency standard, a 4th-grade student in Tennessee must achieve a score that is equivalent to 200 on the NAEP scale. (The minimum NAEP proficiency score is 249.) A student in Massachusetts, however, must achieve a score of at least 255, six points above NAEP's minimum proficiency score, to reach the proficient level.

An area of special concern is the validity of the tests that are being used with students with limited English proficiency (LEP). As pointed out in Chapter 3, NCLB requires LEP students to take an English language proficiency test, and, in addition, the law requires them to meet the same grade-level content proficiency requirements as other students. (Only the scores of recently arrived LEP students—defined as having attended a U.S. school for 1 year or less—do not need to be included in AYP calculations.) Yet, virtually none of the subject-matter tests being used to measure content knowledge of LEPs has been validated for use with this population (Crawford, 2007), and this means that we have virtually no accurate knowledge of the actual levels of proficiency of these students.

Even if a test has been validated for use with the general population, when the test is administered in English to students who are not sufficiently proficient in English, its validity is seriously compromised (AERA et al., 1999). This is because linguistic deficits interfere with a fair assessment of a student's knowledge of the subject matter, and students' test scores, therefore, cannot be considered fair indicators of their actual level of achievement (Butler & Stevens, 2001; Menken, 2000). This point has been substantiated by recent research that indicates that LEP students who score at the highest levels in English proficiency are twice as likely to meet minimum English language arts scores as those with low English proficiency levels. Very few students with low English proficiency score well on state language arts and math assessments (Francis, Rivera, Lesaux, Kieffer, & Rivera, 2006).

Although NCLB permits LEP students to take assessments in their native language for 3 years, plus 2 additional years if deemed necessary, only 11 states make assessments available in native languages statewide (Zehr, 2005). Many states point to the high costs of developing alternative assessments, especially in places where linguistic diversity can require testing of students from up to 130 different linguistic backgrounds (Washington Area School Study Council, 2003). Moreover, it is not even clear that the few native language assessments that are available meet applicable test validation requirements. As Lazarín (2006) points out, merely translating existing tests into another language is not sufficient. For the test to be a valid assessment of LEP students' content knowledge, it must be culturally appropriate, and the skills and knowledge being assessed must be expressed in concepts that are familiar to the student and his or her experiences.

The law permits testing accommodations for LEP students, yet most of the frequently used accommodations, such as allowing extra testing time, reading directions aloud, or administering tests individually, have proved to be of limited benefit to LEP students (Abedi, 2001; Lazarín, 2006). Only one particular accommodation has been shown to narrow the performance gap between LEP and non-LEP students: reducing the complexity of language on test items with excessive language demands (Abedi, 2001).

The core of the design of NCLB rests on fair and accurate assessment of student performance and progress. If the methods used to measure progress toward proficiency are inaccurate or subject to widespread manipulation, the validity and credibility of the entire enterprise is undermined. The lack of professional confidence in the validity of the assessments being used in most states—and particularly in the setting of cut scores and the validity of tests for LEP students—therefore constitutes a veritable crisis for NCLB. Clearly, definitive steps must be taken to boost the integrity of NCLB's assessment regime.

Because of the paucity of substantive analysis on the validity of the tests upon which the NCLB accountability system is based, NCLB should be revised to require each state to undergo an external review of the validity of its tests and of its cut score procedures by an independent agency with expertise in this area from a list of such agencies approved by the secretary of education. The Department of Education should then review this evidence and scrupulously enforce the already existing requirements in the law that these tests be "valid and reliable, and be consistent with relevant, nationally recognized professional and technical standards" (NCLB, 2001, § 111 (b) (3) (C) (iii)).

Given that few validated tests for English language learners exist at the present time, the federal government should take responsibility for developing benchmark tests in all mandated subjects and grade levels in Spanish and at least five other major languages commonly used in American schools. The states should then adapt and align these tests with their own standards. The costs involved in such an endeavor would overtax the resources of any single state and should be borne by the federal government. The states should also be required to use these federally validated tests, or appropriately adapted versions of them, for assessing the content knowledge of their ELL students unless they can demonstrate that they have developed fully validated tests of their own.

SOUND PROGRESS REQUIREMENTS

Under NCLB, states, school districts, and schools must show compliance with the law's mandate that all students be proficient in challenging state standards by 2014 by reaching state-set progress targets each year. Adequate yearly progress calculations that are based on student test scores at the school level are used to judge progress toward proficiency.

Examination of the Problems

A basic problem here is that the concept of "proficiency," which is at the heart of the NCLB accountability system, is inherently elusive. There is no scientific basis for defining "proficient" performance, and "proficiency standards" are really educational/political judgments for encouraging improved performance that have no inherent psychometric authority. Even NAEP's methods for establishing its "basic," "proficient," and "advanced" designations have been repeatedly criticized by a number of federal commissions and the federal government's own General Accounting Office as being "inherently flawed" because they were determined by nonexpert judges whose determinations were not guided by any objective criteria (Rothstein, Jacobsen, & Wilder, 2006, pp. 37–38).

Richard Rothstein and his colleagues explain that "When proficiency criteria were established for NAEP in the early 1990s, the criteria were made unreasonably high because policy makers wanted to spur school reform by demonstrating (or exaggerating) how poorly American students perform" (p. 41). To substantiate this point, Rothstein and colleagues cite a study by Gary Phillips, the former U.S. commissioner of education statistics, linking the NAEP scale to the scale used in the Third International Mathematics and Science Study (TIMSS) developed by the International Association for the Evaluation of Educational Achievement (IEA) to compare student achievement in 46 countries. Phillips found only five countries where the average 8th grader would score at proficient levels according to NAEP. Even in Singapore, the highest-scoring country in the world in TIMSS 8th-grade math and science, 25% of the students would be less than proficient on NAEP's 8th-grade math scale, and 49% would be less than proficient in science (Rothstein et al., 2006).

In addition to the problems stemming from the inherently judgmental nature of the concept of "proficiency," the term *adequate yearly progress* is a misnomer, since the method that is used to make these calculations does not really measure "progress." What it actually measures is the performance status of all students and certain subgroups of students in each school at a certain point in time. To use the running metaphor from earlier in this book, if students must run a 10-minute mile to be considered proficient, AYP would merely tell us the percentage of 8th-grade students running at least a 10-minute mile in a given year. It would not tell us anything about the students who had progressed from a 12-minute mile to a 10:02-minute mile during the past year, nor would it tell us anything about those students who improved their pace from a 9- to a 7-minute mile (or the practices that enabled them to do so). In fact, it wouldn't tell us anything about the progress of any particular students at all because "progress" is not measured in relationship to individual students.

In essence, AYP as currently used is a "status" indicator, which tells us only how fast this year's cohort of 8th graders ran on a particular day in comparison with last year's cohort of 8th graders. The Department of Education makes inferences concerning "progress" by seeing whether more 8th-grade students reached proficiency targets this year than last, but these inferences may not account for a host of factors, other than school quality, that may have affected the actual outcomes. For example, an influx of new immigrants, the exodus of high-scoring students to a new magnet school, and other demographic differences between one cohort and another would affect a school's AYP scores, but would not reflect actual changes in the school's programs or student progress.

A further problem with the current approach to AYP is that schools with diverse populations, which also tend to be those serving large numbers of disadvantaged students, are more likely to face sanctions for failing to make AYP (Goldschmidt & Choi, 2007). Since AYP is calculated not only for the school as a whole, but also on a disaggregated basis for all racial/ethnic subgroups, low-income students, students with disabilities, and English language learners, schools that have more of the subgroups have more opportunities to miss AYP. In addition, the students in such schools are likely to perform at lower initial performance levels than their more advantaged peers, requiring them to make greater progress toward universal proficiency in the same amount of time. Teachers and administrators in these schools are faced with the task of raising achievement at rates never before seen or risk being labeled as failures (Choi, Goldschmidt, & Yamashiro, 2005, p. 132). This provides the best teachers and principals—those who have a choice of employment opportunities—with a perverse incentive to avoid schools in the greatest need of high-quality staffing.

In addition, the complex methodology used to calculate AYP provides many opportunities for states and school districts to manipulate their figures to avoid being subject to sanctions under the act. For example, states are given broad leeway in defining the size of their subgroups. Although many states use 20 students in any subcategory per school as a basic measuring rod, others use 40 or even 100. This means that in the latter states, schools that have 39 or even 99 low-performing racial minority or LEP students can ignore their scores in their disaggregated reporting. States are also given great leeway to manipulate the AYP timetable, and many have done so by minimizing the progress they need to make in the early years and "back-loading" the bulk of their obligations to the years that are closer to the 2014 proficiency date (Popham, 2004; Riddle, 2006a). The fact that some, but not all, states and school districts "game" the system in this way renders it difficult to calculate or compare actual progress among schools and among states in a fair, uniform manner.

The law further allows states wide discretion in the use of statistical concepts such as confidence intervals and standard errors of measurement, in averaging scores over several years, and in the reporting of disaggregated district scores by schooling level (elementary, middle, high school). A state that takes advantage of most or all of these loopholes, like Wisconsin, can show 99.8% of its districts making AYP in 2004–2005, while a state like North Carolina, which provides more complete and transparent data, shows only 7% making AYP (Carey, 2006). In addition, the Department of Education, in an ad hoc manner and without use of uniform regulations, has allowed individual states waivers, or "state accountability plan amendments," that further undermine the integrity of NCLB as a mechanism to ensure accountability for quality education nationwide. For example, Florida has been allowed to use a new designation of "provisional AYP" for schools that met requirements under its state accountability system but did not satisfy normal federal AYP standards, and some states have been allowed to change the starting point or the intermediate goals along their timelines to 100% proficiency (Sunderman, 2006).

Fair assessment of the progress of students with disabilities presents additional problems. NCLB requires most students with disabilities, like all other students, to meet AYP targets and to meet the mandated proficiency targets by 2014. The regulations do specify that students with disabilities are entitled to receive testing accommodations and that students with the most significant cognitive disabilities who cannot participate in their state's general assessment—up to 1% of the total tested population—may be provided an alternate assessment that "differs in complexity from a grade-level achievement standard" (U.S. Department of Education, 2007a). In addition, students with disabilities who can make significant progress but may not reach grade-level achievement standards within the same time frame as other students—up to 2% of the tested population—may be held to "modified" achievement standards, which may reflect reduced breadth or depth of grade-level content (U.S. Department of Education, 2007a).

Even with these exceptions, a serious issue arises as to whether it is reasonable to hold special education students to the standard proficiency and AYP requirements. There is an inherent contradiction between NCLB's demands and the basic thrust of the federal Individuals with Disabilities Act (IDEA), which requires students with disabilities to be educated in accordance with individual education plans that set academic goals in accordance with their particular schooling needs and capabilities. Although including most special education students in the basic AYP calculations does aid the general "mainstreaming" and "inclusion" goals of the IDEA and motivates schools to provide challenging curricula to these students, it is not clear that NCLB's proficiency goals and timelines are attainable for many of these students, since they have been diagnosed as needing special education services precisely because they have a disability that impedes their ability to learn (McLaughlin, 2006).

To the extent that it is not reasonable to hold special education students (beyond the allowed exceptions) to the regular NCLB requirements, schools and school districts with relatively large cohorts of such students are being penalized unfairly. Not surprisingly, therefore, it is school districts and schools with large numbers of special education students that tend to take greatest advantage of the available loopholes in an attempt to exempt as many of these students as possible from AYP calculations. The Center on Education Policy (2005) reported that special education students were not included in the calculation of AYP for 92% of schools in California due to a subgroup size of fewer than 100 students. In an analysis of five states, CEP also found that 80% of schools meeting AYP targets did not include the subgroup of disabled students (McLaughlin, 2006).

Recommended Revisions

To remedy all of these problems and create a set of sound progress requirements, we recommend major revisions in NCLB's approach to "proficiency" determinations and in the manner by which AYP is calculated. The first step that needs to be taken in this regard is to reconsider the NAEP designation of its "basic," "proficient," and "advanced" levels. NAEP serves as an informal national benchmark for judging the validity of the proficiency levels that each of the states has established for its assessments. If NAEP standards are unreasonably high and expert independent analyses sponsored by the federal government itself have repeatedly criticized the methodology that was used to designate NAEP's performance levels, the credibility of the entire system is undermined.

In 1994, Congress itself stated that NAEP's current achievement levels should be used only on a "developmental basis" until the commissioner of education statistics reevaluated them and determined that the levels were reasonable and valid. Buried in the fine print of all NAEP reports since that time have been disclaimers about the validity of the proficiency levels being used (Rothstein et al., 2006). It is time for the long-delayed reevaluation of NAEP proficiency levels to take place. Given the increasing importance that NAEP scores have assumed in recent years as national benchmarks for proficiency, the NAGB and the commissioner of education statistics need promptly to develop and circulate for public comment a sound methodology for establishing NAEP proficiency levels that reflect challenging but attainable levels of achievement for America's students.

Furthermore, to fulfill the critical new role that NAEP would play under our proposed system as the framework that a distinguished panel would use to establish national benchmark standards, the basic content of the NAEP exams, and the extent to which they emphasize higher-order cognitive skills, take on added significance. The procedures for establishing the content and the proficiency levels for these new NAEP exams must also reflect on a continuing basis positive curriculum innovations that are being undertaken by the states. The convening of a distinguished national panel to deal with these matters will provide an appropriate occasion to reconsider the critical standard content and proficiency level issues that are at the heart of NCLB's capacity for ensuring that children are, in fact, being educated in accordance with "challenging," high-quality educational norms.

The final methodology that NAGB and the commissioner use for establishing credible proficiency levels for NAEP should then be widely disseminated to the states. The secretary of education in his or her review of state annual reports should analyze the methodologies used to establish proficiency levels for state assessments and comment on any major deviations between the methodologies used by the states and the methodologies used by NAEP. States whose proficiency levels are not aligned with high-quality state standards—and that cannot offer adequate proof that their proficiency levels have been validated as meeting applicable professional standards by an independent psychometric agency approved by the secretary—should be required to revise their proficiency determinations.

The major reform needed in regard to AYP calculations is to base them on a "growth model" that tracks individual student progress from one year to the next, instead of relying on the current "status" of the school or grade as a whole. A growth model gives schools credit for student improvement over time, and thereby provides a more accurate picture of school performance. Mounting interest in such growth models prompted the Department of Education in 2006 to launch a growth model pilot project (U.S. Department of Education, 2006b). As of May 2007, five states, out of 20 that applied, received approval to implement growth models in the calculation of AYP for the 2006–2007 school year, and two others also received conditional approval (U.S. Department of Education, 2007b).

The conditions that the Department of Education has attached to this pilot growth model project have, however, compromised the potential significance of this experiment. The most serious limitation is that the participating states are still required to adhere to the unattainable mandate for universal proficiency by 2014 and, therefore, they will still be expected to make impossible achievement gains in a short period of time. Furthermore, the states' growth model proposals were required to "set expectations for annual achievement based on meeting grade-level proficiency, not on student background or school characteristics" (U.S. Department of Education, 2006b), thereby perpetuating the implicit assumption of the present system that "it is possible to isolate a school's effect from all other factors that might influence achievement (e.g., student background or inputs outside of a school's control)" (Choi, Goldschmidt, & Yamashiro, 2005, p. 122). Finally, states were required to "validate" pilot growth models by comparing schools that did not meet AYP under the current NCLB model with schools that are operating under the proposed growth model. The implicit criterion reflected in this requirement is that use of a growth model should not yield markedly different results from the present system, so there is little reason to expect the adoption of

U.S. Department of Education–approved growth models to do much to cure present problems (Goldschmidt & Choi, 2007).

We believe that NCLB should be revised not only to allow but to require all states to develop effective growth models that are not tethered to the unattainable mandate for 100% proficiency by 2014, and that take into account student background and school characteristics in determining reasonable expectations for progress in student achievement. Growth models that include a "value-added" component best achieve these ends.

With a "value-added" growth model, individual student progress is tracked, as with a basic growth model, but, in addition, the model uses additional data to determine the unique contribution teachers and schools have made to student learning gains (McCaffrey et al., 2003). In order to isolate the effect of a given year of education, value-added models typically adjust for the effect of student background or prior years of education either implicitly or explicitly (Choi, Goldschmidt, & Yamashiro, 2005). For instance, a model that considers the difference between the learning gains of one teacher's students and the average gain of the entire school district can tell us how much "value" that particular teacher added to those students' learning, *but only* if we can assume there are no differences in resources between schools in the district and no systematic differences in the student populations of classrooms across the district (McCaffrey et al., 2003). We know that these assumptions are not reasonable. To realize the benefits of value-added models fully, a growth model should compare the achievement gains for schools or classrooms that "started out at similar levels of performance (e.g., those that start in the lowest 10%), or that serve similar populations of students (e.g., 85% English language learners)" (Choi, Goldschmidt, & Yamashiro, 2005, p. 131).

The inclusion of student background or school characteristics to the growth equation does not mean holding students with disadvantages to a lower standard. On the contrary, a value-added approach actually strengthens schools' ability to raise student achievement for particular subgroups of students at a faster rate, since it allows schools to use the results as a diagnostic tool to identify and promote school and classroom resources and practices that are particularly effective with different groups of students (Choi, Goldschmidt, & Yamashiro, 2005; Commission on No Child Left Behind, 2007).

Although value-added models provide a more nuanced understanding of school performance than the current status model—for example, they allow us to track the progress of all students at all times, and not only those who are crossing designated proficiency level thresholds at particular points in time—they are technically more complex and, for most states, would require extensive data enhancements. The adoption of a value-added model would require states to implement a data system that, among other things, gives every student in the state an individual identifier; inputs accurately a range of demographic, participation, and performance data about each student on an ongoing basis; provides assessments that produce comparable results from grade to grade and year to year; has a teacher identifier system with the ability to match teachers to students; and includes a built-in audit capacity to confirm the accuracy of the vast amount of information that is being used (Data Quality Campaign, 2005).

Most state data systems are not currently equipped to meet these extensive demands (Choi, Goldschmidt, & Yamashiro, 2005). That is why NCLB should be revised to require the states to augment the capacity of their data systems to allow them to implement a value-added growth model. This requirement should also be accompanied with additional federal funding to defray at least some of the costs involved in these large-scale data system upgrades. A significant added advantage of sophisticated state data systems that are capable of tracking accurate value-added accountability results is that the individual student identifiers and other components of the system will also allow states to track efficiently information about the allocation of resources and the effectiveness of programs and practices, thereby ensuring that all students are truly being provided with a meaningful educational opportunity and contributing to knowledge about the effective use of resources.

There is one major potential drawback to relying on a growth model in the context of a policy imperative to overcome achievement gaps: Many proposed models assume that all students should progress at the same rate. If all students progress at the same rate, those who are presently far behind will never be able to catch up. We think that this challenge can be met by evaluating the states' provision of meaningful educational opportunity to poor and minority children by the extent to which these children progress at rates that will overcome the achievement gaps. As was illustrated by the results of the STAR class size experiment in Tennessee (Kreuger & Whitmore, 2001), because these children by and large are so far behind other students, the rates of growth they achieve when they are provided with meaningful educational opportunities will tend to exceed the rates of progress demonstrated by more advantaged children in the same environments. Feasible benchmark growth targets for low-income and minority students that would accomplish these aims might, for example, tie expected growth rates for those who are currently low-achieving to the rate of progress of the 20% highest-achieving schools in highly affluent and advantaged areas (Linn, 2006). This approach would relate excellence to equity, and would promote high standards and high achievements for all.

Reform of the current AYP system should also include use of fair and consistent criteria for subgroup size, use of confidence intervals and standard errors of measurement, as well as a range of timeline factors. These criteria should be set forth in uniform regulations that apply to all states and school districts and should not be negotiated on an ad hoc basis in the context of a review of a particular state's plan. Substituting demanding, yet realistic, growth targets will encourage school leaders to take AYP calculations seriously and to use them as guidelines for achieving better results, rather than looking for loopholes, gaming the system, or teaching to the test. Additional consideration should be given to growth targets for special education students that challenge them to master the regular curriculum to the extent possible, but do not hold schools responsible for special education achievement goals that are simply not feasible.

Once credible proficiency levels have been established and the data systems to support value-added growth models are in place, more precise and more strategic targets for annual progress can be established. Value-added growth expectations for each school, each school district, and each state should be set in accordance with the present functioning levels of their students and the extent to which the resources to support a meaningful educational opportunity have been put in place. Although schools and school districts with large numbers of students from backgrounds of concentrated poverty may initially need more time to reach desirable proficiency levels, the precision provided by a well-functioning value-added growth model will make it more likely that they will actually reach these goals, since their true needs and their true progress can be accurately gauged.

CHAPTER 8

Building Local Capacity for School Improvement

In light of NCLB's unrealistic 100% proficiency goal and unreasonable AYP demands, it is not surprising that during the 2007–2008 school year, the act will have labeled an estimated 10,000 schools nationwide "Schools in Need of Improvement" (SINI)—or "failing" schools, in common parlance (Schemo, 2007). These numbers are growing rapidly: In Massachusetts, for example, the number of SINI schools rose almost 50%, from 420 to 616, from 2005 to 2006 (Elmore, 2006). And unless major changes are made in the law, these numbers will escalate dramatically, encompassing almost all schools in the nation as we near 2014 and schools and districts are required to make ever larger, and wholly unprecedented, performance gains (Linn, 2004).

Fair, growth-based assessments and sound progress goals would lower these numbers by eliminating many schools that are unfairly and inaccurately identified as failing by the current system. Nevertheless, if all states adopt content standards that are truly challenging, there is no doubt that thousands of American schools will still genuinely be in need of improvement, especially those attended largely by low-income and minority students. SINIs must be identified accurately and fairly, and they must be provided with the assistance necessary to improve. After all, NCLB's insistence on positive results and its expectation that these schools can be dramatically improved gives the act its potency. Unfortunately, the current accountability scheme is not likely to assist schools in meeting these expectations.

From the perspective of ensuring all students a meaningful educational opportunity, NCLB's accountability scheme, which primarily establishes test score targets and identifies and sanctions low-performing schools, is inadequate. What is called for instead is a "next generation" accountability system that is oriented toward building local capacity and school improvement. Such a system may include testing, sanctions, and other traditional accountability concepts, but it incorporates them into an improvement-focused system whose purpose is to improve teaching and learning and hold all levels—federal, state, district, school, and classroom—responsible for student performance (Cohen, 2002; Education Commission of the States, 1998). To improve low-performing schools and to ensure that all of their students receive a meaningful educational opportunity requires adequate systemic funding, sufficient school-based and out-of-school resources in every school, and the professional support needed for local districts and schools to acquire the capacity to strengthen teaching and learning. In previous chapters, we have argued for essential in-school and out-of-school resources and adequate funding; in this chapter, we will argue for revisions of NCLB that will truly support building new district- and school-level capacity for improving teaching and learning.

CURRENT CAPACITY-BUILDING EFFORTS

Policies that support building local capacity for school improvement have been adopted by a number of states, in some cases in response to a court order. State courts ordering finance reforms are increasingly including capacity-building accountability provisions as part of their remedies to ensure that schools actually acquire the resources and capabilities needed to improve student achievement. The 1989 Kentucky Supreme Court decision specifically held that the state must "carefully supervise" the state education system (*Rose v. Council for Better Education*, 1989). In direct response, the legislature enacted the Kentucky Education Reform Act (KERA), which included a range of significant capacity-building and accountability initiatives. Among other reforms, it established a statewide office of education accountability and invested in the expertise to run a comprehensive program of assistance for low-performing schools.

In New Jersey, the *Abbott* decisions have also emphasized building the capacity of the schools to improve teaching and learning and close achievement gaps. These decisions stress that low-performing schools should not simply be labeled "failing" but instead should be provided with the tools needed to improve and sustain improvement—adequate funding, essential programs (including high-quality preschool for all at-risk 3- and 4-year-olds), and early literacy, summer school, and after-school programs. The *Abbott* decisions directly place on the state the obligation to use its statutory, regulatory, and administrative authority to ensure the "effective and efficient" use of all funding to enable students to meet challenging state academic standards (*Abbott v. Burke*, 1990). In more recent *Abbott* decisions, the court went even further by ordering the state to implement an accountability system of baseline data and progress benchmarks to inform decisions about program improvement; a "formal evaluation . . . to verify" whether those efforts are successful; and an external intervention process in low-performing schools that focuses on all aspects of the school (*Abbott v. Burke,* 1998, p. 461).

Maryland's adequacy litigation spurred a new, comprehensive capacity-building accountability scheme that requires every local district to adopt and implement a master plan to ensure that both new and existing revenues are targeted to improve student achievement (Maryland State Department of Education, 2003). In legislation implementing New York's adequacy decision, the legislature adopted significant new capacity-building accountability measures, including the requirement for a "Contract for Excellence" that specifies priority areas for spending new funds to improve low-performing schools and sets benchmarks and indicators by which to judge the success of the new initiatives (McKinney's N.Y. Education Law, 2007).

NCLB's CASCADE OF CONSEQUENCES

NCLB's prescription for low-performing schools is quite different. The law requires states to impose an escalating cascade of consequences and sanctions on schools that repeatedly fail to meet their AYP targets, but puts little emphasis on capacity-building assistance to advance the schools' improvement. As we explained in Chapter 3, schools are designated as being in need of improvement under NCLB if they fail to make adequate yearly progress for 2 years in a row. To review, the cascade of consequences for schools in need of improvement (SINI) unfolds as follows:

Year 1. The school must develop a school improvement plan specifying certain specific actions that will be taken, such as providing increased professional development and fostering greater parental involvement. Students in the school also must be afforded the right to attend non-SINI public schools in the district.

Year 2. The school must use its Title I funds to provide students with the opportunity to access "supplemental educational services" in the form of tutoring or other academic support provided by district-approved vendors.

Year 3. The school must implement "corrective action," such as replacing certain staff or adopting a new curriculum or an extended school day.

Year 4. The district must create plans to "restructure" the school.

Year 5. The district must implement a restructuring plan that calls for entering into a contract to have an outside agency run the school, reopening the school as a charter school, replacing all or most of the school staff, turning the operation of the school over to the state, or undertaking "other major restructuring" of the school's governance.

The mandate for this cascade of consequences is based on the assumption that this specific series of interventions will straighten out wayward schools and propel them onto a pathway to success—and that states have the resources and capacity to carry them out. However, both assumptions are unfounded. The interventions have no clear track record for success, and, even if they did, states and school districts lack the resources and expertise to implement them.

Further, part of the cascade directly undermines the ability of schools to improve. The provisions that allow parents to transfer students to a different school and that compel the district to use Title I money to hire outside vendors to provide tutoring and other services to students, rather than building school capacity to provide a quality education, directly divert energy and resources from schools' efforts. Although some individual students may benefit from the transfer and tutoring provisions, from the perspective of ensuring a meaningful educational opportunity for *all* students, these measures are counterproductive. The savviest parents and the most committed students, those who have most to contribute to a school's rejuvenation, are the most likely to take advantage of the transfer option. Similarly, using school resources to buy instructional services from outside vendors diffuses responsibility for student learning, jeopardizes the coherence of students' learning experience, and does nothing to help build a better climate for teaching and learning in the school. Further, there is little evidence that either of these options is succeeding at improving the outcomes of large numbers of students from low performing schools (Zimmer, Gill, Razquin, Booker, & Lockwood, 2007). All communities need and deserve good local public schools, and families should not have to chase after a decent education for their children. NCLB should create incentives for states and districts to invest in neighborhood schools rather than force families to cobble together alternatives.

Considering this rapid-fire cascade of consequences as a whole, no body of evidence supports the proposition that imposing the specific series of actions that NCLB requires of failing schools on a predetermined multiyear schedule can turn these schools around and substantially improve their students' performance on a sustained basis (Elmore, 2006; Sunderman & Orfield, 2006). Analyses of similar interventions implemented through different state accountability systems, as well as initial experiences in recent years under NCLB, indicate that, although some of these mandates have resulted in improvements in some schools some of the time, the single series of actions mandated by NCLB is not a definitive formula for success.

Ron Brady (2003), former head of New Jersey's office of state-operated school districts, undertook a detailed study of the major state intervention programs implemented in three states: the Schools Under Registration Review process in New York state, the comprehensive school reform program in Memphis, Tennessee, and the reconstitution of schools in Prince George's County, Maryland. He concluded that "the intervention experience is marked more by valiant effort than by notable success" (p. 30). Specifically, he found that a success rate of 50% is high and that most interventions yield positive results at lower rates. Furthermore, he found that it is very difficult to sustain the momentum behind a turnaround effort as political circumstances change. An analysis of other pre-NCLB state efforts to support improvement in low-performing schools by the Civil Rights Project at Harvard University also shows that success was "limited at best" (Sunderman & Orfield, 2006, p. 30).

The Center on Education Policy (CEP) (2007a, 2007c) recently analyzed the initial restructuring efforts under NCLB (years 4 and 5 of the NCLB cascade) in California and Michigan. It found that, in 2005–2006, only 11% of the schools in restructuring in California made AYP (CEP, 2007a). In Michigan, 64% of the schools in restructuring planning or implementation made AYP, but these results may be skewed by changes to the state's testing system and its new way of calculating proficiency levels, which made it easier for schools to make AYP (CEP, 2007c).

THE NEED FOR CAPACITY-BUILDING ASSISTANCE

NCLB does mandate state assistance to schools and districts in need of improvement and sets aside a small amount of funding for this purpose, requiring the states to use 4% of their Title I money for this purpose (overall, 95% of Title I funds must go to local educational agencies; only 5% may be used by the state educational agency to carry out its own responsibilities) (Sunderman & Orfield, 2006). Because of other conflicting federal regulations that give priority to requirements for holding harmless school districts whose numbers of

Title I–eligible students had decreased, most states are not even able to spend the full 4% on intervention support activities. During the 2006–2007 school year, 29 states were unable to access the full amount of the funds set aside for this reason. Although Congress that year, for the first time, provided a separate appropriation of $125 million for school improvement, that appropriation still did not meet the shortfall of about $192 million in federal school improvement funds that resulted from the hold harmless requirement (Center on Education Policy, 2007d).

In any event, the amount that the federal regulations dedicate to school improvement functions is a fraction of the amount that states must set aside for supplementary educational services and the transfer option. Furthermore, this allotment is minimal in relation to the real needs for long-term capacity-building involved in turning failing schools around, and most state education departments simply do not have sufficient resources, sufficient in-house staff, or sufficient expertise to provide meaningful assistance to schools and school districts in need of improvement (Reville, Coggins, Schaefer, & Candon, 2004; Sunderman & Orfield, 2006).

A 2007 study by the Center on Education Policy (2007b) that looked into this specific issue found that only 11 states reported that they were able to provide technical assistance to districts with schools in need of improvement. The biggest problem cited was insufficient numbers of staff capable of carrying out these functions. The lack of federal investment in state school improvement capacity has restricted state roles to monitoring compliance, forced states into a managerial role, and limited the number of schools or districts states can support (Sunderman & Orfield, 2006). The federal mandates in this area are especially unfair, according to Elmore (2006), because NCLB is a regulatory policy nested within a grant-in-aid policy that allows the federal authorities, who are paying less than 10% of the bills for education, to "borrow capacity" from the states and order them to achieve impossible results for which the federal government assumes very little responsibility.

Two states that have invested and been successful in providing technical assistance to local districts are Kentucky and North Carolina. Kentucky's Distinguished Educator Program, created under the 1990 Kentucky Education Reform Act (KERA), sent 55 "Highly Skilled Educators" (HSE) to 84 schools during the 2002–2004 school years. Of these schools, 80 reported an improved academic index. Since the inception of the program, 95% of the schools that have utilized the HSE program have met Kentucky's student achievement standards within two years (Kentucky Department of Education, 2007). North

Carolina's assistance teams have had similar success. The state reports that all but four of the 56 schools that have entered their program since 1997 have been "lifted from the bottom category . . . and more than half have gone to the top" (Tucker & Toch, 2004, p. 34).

Even these successful states, however, lack the resources to extend these services to all of the schools that need them. Although North Carolina's assistance teams had a high success rate with the 56 schools they have assisted over the past 10 years, the number of schools that need improvement under NCLB's current AYP requirements is close to 500, a number whose needs the state cannot come close to meeting (Tucker & Toch, 2004). Similarly, Kentucky's director of assessment reported that he is able to handle "tens of schools" while "NCLB is requiring us to work with hundreds" (p. 34). Thus, NCLB "threatens to overwhelm even those [states] that have made real progress fixing failing schools" (p. 34).

The other part of the capacity equation, of course, is the ability of the schools in need of improvement to follow through on the planning and advice that is given to them by state education department technical assistance teams or highly skilled educators. James H. Lytle (2007), a retired urban school superintendent, describes the "façade of intervention" that he believes is the typical experience of urban schools responding to state assistance teams:

> A team writes a critique based on its review of school programs, staffing and performance data; this is forwarded to the school, to be transformed into a plan for implementation in the coming months. . . . Behind these strategies is the assumption that a school which has been unable to make adequate progress will seize upon a critique, defer to the experts, address all the deficiencies, and make dramatic strides. The question of how the school suddenly develops the capacity or the inclination to do what previously has been unable to do is left unattended. (In my own experience, these corrective action plans may have from 90 to 100 recommendations, but no discussion of funding or strategy.) (p. 28)

Many schools simply do not have the capacity to implement school improvement or corrective action plans, no matter how well conceived. As Elmore (2006) explains,

> Most schools get classified as failing under AYP because *they don't know what to do to get better.* No amount of regulatory enforcement, no matter how cleverly contrived, will rectify this condition. Surrounding failing schools with procedural requirements, as NCLB does, doesn't solve the knowledge problem, and, indeed, can make it worse, by focusing fail-

ing schools on compliance rituals—planning, consulting, issuing no-tices, filing reports—rather than addressing the lack of knowledge and skill that produced the problem in the first place. (p. 11)

State assistance therefore must focus on ensuring that districts and schools "know the right thing to do" rather than merely comply with state requirements or recommendations ("doing the right thing") and, ultimately, that capacity-building efforts focus on improving teaching and learning in every classroom (Elmore, 2003).

The records compiled in the education adequacy cases have estab-lished overwhelmingly that most of the schools that serve low-income and minority students simply do not have the material or human re-sources to provide a meaningful educational opportunity to their stu-dents. If school improvement efforts for schools with large numbers of students from backgrounds of concentrated poverty are to succeed on a broad-based and sustained basis, it is clear that additional funding will be needed to provide these resources, as well as critical out-of-school services (see Chapter 2). Although high expectations and accountabil-ity are important, the bottom line is that adequate resources are neces-sary for quality schooling (Fuhrman, 2001). It is totally unrealistic and unproductive for the federal government to hold schools and school districts to high expectations of proficiency and to impose substantial punitive sanctions on them without providing any effective mecha-nism for ensuring that these schools have the basic resources and sup-ports that they need to succeed in meeting these expectations.

EFFECTIVE STRATEGIES FOR SCHOOL IMPROVEMENT

How many of the 10,000 schools that now are listed as being in need of improvement would quickly emerge from that status if they were suddenly provided with the adequate resources to educate all of their students? We have no doubt that the mere infusion of sufficient funds and a cadre of effective teachers would turn around a large propor-tion of these schools. But we also must acknowledge that adequate school-level resources alone cannot guarantee success, especially for persistently low-performing schools in communities of concentrated poverty. Resources are a *sine qua non* for sustained success, but building a school's capacity to offer each student a meaningful educational op-portunity ultimately depends on long-term strategies for using those resources to create the climate for teaching and learning that is critical for success. What are these strategies?

The literature consistently shows that the key to building successful schools is a "productive school culture" (Patterson, Purkey, & Parker, 1986; Johnson & Birkeland, 2003). A recent review of the research on "What Works with Low-Performing Schools" highlighted three factors that, in essence, are the building blocks for such a culture: a cohesive instructional program, a strong planning process focused on improving student achievement, and a culture of collaboration among the teaching staff and administrators (Corallo & McDonald, 2002). Fullan (2001) observes that "educational change depends on what teachers do and think—it's as simple and as complex as that" (p. 115). He notes that "Collegiality among teachers, as measured by the frequency of communication, mutual support, help, and so forth, [is] a strong indicator of implementation success" (p. 124). Rosenholtz (1989) explains that teacher collaboration inspires greater confidence in teachers, which leads to greater motivation and performance. Creation of a productive school culture, of course, also requires strong administrative leadership and a cadre of effective teachers (Becker, 1992).

Adoption of the measures we have already advocated under the guiding concept of meaningful educational opportunity—that is, adequate funding, increasing the supply and retention of more effective teachers, as well as ensuring other essential school-based and out-of-school resources, and basing school progress requirements on a fair, growth model—would help significantly to foster a climate for teaching and learning. These measures would ensure educators the tools and colleagues they need to ply their craft and would overcome much of the skepticism and opposition to NCLB that stem from perceptions that their school's SINI designation is "unfair, invalid and unrealistic" (Mintrop, 2003). Although 45% of the general public has a favorable opinion of NCLB and 38% views it unfavorably, 75% of high school teachers view it unfavorably and only 19% are positively inclined (Hess & Petrilli, 2006). This is a troublesome indication that the teachers, the individuals on whom the success or failure of NCLB largely rests, are now negatively, not positively, motivated by the law.

Beyond helping to ensure the necessary material and human resources, can federal law do more to help create an effective, collaborative climate for teaching and learning in thousands of schools around the country? Dr. Thomas Sobol (2004), the former New York state commissioner of education, once said that "schools are not like cars that need to be 'fixed' when they break down; rather they are more like gardens—fragile phenomena that need constant care and nurturing to continue to grow." Is there then a way to transform NCLB's current heavy cascade of consequences and sanctions into a supportive scheme that can provide a climate that will help make these gardens grow?

There clearly is. The first step in doing so is to scrap the current cascade of consequences and sanctions and replace it with an effective system for providing technical assistance and accountability for capacity building. NCLB should ensure that high-quality, supportive state services are provided and are made available to all of the districts and schools that need them. The assumption that all state education departments have the funding and the capacity to carry out these responsibilities needs to become a reality. (If AYP is calculated in the rational manner we recommend in Chapter 7, many fewer schools will likely be designated as needing improvement.) Schools must be swiftly supplied with adequate resources, but, afterward, the rigid timetables that now dictate in advance how quickly schools must progress through each stage of improvement should be replaced with challenging but flexible, long-term performance goals based on "practice time" (Elmore, 2006, p. 25), that is, the realities of school improvement, and not abstract regulatory time.

If state assistance is to be more than a "façade of intervention," what form would it take? Kentucky's successful school improvement program provides one model. As part of this program, low-performing schools receive detailed scholastic audits that are performed by a team of state, regional, and local district personnel. The audits provide schools with information from nine school improvement standards on more than 80 indicators related to school success. (Districts with persistently low-performing schools are also subject to audits.) They are so useful that schools that are not low performing voluntarily request and are granted scholastic reviews. Because Kentucky collects data on the same indicators for successful and low-performing schools, it can disseminate best practices by comparing indicators where results vary most from the lowest-performing schools to successful schools (Kentucky Department of Education, 2003).

As mentioned earlier in the chapter, Kentucky enlists "highly skilled educators" to assist low-performing schools. HSE candidates are successful teachers and administrators with at least 5 years of experience who undergo a rigorous selection process. The selection process takes about a year and involves multiple steps, including oral interviews and written assessments, a performance event, site visit, and portfolio presentation and participation in weekend training sessions. Applicants are screened out after each step. Successful candidates receive 135% of their current salaries (Kentucky Department of Education, 2007). These well-qualified and well-trained HSEs work with a team and assist a school in strengthening its curriculum and instruction and assessment practices. Because of the positive reputation this assistance process has garnered, Kentucky HSEs are welcomed into the schools. Faculties credit HSEs with strengthening school leadership and professional development, improving morale, and increasing collaboration among teachers. Part of the success of the Kentucky system seems to stem from the fact that the HSEs do not have the authority to evaluate staff. This leads schools to view HSEs "as a benefit, not a threat" (David, Coe, & Kannapel, 2003, p. 8).

NCLB should ensure as a core requirement that productive state assistance is fully funded and actually put into effect at all schools in need of improvement. The specific forms of assistance that the state representatives provide should, however, be determined by each state and based on needs of the particular school community and on an assessment of how best to work with the people in that community.

Because effective leadership is a threshold requirement for successful school reform, especially for schools with high proportions of educationally disadvantaged students, it may be advisable at the outset that the state representatives make an initial assessment and recommendation to state and district officials of the ability of the current principal to lead the school through an intensive school improvement process. Again, however, this should be a matter for the state technical assistance teams (or perhaps the state education department) to decide, rather than a matter for across-the-board federal regulation. Although teacher effectiveness, like principal effectiveness, is critical to instructional success, abstract strictures to replace all or most of the school staff at certain stages of an intervention process are not useful or productive. If principals are to succeed, state laws must give them the ability to select their staffs and to dismiss teachers who clearly are not performing.

In order to give principals this authority, state laws and collective bargaining agreements in some states will need to be revised to strike a better balance between appropriate job protections for teachers and the circumstances under which they can be dismissed if they are not proving effective. We believe that if teachers are provided with adequate resources and improved working conditions, more of them will be motivated to rise to the challenge of effectively educating students from diverse backgrounds. As we discussed in Chapter 5, we also think that, under the changed circumstances we envision, teacher unions will be willing to negotiate new procedures for eliminating poor performers from the profession so that their colleagues can better fulfill their professional missions.

Federal regulations should not micromanage the details of the state assistance programs. We believe, however, that one aspect of the Kentucky scholastic audit process should be undertaken by state assistance personnel at the outset of their assignment to any school in need of improvement and should be required as a matter of federal regulation because of its centrality to the focus on meaningful educational opportunity that we have recommended. Specifically, before beginning their analysis of the school's programs and their recommendations for reform, state representatives should carry out a "resource audit" as a means of helping to determine whether adequate funding is in place and resources are being distributed equitably. This resource audit should assess the degree to which the school has sufficient staff and basic tools of teaching and learning, such as up-to-date textbooks, computers, supplies, libraries, and laboratories, and the means to ensure adequate in-school and out-of-school programs as needed to provide meaningful educational opportunities for all children in the school.

The collection of such data about essential resources is critical to an improved understanding of how best to use resources to improve student achievement and to build capacity for school improvement. If sufficient resources are not in place, the appropriate school district or state authorities should be held accountable for providing them before major changes in school policies and practices are considered. Although we envision the elimination of the current cascade of consequences, periodic testing and annual progress requirements (undertaken through validated broad-based assessments and value-added growth model calculations) would remain in place. Valid student performance measures are critical for ensuring that professionals and the public alike have accurate data for assessing the efficacy of personnel, success of initiatives, and the adequacy of resources—and the equitable distribution of opportunity and achievement. The precise contours of the accountability systems to emerge under these circumstances would and should vary from state to state. We would expect the laboratory of the states to foster innovations that would advance best practices in areas such as pay for performance, leadership promotion, and tenure reforms.

If the mechanisms for adequate funding and meaningful educational opportunities we recommend are adopted, one critical change is likely to permeate all state accountability systems: These systems are likely to become fairer, more rational, and more "reciprocal." Principals, teachers, and students will be held accountable for their actions and their accomplishments, but so will higher-level school authorities, state officials, and federal officials who are responsible for ensuring adequate funding, essential resources, reasonable regulations, and effective capacity-building support.

CHAPTER 9

Accountability and Credibility: Defining a New Federal–State Partnership

Secretary of Education Margaret Spellings was recently asked how the federal government can maintain its mandate for 100% proficiency by 2014 even though it is now clear that this goal is unattainable. She replied that the Bush administration would not back away from its commitment to NCLB's present approach, but that the department's strategy is to provide "waivers and accommodations" to states that are making good faith efforts to comply with the law (Spellings, 2007). This is essentially an admission by the secretary that the Department of Education's enforcement of NCLB is largely a sham. While the department continues publicly to adhere to the 100% proficiency by 2014 timetable, at the same time, it clearly signals to the states that full compliance is not really expected, that proficiency requirements may be watered down, and that deals will be made to avoid the untenable result of huge and accelerating numbers of schools being labeled "in need of improvement" the closer we get to 2014.

The details of this regulatory charade have been documented in a recent report of the Harvard Civil Rights Project. It found that

> Beginning in 2004 states could submit a request to amend their plans for consideration by ED [the Department of Education]. However, there were no guidelines on the kind of changes states could request or how these requests would be judged and no guarantees that changes approved in one state would be approved in another. Since these amendments were the result of negotiations between individual states and ED, learning about them in other states depended on informal communication among states. . . .
>
> These changes reflect a political strategy by the administration to respond to the growing state opposition to the law by providing relief from some of the law's provisions and reducing, at least temporarily, the number of schools and districts identified for improvement. . . .

> Because this process was politically motivated to respond to growing
> state opposition to the law, ED has not systematically addressed the
> underlying flaws in the law. (Sunderman, 2006, pp. 9–10, 27)

The administration's enforcement policy, which disguises the flaws in
the law and perpetuates the myth that 100% proficiency can really
be attained by 2014, actually impedes achievement of NCLB's vital
goals. The law's basic aims—providing meaningful educational opportunity, eliminating the achievement gaps, and promoting higher
achievement for all students—are critically important, and they are
attainable—but only if we systematically address the law's defects and
take decisive action to correct them.

The key difference between NCLB and prior incarnations of the Elementary and Secondary Education Act is that the new law has insisted on accountability for results. In exchange for federal aid to support
their programs to benefit students from disadvantaged backgrounds,
NCLB requires states to test their students, show dramatic improvement, and apply sanctions when sufficient academic progress has not
been achieved. The experience of the past 5 years has shown, however,
that this simplistic concept of accountability is unproductive. Insisting on definitive and demanding outcomes without ensuring that
schools have the capacity to achieve these results has substantially
undermined the law's effectiveness and credibility.

Defining desired outcomes and creating expectations that all students can achieve them are important advances for accountability and
equity. This was an essential insight of the state standards movement on
which NCLB was based. But, as the numerous state court education adequacy cases have demonstrated, schools and school districts can only be
productively held accountable for results when they have the resources
and tools to achieve them. Without the means to achieve improvements, schools, districts, and states (not to mention the Department of
Education itself) have resorted to gaming the system by back-loading
AYP commitments, lowering cut scores, manipulating subgroup sizes,
and simply neglecting to enforce key provisions of the law. As 2014 approaches, the perverse incentives created by the law may, in fact, lead
to a race to the bottom to avoid impending sanctions, a decline in real
proficiency, and a reinforcement of the achievement gaps.

CREATING AN INFRASTRUCTURE FOR OPPORTUNITY

Having adopted high achievement for all and elimination of achievement gaps as the country's national educational goals, the federal

government must now ensure that meaningful educational opportunities are in place so that students have realistic prospects for attaining these goals. To do this, NCLB must be revised to ensure that each state puts into place an opportunity infrastructure that will allow all students to make significant achievement gains. This would include ensuring that every school provides the school-based resources, such as effective teachers, small classes, support services, extra learning time, and sufficient books, computers, and laboratories, that are critically necessary for children's educational progress—and that most students in our country can take for granted. In addition, it is clear that, to succeed in school, children from backgrounds of concentrated poverty and others at risk will also need early childhood education programs and health, family support, and other out-of-school resources. NCLB's lack of emphasis on necessary resources and learning opportunities and its gross neglect of the need for adequate funding to obtain these have significantly limited the ability of millions of students to meet NCLB's proficiency expectations and perpetuated the achievement gaps.

Although more money alone will not close our nation's opportunity and achievement gaps, fair and adequate funding for necessary resources is a basic ingredient of educational progress. How much additional money is needed to achieve the results that NCLB has mandated? The honest answer is that no one knows. In enacting NCLB, Congress irresponsibly raised expectations about dramatically increased opportunities and outcomes; it required the states to revamp their education systems extensively without knowing how much this would cost or who would pay for it. When asked to respond to analogous failures of state legislatures to fund the standards-based reforms they had enacted, more than two dozen state courts insisted that enhanced educational expectations could not be met without adequate funding. The federal government must apply that logic on a national scale, if we are to achieve NCLB's challenging and vital goals.

As a first step in making sure our schools are equipped to undertake the reforms that are now required of them, the federal government should undertake a series of national cost studies to determine what level of resources, based on cost-effective best practices, is needed to provide all students with a meaningful educational opportunity to reach national goals. Once realistic estimates of the costs are available, policymakers and the public can engage in real debate about the magnitude of necessary increases and the appropriate federal and state shares. Although we anticipate that education funding will largely remain a state obligation, given the important national interests at stake and the federal government's access to a larger and more progressive tax base, we would expect the federal government's role in educational funding to increase markedly. At a minimum, increased federal aid will be required to ensure that states that lack sufficient resources can meet their obligations to ensure the availability of basic quality services in all of their schools. Realistic cost studies will also provide an important touchstone for the states to use in establishing the spending levels they need to afford essential resources for all of their students.

RECONSIDERING THE FEDERAL AND STATE ROLES

By establishing concrete national educational goals and imposing on the states detailed requirements for achieving them, NCLB has more than ever before defined education as a joint federal–state venture. Although the federal role in education has been expanding steadily over the past half century, its extensive involvement in NCLB and the national security and global competitiveness concerns that are cited to justify these changes constitute a profound shift away from the traditional understanding that education is virtually an exclusive state domain. Legally, this broad application of Congress's spending authority appears unassailable (Heise, 2006), and politically, the combined support for an enhanced federal role by civil rights groups, business groups, and a strong bipartisan coalition in Congress means that the federal partnership with the states in educational policymaking is not likely to be undone.

If this new partnership is to work, the appropriate responsibilities of each level of government must be clarified and respected. The federal government and the state governments must "borrow strength" from each other by leveraging the capacities that each of them can bring to bear on the issues (Manna, 2006, p. 5). In our complex federal system, the states are entrusted with basic operating responsibility for public education, and, even when the federal government rightfully asserts overarching national policies of equity and economic competitiveness, effective implementation of these policies depends on their execution at the local level. We have used Justice Brandeis's metaphor of the laboratory of the states to convey the important truth that, especially in an area like education in which there is as yet no definitive "scientific evidence" of practices that work in all situations, effective reform depends on the creative efforts of the states to develop a range of programs and practices that relate the general policy to local needs.

To achieve NCLB's ambitious goals, the experience and the efforts of the states are of particular significance. The impetus for using higher standards to promote both excellence and equity emerged from the joint agreement of all 50 governors and the first President Bush at the National Education Summit in 1989, and virtually all of the states quickly moved ahead to put the agreed-upon national goals into practice (albeit with varying degrees of quality) through their standards-based initiatives. Years before NCLB was adopted, the states were "committed to improving learning for all students and closing the achievement gap" (National Conference of State Legislatures, 2005, p. 4). Where those commitments were not accompanied by sufficient funding for resources to realize these goals, many of the state courts issued decisions that required the legislatures to revise their state education finance systems to ensure the availability of adequate resources.

In these decisions, the courts also analyzed in depth the skills and knowledge that students need for citizenship, for work, and for higher education, and the relationship between specific resources and effective educational outcomes. Past and present efforts of the states (like the work now being done by the consortium of states working with the American Diploma Project [2004, 2007] to develop high school exit standards that relate the outcome of K–12 education to realistic contemporary demands of work and higher education) have contributed enormously to progress toward equity and excellence. These distinctive contributions of the states need to be endorsed and incorporated into the NCLB framework.

Ultimately, however, what is at stake here is fulfillment of the nation's historic commitment to equal educational opportunity and the vital national interests in having competent citizens and being able to compete in the global economy. With such stakes, strong federal efforts are needed to ensure a systematic and sustained pursuit of these goals on a national level. In sum, then, for NCLB to succeed, there must be an effective balancing of both the state and federal roles. NCLB in its current version, however, tilts too far in the direction of unwarranted federal intrusion in some areas and too far toward regulatory laxity in others. This imbalance needs to be rectified.

A more proactive federal role is needed to ensure the integrity and quality of state academic content and performance standards, and to guarantee the validity of the assessments used to measure student performance, including the assessments used for limited English proficient students. The best way to do this in the context of a federal–state partnership is for the federal government to develop national standards and assessments that states may adopt or use as benchmarks for developing their own standards and assessments, which then can be reviewed and compared with the national benchmarks by the secretary of education. These standards and assessments should, at least in the higher grades, cover all the major subject areas needed to prepare students to function productively as citizens, compete in the global marketplace, and lead fulfilled adult lives. States that the secretary determines to be using low-quality standards or setting unreasonably low proficiency requirements, as measured through improved and validated NAEP proficiency standards, should be required to adopt the national benchmark standards or bring their own standards up to par.

The federal government also should continue to require states to report annually on the progress of each school and each school district, in a disaggregated format that illustrates the progress that is being made by each racial and ethnic group, and by low-income students, English language learners, and students with disabilities. These progress indicators should be calibrated not against the unrealistic goal of 100% proficiency by 2014, but on the amount of sustained improvement that will allow low-income and minority students to overcome achievement gaps, at the same time that continued growth in accordance with high-quality standards is also being maintained in schools for more advantaged students. The federal government should also require and support the expansion of state data systems that will allow annual progress measures to be based on value-added growth models, rather than static cohort performance statistics. Clear, uniform criteria for enforcing these requirements need to be articulated and applied fairly—and without politically motivated "waivers and accommodations."

NCLB should also require the states to include in their state plans specific information on the resources that are being expanded and the practices being used to provide all students with a meaningful educational opportunity. In addition, the states should include in their annual report cards information on the extent to which equitable distribution of resources and quality of services has been achieved in each essential category. The Department of Education should analyze the state plans and annual report cards and issue an annual report of its own that highlights the levels of resources and educational practices of those states that have proven most effective in promoting improvement in the performance of all of their students and in narrowing achievement gaps.

These reports will inform state policymakers and the interested public of the level of resources and the educational practices their state is devoting to its children, and the results that are being achieved with these efforts, in a manner that will allow for direct comparisons with efforts and accomplishments of other states. Presumably, education officials and policymakers in states that are failing to provide appropriate resources and appropriate conditions of learning for their students and are obtaining poor results will be pressed by their constituents to provide more resources and to improve their practices. At the beginning of the next reauthorization period, states that are substantially underperforming may be required by the federal government to adopt model resource allocation methodologies and effective practices that have been developed by the successful states.

Offsetting these enhancements of the federal role should be a reduction in federal involvement in improvement directives to low-performing schools. Although the Department of Education should provide information on best practices for building instructional capacity in underperforming schools, given the lack of evidence for prescribing a particular approach to this problem, there is no justification for the federal government to mandate specific mechanisms for dealing with schools in need of improvement. These issues of technical assistance, incentives, and sanctions should be left to the states. (NCLB should, however, require each state to conduct a "resource audit" of each school in need of improvement to ensure that all necessary resources are in place before corrective action plans or other remedies are put into effect.)

The new, reciprocal accountability scheme we recommend balances a limited expansion of federal authority in promoting quality in standards and assessments and in supporting meaningful educational opportunities for all children with an expansion of the authority and responsibility of the states to determine how best to improve practices in low-performing schools. Such a federal–state partnership would give primacy of place to state efforts to develop creative local approaches to improving proficiency and closing achievement gaps, but if, at a certain point, these efforts prove unsuccessful, the interests of the students in the state, and the national interest, call for the federal government to take a more forceful stance in regard to standards and resource allocation.

We do not anticipate extensive use of this ultimate federal authority. The reciprocal accountability model of joint federal–state involvement that we advocate should maximize the role of the states in devising effective methods for providing their students with a meaningful educational opportunity. In addition, it should increase the flow of information to parents, civic and business leaders, and the interested public in each state, allowing them to play a greater role in inducing their school officials and policymakers to develop and implement effective policies. The Department of Education's ultimate sanction against recalcitrant states would be to invoke its authority to terminate the state's federal funding, a power that the department rarely actually employs (Pollock, in press; Rebell & Block, 1985). Currently, NCLB precludes citizen suits in federal court to enforce its provisions, and we have no expectation that a private right of action that would facilitate litigation in the federal courts is likely to be adopted by Congress in the foreseeable future.

The broader dissemination of information about each state's resource allocations and instructional practices and the increase in comparative knowledge of national models may, however, allow the state courts to be more effective in their enforcement efforts in future education adequacy litigations. Although the state courts do not have direct jurisdiction to enforce NCLB's statutory requirements or regulations, some state courts, like the trial judge in the recent Kansas decision (*Montoy v. State,* 2003), have acknowledged the relevance of NCLB criteria to their decisions on state constitutional standards. More generally, NCLB obligations have become embedded in state laws and regulations, which are enforceable by the state courts.

Some may bristle at the thought of further judicial involvement in the standards-reform domain, but the fact is that the state courts do have a vital role to play in ensuring the equity and adequacy of state education systems (Rebell, 2007b). Their direct or indirect adoption or enforcement of NCLB opportunity, achievement, and accountability standards will further advance an effective federal–state partnership in promoting equity and excellence, since these courts will apply the federal criteria with an intimate knowledge of local conditions and a sensitivity to local needs.

CONCLUSION

We have endeavored throughout this book to undertake a frank and thorough appraisal of both the strengths and the weaknesses of the No Child Left Behind Act. We have argued that NCLB constitutes landmark legislation that has reinvigorated America's egalitarian heritage and has adopted as the nation's preeminent educational policy a commitment to implement—finally and fully—the vision of equal educational opportunity articulated more than half a century ago in *Brown v. Board of Education.* At the same time, we have pulled no punches in identifying the political hype that permeates the act, such as calling minimally qualified teachers "highly qualified"; proclaiming that states will be held to high standards, but precluding effective enforcement of that requirement; and demanding miraculous progress in overcoming the barriers to learning in the lives of millions of low-performing students without providing the resources and capacity necessary to accomplish this end. Most insistently, we have proclaimed what others know but most have only whispered: that the mandate for 100% proficiency by 2014 that drives NCLB's accountability scheme is untenable, and that adherence to this impossible scheme is undermining the credibility and the efficacy of the act at an accelerating rate.

Many of the act's other supporters are reluctant to join us in proclaiming that the emperor has no clothes because they see the 100% proficiency mandate as an important motivator and a useful device for focusing attention on the broad learning needs of low-income and minority children. This, however, is a perilous strategy because, at some point, the nakedness of the act's major mandate will be unveiled and its authority will be undone—and the closer we come to 2014, the more imminent is that day of reckoning.

Setting, in its stead, the provision of meaningful educational opportunity for all children and the expectation that schools for low-income and minority students will progress at rates sufficient to overcome achievement gaps, at the same time that continued growth in accordance with quality standards is also being maintained in schools for more advantaged students, poses an immense challenge, requiring a national effort similar perhaps our country's response to the *Sputnik* challenge of the 1950s. These goals, though unprecedented, are achievable. Their attainment would allow the United States truly to realize both excellence and equity and to meet the challenges of global competitiveness that have been repeatedly emphasized by our presidents, governors, and business leaders for the past 2 decades, as well as firming the foundation for productive citizenship in our increasingly diverse democracy in the 21st century.

Our effort to tackle NCLB's core problems head on has required us candidly to confront two major issues that federal policymakers seem eager to avoid: 1) the need for a stronger federal role in a federal–state partnership for creating educational equity, and 2) the need for adequate funding to provide the resources that children from poverty and others at risk will need to succeed. To fulfill our national promise to provide equal opportunity and to overcome achievement gaps, both of these issues need to be faced now rather than later.

Although we acknowledge that, in our federal system, the basic management of the public schools is and must remain under state and local control, enforcement of equity imperatives is a federal responsibility. Simply stated, if the nation is to achieve the paramount goals of providing equal educational opportunity, promoting higher achievement for all, and eliminating achievement gaps, then federal authority must be asserted where necessary to achieve these goals. We have proposed a federal–state partnership model that protects and promotes the role of the states in the standards-based reform enterprise, but we also argue that if particular states fail to meet their children's educational needs, the federal authorities must act to enforce the children's rights and the nation's needs.

In 1973, at a critical point in the enforcement of racial desegregation, the U.S. Supreme Court weighed the competing values of local control and educational equity in determining whether nearby suburbs would have to be included in a plan to undo racial segregation in Detroit's schools, and it held that equity must yield to local control (*Milliken v. Bradley*, 1974). This massive restriction on metropolitan area desegregation remedies has effectively stymied all real progress toward desegregation of the schools since that time (Frankenberg et al., 2003; Rebell, 2007b). Ironically, in its recent decision in *Parents Involved v. Seattle School District*, the Supreme Court overrode local sentiments and voluntary local desegregation plans to enforce a new constitutional stance against race-based school attendance plans.

Congress, in enacting NCLB, has, in effect, picked up the baton of federal equity enforcement that the Supreme Court dropped in *Milliken*. In light of the *Seattle* decision, what it does with that baton is all the more important. If we are now to reach our long-proclaimed equity goals, Congress will have to insist clearly that, when push comes to shove, meaningful equity initiatives must prevail over inconsistent assertions of local control. The state standards-based reform movement has already diluted the tradition of local control. Local school boards and school districts, which traditionally established their own educational policies with little interference from state officials, are now obliged to follow strict state regimens in regard to curriculum, funding, teacher training, testing, and many other policy areas. As indicated above, the Supreme Court itself has also now weakened the foundations of the pillars of local control that it had protected in its earlier decisions. We have outlined a workable federal–state partnership that will create the necessary division of labor to promote educational equity. If states do not or cannot hold up their end, however, the federal government must act assertively to enforce children's rights.

With regard to funding, although no one knows how much additional spending will be required to provide real educational opportunities to all children, it is likely that substantial additional revenues will be required. We expect, though, that the additional costs of providing adequate resources in earlier years can largely be negated by the savings they produce in later years, and that the savings in other costs and recouped taxes from a more productive citizenry will, in the long run, more than offset any additional investment in education. A critical point here is that the American public is also well aware that additional funding will be necessary to meet the educational needs of disadvantaged students in poor urban and rural areas, and, in poll after poll, strong majorities have repeatedly agreed that they would pay higher taxes for the education of these students—if they were convinced that their dollars would really result in demonstrable improvements in student achievement.

We believe that there has been a growing egalitarian imperative throughout American history and that the noble goals embodied in the No Child Left Behind Act are a manifestation of a deep and continuing commitment to equity and fairness. Now that the equity objectives of bringing all students to high achievement levels and eliminating achievement gaps have been adopted as our paramount national educational policy, we need to probe the depths of the nation's commitment to these goals by fully and faithfully pursuing this equity agenda. The convergence at this point in time of the nation's equity ideals with its economic interest in educating its rapidly expanding minority population to be competitive workers and its political interest in having an educated, engaged citizenry increases the likelihood that an honest assessment of our schools' funding needs will receive broad public support.

Ultimately, in our democratic society, the extent of public awareness and the depth of public commitment will determine how actively public officials will implement and enforce the expectations and requirements of NCLB and what level of funding the nation will be willing to accept (Hess, 2006). That is why candid discussions of the importance of the real objectives of NCLB, critical analyses of the mechanisms needed to accomplish them, and honest appraisals of the costs involved are of critical importance.

We have referred several times in this book to the fact that plaintiffs have prevailed in 20 of the 28 (71%) state education adequacy cases that have been decided on a final basis since 1989. This is an astounding litigation success rate. In the eight cases in which plaintiffs did not succeed, the cases were dismissed for technical "justiciability" reasons or because of abstract separation of powers or other concerns before the issues could be fully assessed at a trial. This means that in every case where the courts closely examined the facts, they determined that poor and minority children were being denied a basic educational opportunity and that steps must be taken to remedy this grave injustice.

We think that policymakers and the American people at large, once they closely consider the facts, will similarly agree that strong, effective action, in accordance with the recommendations set forth in this book, must be taken to respond to the needs of millions of disadvantaged children throughout the country who continue to be subjected to substandard schooling. Half a century after the Supreme Court proclaimed in *Brown v. Board of Education* the reality that "it is doubtful that any child may reasonably be expected to succeed in life if he is denied the opportunity for an education," it clearly is time to ensure that *meaningful* educational opportunities are no longer a dream or a vision, but a reality for every child in the United States of America.

Summary of
Moving Every Child Ahead
Recommendations

By enacting the No Child Left Behind Act, U.S. policymakers have reinvigorated America's egalitarian heritage with a pledge to implement—finally and fully—the vision of equal educational opportunity articulated more than half a century ago in *Brown v. Board of Education.* However, the current version of NCLB is riddled with political hype, such as calling minimally qualified teachers "highly qualified"; proclaiming that states will be held to high standards, but prohibiting enforcement of that requirement; and demanding miraculous progress in overcoming the barriers to learning in the lives of millions of low-performing students without providing the resources necessary to accomplish this end.

In its statement of purpose, NCLB sets its two primary goals as ensuring that "all children have a fair, equal and significant opportunity to obtain a high quality education and reach, at a minimum, proficiency on challenging state academic achievement standards and state academic assessments." Currently, attainment of the proficiency goal is stressed, with little attention to the opportunity goal. In this book we argue that this emphasis should be inverted. Greater immediate emphasis on the opportunity goal will lead to higher, more rapid, and more sustained student achievement.

The mandate for 100% proficiency by 2014 that drives NCLB's accountability system is untenable, and adherence to this impossible scheme is undermining the credibility and the efficacy of the act at an accelerating rate. To overcome the historical disadvantages that put a quality education out of reach of so many American children, NCLB should be revised to eliminate this mandate and require instead that the states provide all children with the essential elements of a *meaningful educational opportunity,* the indispensable prerequisite for significant improvements in student achievement and lasting progress toward proficiency. To achieve this, our book makes specific recommendations in eight areas.

Meaningful Educational Opportunity

The roots of America's achievement gaps are significant opportunity gaps endured by millions of low-income and minority students. Because NCLB mainly concentrates on accountability for results but largely neglects the resources and supports that students need to achieve those results, it is falling far short of achieving its goals. States have felt no federal pressure or incentive to deliver any particular level of resources or school quality, and enormous inequities persist between schools that serve affluent, White communities and those that serve low-income and minority communities.

- To maximize student proficiency and minimize achievement gaps, Congress should revise NCLB to eliminate the mandate for 100% proficiency by 2014 and instead require that the states provide *meaningful educational opportunity* for all their public school children by that date.
- Drawing on the legislative history of NCLB, as well as the experiences of the state courts in the education adequacy litigations, Congress should define specific meaningful opportunity expectations.
- Specifically, requirements should be added to the law covering eight categories of in-school educational essentials:
  1. effective teachers, principals, and other personnel
  2. appropriate class sizes
  3. adequate school facilities
  4. rich and rigorous curricula
  5. a full platform of services, including guidance services, after-school, summer, and weekend programming, tutoring, and additional time on task for students from backgrounds of poverty
  6. appropriate programs and services for English language learners (ELLs) and students with disabilities
  7. instrumentalities of learning, including, but not limited to, up-to-date textbooks, libraries, laboratories, and computers
  8. a safe, orderly learning environment

  and five categories of out-of-school educational essentials:

1. high-quality early childhood education
2. necessary levels of nutrition and physical activity
3. physical and mental health care
4. home, family, and community support for student academic achievement
5. access to arts, cultural, employment, community service, civic, and other critical nonacademic experiences

-   In their annual report cards, the states should be required to demonstrate that adequate and appropriate resources and opportunities for essential school-based and out-of school resource areas are being provided, including the extent to which equitable distribution of resources and quality of services has been achieved in each essential category. How these resources and opportunities are actually provided should be left to the states.
-   The Department of Education (ED) should issue an annual report that highlights the levels of resources and educational practices of those states that have proven most effective in promoting improvement in the performance of all of their students and in narrowing achievement gaps.

Effective Teachers

Of the essential elements of a meaningful educational opportunity outlined above, teacher quality is the sole resource presently mandated by NCLB. Quality teaching is a *sine qua non* of meaningful educational opportunity, but this resource alone is not enough, especially for at-risk students. Students must be provided with the full range of school-based and out-of-school resources as described above.

NCLB has increased the number of state-certified teachers in hard-to-staff schools; however, the law has not ensured that these children are being taught by teachers who are really *highly* qualified to meet their needs. By using hyperbole, NCLB conveys the misleading impression that *minimally* qualified teachers are *highly* qualified.

-   NCLB must be revised to require states to identify the qualifications of their teaching corps accurately, and to distinguish among three categories of teachers: "provisionally qualified teachers," "qualified teachers," and "highly effective teachers":

Provisionally qualified teachers should be defined as teachers-in-training who meet the state's alternative certification requirements.

Qualified teachers should be defined as those who have a college degree with a major in a field directly related to the subject area in which they are teaching, and who meet the state's entry level certification requirements.

Highly effective teachers should be defined as teachers who have deep subject matter knowledge, a thorough understanding of state academic content standards and proficiency requirements, and a demonstrated ability to impart effectively the knowledge and skills required by state standards to students from diverse backgrounds and with diverse needs.

- NCLB's current requirements for equitable distribution of "highly qualified" teachers should be applied to these categories; low-income and minority students should not be disproportionately assigned to teachers who are inexperienced or less than highly effective.
- States should be required to articulate methods for maximizing effective teachers and to provide relevant information on the rigor of their certification requirements, the accreditation standards for their schools of education, and their induction, mentoring, and professional development practices in their annual report cards to the public and in the state plans they submit to ED.

Adequate Funding

NCLB grossly neglects the need to ensure that adequate levels of funding are in place to allow students a meaningful opportunity to make solid academic progress, much less the unprecedented results demanded by the law. The current level of NCLB funding does not cover the costs of its own requirements.

- The federal government should be responsible for identifying the true costs of compliance with NCLB and determining a fair allocation of funding responsibility between the federal government and the states.
- To identify the actual costs of providing all students a meaningful educational opportunity, Congress should

authorize comprehensive studies of the costs to states and local districts of complying with NCLB, achieving its goals, and closing achievement gaps.

- This analysis should consider the costs not only of school-based resources but also of the out-of-school resources most important for the academic success of at-risk students. The study should incorporate best practices to overcome achievement gaps in a cost-effective manner.
- States should be held responsible for ensuring that school districts with low tax bases and high needs receive sufficient state aid to meet the basic requirements for providing all of their students with a meaningful educational opportunity. Federal aid to the states should, at a minimum, ensure that states that lack sufficient resources to ensure the availability of essential resources and services to all of their students receive sufficient federal assistance to meet these obligations.
- NCLB should require state plans to include information on present and projected funding levels and to describe states' efforts to ensure equity in funding.

Challenging Standards

Challenging state standards that provide American students with the knowledge and skills they need to succeed in life in the 21st century are critical to efforts to provide all children meaningful educational opportunities and to secure our national welfare, both economically and socially. NCLB requires every state to adopt challenging content standards; however, it explicitly prevents ED from reviewing the standards adopted by each state to ensure their quality. For NCLB to be effective—and for proficiency to have reliable, substantive content—the federal government must take a more proactive role to ensure the quality of all state academic content standards.

- Along with the Aspen Institute's Commission on No Child Left Behind, we call for model national content and performance standards and tests to be created by a commissioned expert panel based on NAEP frameworks. With the Commission, we recommend that states be given a choice of (1) adopting the national model standards and tests as their own; (2) building their own assessment instruments based on the national model standards; or (3) keeping their existing standards or tests (or revamping them in response to the national model standards and tests).

- Departing from the Commission, we recommend that model standards extend beyond the core subjects of English language arts, math, and science. A basic consensus has emerged from the state court adequacy cases about the broad knowledge and skills that students need to be prepared for competitive employment and to function productively in a democratic society. NCLB should adopt this consensus to provide a solid floor of quality for the proficiency requirements and to guard against a narrow interpretation of the educational opportunities that schools need to provide.
- Standards and state exit examinations must also properly emphasize the higher order cognitive skills that students need to succeed in college and in the world of work. NCLB must rectify the current imbalance in subject matter emphases and between basic skills and advanced conceptual thinking by highlighting the importance of students gaining deep knowledge and skills in a broad range of subject areas by the time they graduate from high school.
- The U.S. secretary of education should periodically issue reports comparing the quality of all state standards with the national model and tests.
- States using low-grade standards or setting unreasonably low proficiency requirements should be required to adopt the model standards or bring their own standards up to a satisfactory level of quality.

Valid Assessments

Most state tests used to measure progress under NCLB are neither aligned with state content standards nor valid in accordance with applicable professional standards. In addition, there is rampant manipulation of cut scores to inflate the number of students designated as "proficient" and dramatic variation from state to state in cut scores used to define "proficiency." An area of special concern is that virtually none of the subject matter tests being used to measure content knowledge of students with limited English proficiency has been validated for use with this population, with the result that there is almost no accurate data on the actual proficiency of these students.

- NCLB should be revised to require each state to undergo an external review of the validity of its tests and of its cut score procedures by an ED-approved independent agency with expertise in this area.
- Given that few valid tests for English language learners exist at present, ED should develop model tests in all mandated subjects and grade levels in Spanish and at least five other languages most commonly used in American schools. The costs involved in such an endeavor should be borne by the federal government. The states should be required to use these federally validated tests for assessing the content knowledge of their ELL students unless they can demonstrate that they have developed fully validated tests of their own.

Sound Progress Requirements

NCLB should be revised in the following ways to ensure fair and valid measurement of student progress.

- Ambitious but realistic progress requirements must be substituted for the present mandate of 100% proficiency by 2014.
- Given the importance of NAEP scores as national benchmarks for proficiency, NAEP's content and proficiency levels should be reconsidered and validated.
- NCLB should be revised to base Adequate Yearly Progress (AYP) on a value-added growth model that gives schools credit for student improvement over time and provides a more accurate picture of school performance.
- States should be required to augment the capacity of their data systems to allow them to implement a value-added growth model and assess the adequacy of resources.
- Reform of the current AYP system should also include use of fair and consistent criteria for subgroup size, use of confidence intervals and standard errors of measurement, as well as a range of timeline factors. Additional consideration should be given to growth targets for special education students that challenge them to master the regular curriculum to the extent possible, but do not hold schools responsible for special education achievement goals that are simply not feasible.
- Once credible proficiency levels have been established and the data systems to support value-added growth models are

in place, more precise and more strategic targets for annual progress can be established.

Local Capacity for School Improvement

NCLB requires states to impose an escalating cascade of consequences on schools that repeatedly fail to meet their AYP targets, but it puts little emphasis on providing capacity-building assistance to advance the schools' improvement. Most of the schools that serve low-income and minority students do not have the material or human resources to provide a meaningful educational opportunity to their students, and many schools do not have the capacity to implement school improvement or corrective action plans, no matter how well conceived.

- NCLB's current cascade of consequences and sanctions should be replaced with an effective system for providing technical assistance and accountability for capacity building in low-performing schools. NCLB should ensure that high-quality, supportive state services are provided and made available to all of the schools that need them.
- To help determine whether adequate funding is in place and resources are being distributed equitably, each state should carry out a "resource audit" to assess the degree to which a school in need of improvement has sufficient staff and basic tools, such as up-to-date textbooks, computers, libraries, and laboratories, and the means to mount adequate in-school and out-of-school programs as needed to provide meaningful educational opportunities for all of their students.
- NCLB should ensure that productive state technical assistance is fully funded and actually put into effect at *all* schools in need of improvement. The specific forms of assistance that the state representatives provide should, however, be determined by each state and based on needs of the particular school community.
- The rigid timetables that now dictate in advance how quickly schools must progress through each stage of improvement should be replaced with flexible, long-term performance goals.

A New Federal–State Partnership

By establishing concrete national educational goals and imposing on the states detailed requirements for achieving them, NCLB has more than ever before defined education as a joint federal–state venture. If this new partnership is to work, the appropriate responsibilities of each level of government must be clarified and respected. NCLB, however, tilts too far in the direction of unwarranted federal intrusion in some areas and too far toward regulatory laxity in others. This imbalance needs to be rectified.

- A more proactive federal role is needed to ensure the integrity and quality of state academic content and performance standards, and to guarantee the validity of the assessments used to measure student performance, including the assessments used for limited English proficient students.
- The federal government should continue to require states to report annually on the progress of each school and each school district, in a disaggregated format that illustrates progress being made by each racial and ethnic group, and by low-income students, English language learners, and students with disabilities.
- The federal government should also require and support the expansion of state data systems that will allow annual progress measures to be based on value-added growth models, rather than static cohort performance statistics.
- Clear, uniform criteria for enforcing these requirements need to be articulated and applied fairly—and without politically motivated "waivers and accommodations."
- Federal involvement in improvement directives to low-performing schools should be substantially reduced. These issues of technical assistance, incentives, and sanctions should be left to the states.
- This federal–state partnership should maximize the role of the states in devising effective methods for providing their students a meaningful educational opportunity. If these efforts prove unsuccessful, the federal government must take a more forceful stance in regard to standards and resource allocation.

References

Abbeville County School District v. State, 93-CP-31-0169 (S.C. Ct. Com. Pl. Dec. 29, 2005).

Abbott v. Burke, 575 A.2d 359, 397 (N.J. 1990).

Abbott v. Burke, 710 A. 2d 450 (N.J. 1998).

Abedi, J. (2001). *Assessment and accommodations for English language learners: Issues and recommendations.* Los Angeles: National Center for Research on Evaluation, Standards, and Student Testing.

Achieve. (2002). *Staying on course: Standards-based reform in America's schools: Progress and prospects.* Washington, DC: Author.

Allgood, W. C. (2006, August). *The need for adequate resources for at-risk children* [EPI working paper No. 277]. Washington, DC: Economic Policy Institute.

American Diploma Project. (2004). *Ready or not: Creating a high school diploma that counts.* Washington, DC: Author.

American Diploma Project. (2007). *Closing the expectations gap 2007: An annual 50-state progress report on the alignment of high school policies with the demands of college and work.* Washington, DC: Author.

American Educational Research Association, American Psychological Association, & National Council on Measurement in Education. (1999). *The standards for educational and psychological testing.* Washington, DC: AERA.

American Federation of Teachers. (2001). *Making standards matter 2001: A fifty-state report on efforts to implement a standards-based system.* Washington, DC: Author.

American Federation of Teachers. (2006, July). *NCLB: Let's get it right. AFT's recommendations for No Child Left Behind.* Washington, DC: Author.

American Heritage Dictionary. (1997). Boston, MA: Houghton Mifflin Company.

American Institutes for Research (AIR). (2004). *New York adequacy study: Providing all children with full opportunity.* Washington, DC: Author.

Americans willing to pay for improving schools. (1999). Retrieved May 21, 2007, from http://www.npr.org/about/press/990920.edpoll.html

Anyon, J. (2005). *Radical possibilities: Public policy, urban education, and a new social movement.* New York: Routledge.

Anyon, J., & Greene, K. (2007). No Child Left Behind as an anti-poverty measure. *Teacher Education Quarterly, 34*(2), 157–162.

Aspen Institute. (2006). *Growth models: An examination within the context of NCLB.* Washington, DC: Author.

Barnett, S. W. (1995, Winter). Long-term effects of early childhood programs on cognitive and school outcomes. *The Future of Children, 5*(3), 25–50.

Barton, P. E. (2003, October). *Parsing the achievement gap.* Princeton, NJ: Educational Testing Service.

Becker, M. (1992). *An effective schools primer.* Arlington, VA: American Association of School Administrators.

Belfield, C. (2005, October 24–25). *The promise of early childhood education.* Paper prepared for the Social Costs of Inadequate Education Symposium, Teachers College, Columbia University.

Belfield, C., & Levin, H. (2007). *The price we pay: The social and economic costs of inadequate education.* Washington, DC: Brookings Institution Press.

Berliner, D. C. (2005). Our impoverished view of educational reform [electronic version]. *Teachers College Record.* Retrieved June 27, 2007, from www.tcrecord.org

Bernstein, J., & Gould, E. (2006, August). *Income picture.* Washington, DC: Economic Policy Institute. Retrieved August 16, 2007, from www.epi.org/content.cfm/webfeatures_econindicators_income20060829

Berry, B. (2004). Recruiting and retaining "highly qualified teachers" for hard-to-staff schools. *NASSP Bulletin, 88*(638), 5–27.

Berry, B., Hoke, M., & Hirsch, E. (2004). The search for highly qualified teachers. *Phi Delta Kappan, 85*(9), 684–689.

Berstein, J., Brocht, C., & Spade-Aguilar, M. (2000). *How much is enough? Basic family budgets for working families.* Washington, DC: Economic Policy Institute.

Blank, M. J. (2004). How community schools make a difference. *Educational Leadership, 61*(8), 62–64.

Boushey, H., & Weller, C. E. (2005). What the numbers tell us. In J. Lardner & D. A. Smith (Eds.), *Inequality matters: The growing economic divide in America and its poisonous consequences.* New York: New Press.

Brady, R. (2003). Can failing schools be fixed? Retrieved June 21, 2007, from http://www.edexcellence.net/institute/publication/publication.cfm?id=2&pubsubid=18

Brooks-Gunn, J., & Duncan, G. J. (1997). The effects of poverty on children. *The Future of Children, 7*(2), 55–71.

Brown v. Board of Education, 347 U.S. 483 (1954).

Bush, G. W. (2001a). No Child Left Behind. Retrieved January 28, 2007, from http://www.Whitehouse.gov/news/reports/no-child-left-behind.html

Bush, G. W. (2001b). President discusses education at national urban league conference. Retrieved January 28, 2007, from http://www.Whitehouse.gov/news/releases/2001/08/text/20010801-1.html

Butler, F. A., & Stevens, R. (2001). Standardized assessment of the content knowledge of English language learners K–12: Current trends and old dilemmas. *Language Testing, 18*(4), 409–427.

Campaign for Fiscal Equity v. State of New York, 719 N.Y.S.2d 475 (S.Ct N.Y.Co 2001).

Campaign for Fiscal Equity v. State of New York (CFE II), 801 N.E.2d 326 (N.Y. 2003).

Carey, K. (2006, May). *Hot air: How states inflate their educational progress under NCLB*. Washington, DC: Education Sector.

Cavanagh, S. (2007, May 16). Students' mastery of NAEP history and civics mixed. *Education Week*, p. 16.

Center on Education Policy. (2005). *From the capital to the classroom: Year 3 of the No Child Left Behind Act*. Washington, DC: Author.

Center on Education Policy. (2006). *Title I funds—Who's gaining and who's losing: School year 2006–07 Update*. Washington, DC: Author.

Center on Education Policy. (2007a). *Beyond the mountains: An early look at restructuring results in California*. Washington, DC: Author.

Center on Education Policy. (2007b, May 9). *Educational architects: Do state education agencies have the tools necessary to implement NCLB?* Washington, DC: Author.

Center on Education Policy. (2007c, March 1). *Lessons from Michigan about restructuring schools and next steps under NCLB*. Washington, DC: Author.

Center on Education Policy. (2007d). *Title I funds—Who's gaining and who's losing: School year 2007–2008 update*. Washington, DC: Author.

Children's Defense Fund. (2005). *The state of America's children, 2005*. Washington, DC: Author.

Child Trends DataBank (2006a). *Long-term poverty*. Retrieved November 28, 2006, from www.childtrendsdatabank.org/indicators/61LongTermPoverty.cfm

Child Trends DataBank. (2006b). *Percentage of related children in the United States under age 18 living below the poverty level, selected years: 1960–2005*. Retrieved August 16, 2007, from www.childtrendsdatabank.org/tables/4_Table_2.htm

Choi, K., Goldschmidt, P., & Yamashiro, K. (2005). Exploring models of school performance: From theory to practice. *Yearbook of the National Society for the Study of Education, 104*(2), 119–146.

Clinton, H. R. (2005). Brown at fifty: Fulfilling the promise. *Yale Law and Policy Review, 23*(1), 213–224.

Clotfelter, C., Glennie, E., Ladd, H., & Vigdor, J. (2006). *Would higher salaries keep teachers in high-poverty schools? Evidence from a policy intervention in North Carolina* (working paper No. 12285). Cambridge, MA: National Bureau of Economic Research.

Cohen, M. (2002, May). Emerging issues in the design of next generation accountability models. *ECS Briefing Paper*. Denver, CO: Education Commission of the States.

Coleman, J. S. (1966). *Equality of educational opportunity*. Washington, DC: U.S. Department of Health, Education, and Welfare.

Coleman, J. S. (1974). The meaning of equal educational opportunity. In L. P. Miller & E. W. Gordon (Eds.), *Equality of educational opportunity: A handbook for research* (pp. 3–27). New York: AMS Press.

Coleman, J. S. (1990). *Foundations of social theory*. Cambridge, MA: Harvard University Press.

Comer, J. P. (1997). *Waiting for a miracle: Why schools can't solve all of our problems—And how we can.* New York: EP Dutton & Co.

Comer, J. P. (2004). *Leave no child behind: Preparing today's youth for tomorrow's world.* New Haven, CT: Yale University Press.

Commission on No Child Left Behind. (2007). *Beyond NCLB: Fulfilling the promise to our nation's children.* Washington, DC: Aspen Institute.

Connecticut v. Spellings, No. 05-1330 (D. Conn. Sept. 27, 2006).

Corallo, C., & McDonald, D. H. (2002). *What works with low-performing schools: A review of research.* Charleston, WV: AEL.

Crawford, J. (2007, June 6). A diminished vision of civil rights. *Education Week,* pp. 31, 40.

Cremin, L. (1970). *American education: The colonial experience, 1607–1783.* New York: Harper & Row.

Cremin, L. (1980). *American education: The national experience, 1783–1876.* New York: HarperCollins.

Cronin, J., Dahlin, M., Adkins, D., & Kingsbury, G. G. (2007, October). *The proficiency illusion.* Washington, DC: Thomas B. Fordham Institute.

Cross, C. T. (2004). *Political education: National policy comes of age.* New York: Teachers College Press.

Cross, R. W., Rebarber, T., & Torres, J. (Eds.). (2004). *Grading the systems: The guide to state standards, tests, and accountability practices.* Washington, DC: Fordham Foundation.

Cubberley, E. P. (1934). *Public education in the United States.* Boston: Houghton Mifflin Co.

Darling-Hammond, L. (1993). Creating standards of practice and delivery for learner-centered schools. *Stanford Law and Policy Review, 4,* 37–52.

Darling-Hammond, L. (2002). *Access to quality teaching: An analysis of inequality in California's public schools.* Los Angeles: UCLA's Institute for Democracy, Education, & Access (IDEA).

Darling-Hammond, L., & Sykes, G. (2003). Wanted: A national teacher supply policy for education: The right way to meet the "highly qualified teacher" challenge [electronic version]. *Education Policy Analysis Archives, 11*(33). Retrieved May 30, 2007, from http://epaa.asu.edu/epaa/v11n33/v11n33.pdf

Darling-Hammond, L., & Youngs, P. (2002). Defining "highly qualified teachers": What does "scientifically-based research" actually tell us? *Educational Researcher, 31*(9), 13–25.

Data Quality Campaign. (2005). *Creating a longitudinal data system: Using data to improve student achievement.* Washington, DC: Achieve, Inc.

David, J., Coe, P., & Kannapel, P. (2003). *Improving low-performing schools: A study of Kentucky's highly skilled educator program.* Prepared for the Partnership for Kentucky Schools.

Davis, S. L., & Buckendahl, C. W. (2007, April). *Evaluating NCLB's peer review process: A comparison of state compliance decisions.* Paper presented at the annual meeting of the National Council on Measurement in Education, Chicago.

Dawson, H. A. (1938). The federal government and education. *Journal of Educational Sociology, 12*(4), 226–243.

Debra P. v. Turlington, 633 F. 2nd 397 (5th Cir. 1981).

DeBray, E. H. (2006). *Politics, ideology, and education: Federal policy during the Clinton and Bush administrations*. New York: Teachers College Press.

Denavas-Walt, C., Proctor, B. D., & Lee, C. H. (2006, August). *Income, poverty, and health insurance coverage in the United States: 2005*. Washington, DC: U.S. Census Bureau.

DeRolph v. State of Ohio, No. 22043. Findings of Fact. (Ohio C.P., Perry County 1994).

DeRolph v. State of Ohio, 677 N.E.2d 733, 744-47 (Ohio 1997).

DeRolph v. State of Ohio. 89 Ohio St.3d 1. (2000).

Douglas-Hall, A., & Koball, H. (2006, August). *The new poor: Regional trends in child poverty since 2000*. New York: National Center for Children in Poverty.

Driscoll, W., & Fleeter, H. (2003). *Projected costs of implementing the federal "No Child Left Behind Act" in Ohio*. Columbus, OH: Ohio General Assembly.

Duncombe, W. (2006). Responding to the charge of alchemy: Strategies for evaluating the reliability and validity of costing-out research. *Journal of Education Finance, 32*(2), 137–169.

Eaton, S. (2007). *The children in room E4: American education on trial*. Chapel Hill, NC: Algonquin Books.

Edgewood Independent School District v. Kirby, 777 S.W. 2d 391 (Tex, 1989).

Education Commission of the States (ECS). (1998, March). *Designing and implementing standards-based accountability systems*. Denver, CO: Author.

Education Commission of the States. (2007). *Recent state policies/activities: teaching quality—induction and mentoring*. Retrieved June 27, 2007, from http://www.ecs.org/ecs/ecscat.nsf/WebTopicView?OpenView&count=-1& RestrictToCategory=Teaching+Quality--Induction+and+Mentoring

Education Trust. (1999). *Not good enough: A content analysis of teacher licensing examinations*. Washington, DC: Author.

Education Trust. (2003a). *African American achievement in America*. Retrieved December 1, 2006, from http://www2.edtrust.org/NR/rdonlyres/ 9AB4AC88-7301-43FF-81A3EB94807B917F/0/AfAmer_Achivement.pdf

Education Trust. (2003b). *Latino achievement in America*. Retrieved on December 1, 2006, from http://www2.edtrust.org/NR/rdonlyres/ 7DC36C7E-EBBE-43BB-8392-CDC618E1F762/0/LatAchievEnglish.pdf

Education Trust. (2006). *Missing the mark: An Education Trust analysis of teacher equity plans*. Washington, DC: Author.

Elementary and Secondary Education Act (ESEA) of 1965. (1965). § 6301 et seq.

Elmore, R. (2003). *Knowing the right thing to do: School improvement and performance-based accountability*. Washington, DC: NGA Center for Best Practices.

Elmore, R. (2006, November 13–14). *The problem of capacity in the (re)design of educational accountability systems*. Paper presented at the second annual Equity Symposium, Examining America's Commitment to Closing Achievement Gaps—NCLB and Its Alternatives, Teachers College, Columbia University.

Elmore, R., & Fuhrman, S. H. (1995). *Opportunity to learn and the state role in education.* New Brunswick, NJ: Consortium for Policy Research in Education (CPRE).

Evans, W. N., Murray, S. E., & Schwab, R. M. (1999). The impact of court-mandated school finance reform. In H. F. Ladd, R. Chalk, & J. S. Hansen (Eds.), *Equity and adequacy in education finance: Issues and perspectives* (pp. 72–98). Washington, DC: National Academies Press.

Fagan, T. W., & Kober, N. L. (2004). *Title I funds: Who's gaining and who's losing.* Washington, DC: Center on Education Policy.

Ferguson, R. F. (1998). Can schools narrow the black-white test score gap? In C. Jencks & M. Phillips (Eds.), *The black-white test score gap* (pp. 318–374). Washington, DC: Brookings Institution.

Ferguson, R. F. (2005, October). *Toward skilled parenting and transformed schools: Inside a national movement for excellence with equity.* Prepared for the Achievement Gap Initiative (AGI), the O'Connor Project at Harvard University, and the first annual Equity Symposium of the Campaign for Educational Equity at Teachers College, Columbia University.

Ferguson, R. F. (2006, June). *Racial and ethnic disparities in home intellectual climates.* Presentation prepared for the 2nd annual conference of the Harvard Achievement Gap Initiative, Defining the Achievement Gap Challenge, Cambridge, MA.

Finn, C. E., Julian, L., & Petrilli, M. J. (2006). *To dream the impossible dream: Four approaches to national standards and tests for America's schools.* Washington, DC: Thomas B. Fordham Foundation.

Finn, C. E., & Petrilli, M. J. (2000). *The state of state standards 2000.* New York: Thomas B. Fordham Foundation.

Finn, C. E., Petrilli, M. J., & Vanourek, G. (1998). *The state of state standards.* New York: Thomas B. Fordham Foundation.

Finn, J. D., Gerber, S. B., Achilles, C. M., & Boyd-Zacharias, J. (2001). The enduring effects of small classes. *Teachers College Record, 103*(2), 145–183.

Fisher, G. M. (1992). *The development of the Orshansky poverty thresholds and their subsequent history as the official U.S. poverty measure. A poverty measurement working paper.* Washington, DC: U.S. Census Bureau.

Francis, D., Rivera, M., Lesaux, N., Kieffer, M., & Rivera, H. (2006). Research-based recommendations for the use of accommodations in large-scale assessments. Retrieved June 21, 2007, from http://www.ed.gov/about/inits/ed/lep-partnership/assessments.pdf

Frankenberg, E., Lee, C., & Orfield, G. (2003). *A multiracial society with segregated schools: Are we losing the dream?* Cambridge, MA: Civil Rights Project, Harvard University.

Friedman. T. L. (2005). *The world is flat: A brief history of the twenty-first century.* New York: Farrar, Straus and Giroux.

Fryer, R. G., Jr., & Levitt, S. (2006, June). *Testing for racial differences in the mental ability of young children.* Paper presented at the 2nd Annual Conference of the Harvard Achievement Gap Initiative, Cambridge, MA.

Fuhrman, S. H. (Ed.). (1993). *Designing coherent educational policy: Improving the system.* San Francisco: Jossey-Bass.

Fuhrman, S. H. (Ed.). (2001). *From the capitol to the classroom: Standard-based reform in the states.* Chicago: University of Chicago Press.

Fullan, M. (2001). *The new meaning of educational change.* New York: Teachers College Press.

Fuller, B., Gesicki, K., Kang, E., & Wright, J. (2006). *Is the No Child Left Behind Act working? The reliability of how states track achievement.* Berkeley: Policy Analysis for California Education.

Gandal, M. (1997). *Making standards matter, 1997: An annual fifty-state report on efforts to raise academic standards.* Washington, DC: American Federation of Teachers.

Goals 2000: Educate America Act. (1994). 20 U.S. C. A. § 5801 et seq.

Goe, L. (2002). *Legislating equity: The distribution of emergency permit teachers in California.* Berkeley: Graduate School of Education, University of California, Berkeley.

Goldhaber, D. D. (2004). Why do we license teachers? In F. M. Hess, A. J. Rotherham, & K. Walsh (Eds.), *A qualified teacher in every classroom: Appraising old answers and new ideas* (pp. 81–100). Cambridge, MA: Harvard University Press.

Goldschmidt, P., & Choi, K. (2007). *The practical benefits of growth models for accountability and the limitations under NCLB* (No. 9). Los Angeles: National Center for Research on Evaluation, Standards, and Student Testing.

Gordon, E. W. (1999). *Education and justice: A view from the back of the bus.* New York: Teachers College Press.

Gordon, E. W. (2005). The idea of supplementary education. In E. Gordon, B. L. Bridglall, & A. S. Meroe (Eds.), *Supplementary education: The hidden curriculum of high academic achievement.* Lanham, MD: Rowman & Littlefield.

Gordon, E. W., & Bridglall, B. L. (Eds.). (2006). *Affirmative development: Cultivating academic ability.* Lanham, MD: Rowman & Littlefield.

Gordon, E. W., Bridglall, B. L., & Meroe, A. S. (Eds.). (2005). *Supplementary education: The hidden curriculum of high academic achievement.* Lanham, MD: Rowman & Littlefield.

Green v. County School Board, 391 U.S. 430, 439 (1968).

Grigg, W., Donohue, P., & Dion, G. (2007). *The nation's report card: 12th-grade reading and mathematics 2005* (NCES 2007-468). U.S. Department of Education, National Center for Education Statistics. Washington, DC: U.S. Government Printing Office.

Guthrie, J. W. (2007). Implications for policy: What might happen in American education if it were known how much money actually is spent? In L. O. Picus & J. L. Wattenberger (Eds.), *Where does the money go? Resource allocation in elementary and secondary schools.* Thousand Oaks, CA: Corwin Press.

Hancock v. Driscoll, 2005, p. 1166 822 N.E. 1134 (MA, 2005).

Hanushek, E. A. (Ed.). (2006). *Courting failure: How school finance lawsuits exploit judges' good intentions and harm our children.* Stanford, CA: Education Next Books.

Hanushek, E. A., Kain, J. F., & Rivkin, S. G. (1999). *Do higher salaries buy better teachers?* Working paper 7082. Cambridge, MA: National Bureau of Economic Research.

Hanushek, E., Kain, J., & Rivkin, S. (2005). Teachers, schools, and academic achievement. *Econometrica, 73*(2), 417–458.

Hart, B., & Risley, T. R. (2003). The early catastrophe: The 30 million word gap by age 3. *The American Educator, 27*(1), 4–9.

Hartz, L. (1955). *The liberal tradition in America: An interpretation of American political thought since the revolution.* New York: Harcourt Brace.

Haycock, K. (1998). Good teaching matters . . . a lot. *Thinking K–16: A Publication of the Education Trust, 3*(2), 3–14.

Heise, M. (2006). The political economy of education federalism. *Emory Law Journal, 55*(1), 125–157.

Henke, R., Chen, X., & Geis, S. (2000). *Progress through the teacher pipeline: 1992-93 College graduates and elementary/secondary school teaching as of 1997.* Retrieved May 30, 2007, from http://nces.ed.gov/pubsearch/pubsinfo.asp?pubid=2000152

Hess, F. M. (2006). Accountability without angst? Public opinion and No Child Left Behind. *Harvard Educational Review, 76*(4), 587–610.

Hess, F. M., & Petrilli, M. J. (2006). *No Child Left Behind primer.* Peter Lang.

Hickrod, G. A., Hines, E. R., Anthony, G. P., & Dively, J. A. The effect of constitutional litigation on education finance: A preliminary analysis. *The Journal of Education Finance, 18*(2), 180–210.

Hirschland, M. J., & Steinmo, S. (2003). Correcting the record: Understanding the history of federal intervention and failure in securing U.S. educational reform. *Educational Policy, 17*(3), 343–364.

Hochschild, J. L. (1995). *Facing up to the American dream: Race, class, and the soul of the nation.* Princeton, NJ: Princeton University Press.

Hochschild, J. L., & Scovronick, N. (2003). *The American dream and the public schools.* New York: Oxford University Press.

Hoff, D. J. (2002, October 9). States revise the meaning of "proficient." *Education Week,* pp. 1, 24–25.

Hoke County Board of Education v. State, No. 95CVS1158, 2000 WL 1639686 (N.C. Super. Ct. Oct. 12, 2000).

Hunter, M. A. (2003). *Plaintiff witnesses decry conditions in South Carolina schools, seeking opportunity 50 years after* Brown v. Board of Education. New York: National Access Network. Retrieved August 18, 2007, from http://www.schoolfunding.info/states/sc/10-14-03Abbeville.php3

Hunter, M. (2006, July 31). *Kansas Supreme Court: Legislature has complied with Montoy orders.* Retrieved June 27, 2007, from http://www.schoolfunding.info/news/litigation/7-31-06kansasdecision.php3

Hunter, M. (2007, April 10). *Litigation into law and public engagement into policy: CFE money flowing to New York districts this year.* Retrieved June 21, 2007, from http://www.schoolfunding.info/news/policy/4-10-07newyork.php3

Imazeki, J., & Reschovsky, A. (2006). Does No Child Left Behind place a fiscal burden on states? Evidence from Texas. *Education Finance and Policy, 1*(2), 217–246.

Improving America's Schools Act of 1994, Pub. L. No. 103-382 § 1001 et seq.

Individuals with Disabilities Education Act of 1997, 20 U.S.C.A § 1401 et seq.

Ingersoll, R. (2001). Teacher turnover and teacher shortages: An organizational analysis. *American Educational Research Journal, 38*(3), 499–534.

Ingersoll, R. (2003). *Is there really a teacher shortage?* Seattle: Center for the Study of Teaching and Policy and the Consortium for Policy Research in Education.

Interstate New Teacher Assessment and Support Consortium (INTASC). (1992). *Model standards for beginning teacher licensing, assessment, and development: A resource for state dialogue.* Retrieved May 30, 2007, from http://www.ccsso.org/content/pdfs/corestrd.pdf

Iverson, D. (2005). Schools uniting neighborhoods: The SUN initiative in Portland, Oregon. In J. Dryfoos & J. Quinn (Eds.), *Community schools: A strategy for integrating youth development and school reform.* San Francisco: Jossey-Bass.

Jennings, J. (2000). Title I: Its legislative history and its promise. *Phi Delta Kappan, 81*(7), 516–522.

Jennings, J. (2006). *Ten big effects of the No Child Left Behind Act on public schools.* Washington, DC: Center on Education Policy.

Jennings, J. (2007, March 14). Statement of Jack Jennings, President of the Center on Education Policy, before the Subcommittee on Labor, Health and Human Services, Education, and Related Agencies, U.S. Senate Committee on Appropriations.

Jerald, C. (2002). *All talk, no action: Putting an end to out-of-field teaching.* Washington, DC: The Education Trust.

Johnson, L. (1971). *The vantage point: Perspectives of the presidency, 1963–1969.* New York: Holt, Rinehart and Winston.

Johnson, S. M., & Birkeland, S. E. (2003). Pursuing a "sense of success": New teachers explain their career decision. *American Education Research Journal, 40*(3), 581–617.

Joint Organizational Statement on the No Child Left Behind (NCLB) Act. (2004). Retrieved June 28, 2007, from http://www.fairtest.org/joint%20statement%20civil%20rights%20grps%2010-21-04.html

Junn, J. (2005, October). *The political costs of unequal education.* Paper presented at the first annual Equity Symposium on the Social Costs of Inadequate Education, Teachers College, Columbia University, New York.

Kaestle, C. F. (2001). Federal aid to education since World War II: Purposes and politics. In J. Jennings (Ed.), *The future of the federal role in elementary and secondary education.* Washington, DC: Center on Education Policy.

Kagan, S. L. (2006, September). *American early childhood education: Preventing or perpetuating inequity?* New York: Campaign for Educational Equity, Teachers College, Columbia University.

Kain, J. F. & Singleton, K. (1996, May–June). Equality of educational opportunity revisited. *New England Economic Review,* 87–111.

Kane, M., Berryman, S., Goslin, D., & Meltzer, A. (1990). *Identifying and describing the skills required by work.* Washington, DC: The Secretary's Commission on Achieving Necessary Skills.

Karoly, L., Greenwood, P., Everingham, S., Hoube, J., Kilburn, R., Rydell, P., Sanders, M., & Chiesa, J. (1998). *Investing in our children: What we know and don't know about the costs and benefits of early childhood interventions.* Santa Monica: RAND.

Kennedy, J. F. (1961). Message to the members of the National Education Association meeting in Atlantic City. Retrieved April, 2007, from http://www.presidency.ucsb.edu/ws/index.php?pid=8206

Kentucky Department of Education. (2003). *The scholastic audit 2003: A report on school improvement in Kentucky.* Frankfort: Kentucky Department of Education.

Kentucky Department of Education. (2007). New highly skilled educators selected. *News Release 07-034.* Retrieved on June 28, 2007, from www.kde.state.ky.us/KDE/HomePageRepository/News+Room/Current+Press+Releases+and+Advisories/07-034.htm

Keyes v. School District No. 1, 413 U.S. 189, 200-03 (1973).

Kingsbury, G. G., Olson, A., Cronin, J., Hauser, C., & Houser, R. (2003). *The state of state standards: Research investigating proficiency levels in fourteen states.* Lake Oswego, OR: Northwest Evaluation Association.

Kirby, S. N., Berends, M., & Naftel, S. (1999). Supply and demand of minority teachers in Texas: Problems and prospects. *Educational Evaluation and Policy Analysis, 21*(1), 47–66.

Kirst, M. W. (1993). Financing school-linked services. *Education and Urban Society, 25*(2), 166–174.

Krueger, A., & Whitmore, D. (2001). The effect of attending a small class in the early grades on college-test taking and middle school test results: Evidence from Project STAR. *Economic Journal, 111*(468), 1–28.

Laird, J., DeBell, M., & Chapman, C. (2006, November). *Dropout rates in the United States: 2004.* Washington, DC: U.S. Department of Education, National Center for Education Statistics. Retrieved on June 28, 2006, from http://nces.ed.gov/pubs2007/2007024.pdf

Lake View School District No. 25 v. Huckabee, No. 1992-5318 (Pulaski County Chancery Court, May 25, 2001).

Lareau, A. (2003). *Unequal childhoods: Class, race and family life.* Berkeley: University of California Press.

Lau v. Nichols, 414 U.S. 563, 566 (1974).

Lazarín, M. (2006). *Improving assessment and accountability for English language learners in the No Child Left Behind Act.* Washington, DC: National Council of La Raza.

Lee, G. C. (1949). *The struggle for federal aid. First phase: A history of the attempts to obtain federal aid for the common schools, 1870–1890.* New York: Bureau of Publications, Teachers College, Columbia University.

Lee, J. (2006). *Tracking achievement gaps and assessing the impact of NCLB on the gaps: An in-depth look into national and state reading and math outcome trends.* Cambridge, MA: The Civil Rights Project, Harvard University.

Lee, V. E., & Burkam, D. T. (2002). *Inequality at the starting gate: Social background differences in achievement as children begin school.* Washington, DC: Economic Policy Institute.

Leichter, H. (1975). *Families as educators.* New York: Teachers College Press.

Levine, A. (2006, September). *Educating school teachers.* Washington, DC: The Education Schools Project.

Linn, R. L. (2003). Accountability, responsibility and reasonable expectations. *Education Researcher, 32*(7), 3–13.

Linn, R. L. (2004, July 28). *Rethinking the No Child Left Behind accountability system.* Paper prepared for a forum on No Child Left Behind sponsored by the Center on Education Policy, Washington, DC.

Linn, R. L. (2006, November 13–14). *Improving the accountability provisions of NCLB.* Paper presented at the second annual Equity Symposium, Examining America's Commitment to Closing Achievement Gaps—NCLB and Its Alternatives, Teachers College, Columbia University.

Liu, G. (2006). Interstate inequality in educational opportunity, *NYU Law Review, 81*(6), 2044–2128.

Loeb, S., Bryk, A., & Hanushek, E. (2007, March). *Getting down to facts: School finance and governance in California.* Palo Alto, CA: Stanford University.

Loeb, S., & Miller, L. (2006, November 13–14). *A federal foray into teacher certification: Assessing the "highly qualified teacher" provisions of NCLB.* Paper presented at the second annual Equity Symposium, Examining America's Commitment to Closing Achievement Gaps—NCLB and Its Alternatives, Teachers College, Columbia University.

Louis, K. S., Marks, H. M., & Kruse, S. (1996). Teachers' professional community in restructuring schools. *American Educational Research Journal, 33*(4), 757–798.

Lytle, J. H. (2007, February 7). A snake in the "No Child Left Behind" woodpile. *Education Week, 26*(22), 39.

Manna, P. (2006). *School's in: Federalism and the national education agenda.* Washington, DC: Georgetown University Press.

Maryland State Department of Education. (2003). *Bridge to Excellence in Public Schools Act: Final guidance on developing the five year comprehensive master plan.* Baltimore, MD: Author.

Mathis, W. J. (2004, April 21). Two very different questions. *Education Week,* pp. 33, 48.

McCaffrey, D. F., Lockwood, J. R., Koretz, D. M., & Hamilton, L. S. (2003). *Evaluating value-added models for teacher accountability.* Santa Monica, CA: Rand Corporation.

McCullough, D. (2001). *John Adams.* New York: Simon & Schuster.

McDonnell, L. M. (1995). Opportunity to learn as a research concept and a policy instrument. *Educational Evaluation and Policy Analysis, 17*(3), 305–322.

McDonnell, L. M. (2005). No Child Left Behind and the federal role in education: Evolution or revolution? *Peabody Journal of Education, 80*(2), 19–38.

McDuffy v. Secretary of Education, 615 N.E.2d 516, 554 (Mass. 1993).

McGuinn, P. J. (2006). *No Child Left Behind and the transformation of federal education policy, 1965–2005.* Lawrence: Kansas University Press.

McKinney's N.Y. Education Law. (2007). § 211-d ("Contract for Excellence").

McLaughlin, M. M. (1975). *Evaluation and reform: The Elementary and Secondary Education Act of 1965, Title I.* Cambridge, MA: Ballinger.

McLaughlin, M. (2006, November 13–14). *Closing the achievement gap and students with disabilities: The new meaning of a "free and appropriate public education."* Paper presented at the second annual Equity Symposium, Examining America's Commitment to Closing Achievement Gaps—NCLB and Its Alternatives, Teachers College, Columbia University.

McLaurin v. Oklahoma State Board of Regents, 339 U.S. 637, 641-42 (1950).

Menken, K. (2000). *What are the critical issues in wide-scale assessment of English language learners?* (No. 6). Washington, DC: National Clearinghouse for Bilingual Education.

Mercer, J. R. (1973). *Labeling the mentally retarded: Clinical and social system perspectives on mental retardation.* Berkeley: University of California Press.

Milanowski, A. (2003). The varieties of knowledge and skill-based pay design: A comparison of seven new pay systems for K–12 teachers [electronic version]. *Education Policy Analysis Archives, 11*(4). Retrieved June 28, 2007, from http://epaa.asu.edu/epaa/v11n4/

Miller, L. S. (1995). *An American imperative: Accelerating minority educational advancement.* New Haven, CT: Yale University Press.

Milliken v. Bradley, 418 U.S. 717-18 (1974).

Mintrop, H. (2003). *The limits of sanctions in low-performing schools: A study of Maryland and Kentucky schools on probation* [electronic version]. Retrieved May 10, 2007, from http://epaa.asu.edu/epaa/v11n3.html

Mishel, L., Bernstein, D. C., & Allegretto, S. (2005). *The state of working America 2004/2005.* Washington, DC Economic Policy Institute; Ithaca, NY: Cornell University Press.

Mishel, L., Bernstein, D. C., & Allegretto, S. (2007). *The state of working America, 2006/2007.* Washington, DC: Economic Policy Institute; Ithaca, NY: Cornell University Press.

Montoy v. State, 99-C-1738, 2003 WL 22902963.

Moretti, E. (2005, October 24–25). *Does education reduce participation in criminal activities?* Paper presented at the first annual Equity Symposium, The Social Costs of Inadequate Education, Teachers College, Columbia University.

Muennig, P. (2005, October 24–25). *The economic value of health gains associated with education interventions.* Paper presented at the first annual Equity Symposium, The Social Costs of Inadequate Education, Teachers College, Columbia University.

Murphy, J. (1991). Title I of ESEA: The politics of implementing federal education reform. In A. R. Odden (Ed.), *Education policy implementation.* Albany: State University of New York Press.

National Access Network. (2006, September 18). *"Equity" and "adequacy" school funding court decisions.* Retrieved June 27, 2007, from http://www.schoolfunding.info/litigation/equityandadequacytable.pdf

National Assessment Governing Board (NAGB). (2006, August 4). *The future of 12th grade NAEP: Report of the ad hoc committee on planning for NAEP 12th grade assessments in 2009.* Washington, DC: Author.

National Center for Education Statistics. (2006a). *The condition of education 2006* (NCES 2006-071). Washington, DC: U.S. Government Printing Office.

National Center for Education Statistics. (2007a). *Mapping 2005 state proficiency standards onto the NAEP scales* (NCES 2007-482). Washington, DC: U.S. Government Printing Office.

National Center for Education Statistics. (2007b). *National Assessment of Educational Progress (NAEP). The nation's report card: Mathematics 2007.* Washington, DC: U.S. Government Printing Office.

National Center for Education Statistics. (2007c). *National Assessment of Educational Progress (NAEP). The nation's report card: Reading 2007.* Washington, DC: U.S. Government Printing Office.

National Center on Education and the Economy. (1990). *America's choice: High skills or low wages.* Washington, DC: Author.

National Center on Education and the Economy. (2007). *Tough choices or tough times: The report of the new commission on the skills of the American workforce.* Washington, DC: Author.

National Conference of State Legislatures. (2005). *Delivering the promise: State recommendations for improving No Child Left Behind.* Denver, CO: Author.

National Council on Education Standards and Testing. (1992). *Raising standards for American education. A report to Congress, the Secretary of Education, the National Education Goals Panel, and the American people.* Washington, DC: U.S. Government Printing Office.

National Council on Teacher Quality. (2004). *Searching the attic: How states are responding to the nation's goal of placing a highly qualified teacher in every classroom.* Washington, DC: Author.

National Education Association. (2006, July). *ESEA: It's time for a change! NEA's positive agenda for the ESEA reauthorization.* Washington, DC: Author.

National Governors Association. (1996, March). *National Education Summit policy statement.* Washington, DC: Author.

Nave, G., Woo, A., Kruger, R., & Yap, K. O. (2006). *Multnomah County Department of Schools and Communities SUN service system 2004–05 evaluation report.* Portland: Northwest Regional Educational Laboratory.

Nettles, M. T., Millett, C. M., & Oh, H. (2006, October 24–25). *The challenge and opportunity of African American educational achievement in the United States.* Paper presented at the second annual Equity Symposium, Examining America's Commitment to Closing Achievement Gaps—NCLB and Its Alternatives, Teachers College, Columbia University.

New State Ice Co. v. Liebmann, 285 U.S. 262, 311 (1932) (Brandeis, J., dissenting).

New York State Department of Education. (2005). *The state of learning: Statistical profiles of public school districts.* New York: Author.

No Child Left Behind Act of 2001, 20 U.S.C. § 6301 et seq. (2001).

No Child Left Behind Regulation, 34 C.F.R. § 200.56 (2007).

Noddings, N. (2005). What does it mean to educate the whole child? *Educational Leadership, 63*(1), 8–13.

O'Day, J. A., & Smith, M. S. (1993). Systemic school reform and educational opportunity. In S. H. Fuhrman (Ed.), *Designing coherent education policy: Improving the system.* San Francisco: Jossey-Bass.

Odden, A., Kellor, E., Heneman, H., & Milanowski, A. (1999). *School-based performance award programs: Design and administration issues synthesized from eight programs.* Madison: University of Wisconsin-Madison Center for Education Research, Consortium for Policy Research in Education.

Oklahoma City Public Schools v. Dowell, 498 U.S. 237, 249-50 (1991).

Oregon Quality Education Commission. (2004). *Quality education model: Final report.* Salem, OR: Oregon Department of Education.

Orfield, G., & Lee, C. (2005, January). *Why segregation matters: Poverty and educational inequality.* Cambridge, MA: Harvard Civil Rights Project.

Orfield, M. (2002). *American metropolitics: The new suburban reality.* Washington, DC: Brookings Institution Press.

Organisation for Economic Co-operation and Development. (2004). *Education at a glance: OECD indicators.* Paris, France: Author.

Paley, A. R. (2007). "No Child" target is called out of reach: Goal of 100% proficiency debated as Congress weighs renewal. *Washington Post*, p. A1.

Parents Involved in Community Schools v. Seattle School Dist. No. 1, 551 U.S. (2007).

Patterson, J. L., Purkey, S. C., & Parker, J. V. (1986). *Productive school systems for a nonrational world.* Alexandria, VA: Association for Supervision and Curriculum Development.

Phi Delta Kappan. (2006). 38th Annual *Phi Delta Kappan*/Gallup poll of the public's attitudes toward the public schools. Retrieved May 30, 2007, from http://www.pdkintl.org/kappan/k0609pol.htm

Pole, J. R. (1978). *The pursuit of equality in American history.* Los Angeles: University of California Press.

Pollock, M. (in press). *Because of race: How Americans debate harm and opportunity in our schools.* Princeton: Princeton University Press.

Pontiac School District et al. v. Spellings, No. 09-71535 (E.D. Mich. Nov. 23, 2005).

Popham, J. W. (2004). *America's failing schools: How parents and teachers can cope with No Child Left Behind.* New York: Routledge.

Porter, A. (1993). School delivery standards. *Education Researcher, 22*(5), 24–30.

Porter, A. (1995). The uses and misuses of opportunity-to-learn standards. *Educational Researcher, 24*(1), 21–27.

Porter, A. C., Garet, M. S., Desimone, L., Yoon, K. S., & Birman, B. F. (2000). *Does professional development change teaching practice? Results from a three-year study.* Washington, DC: U.S. Department of Education.

Pressley, M. (2005, December 14). The rocky year of Reading First: Another chapter in the long history of complaints about federal reading efforts. *Education Week*, pp. 24–25.

Price, C. D. (2002). *Higher pay in hard-to-staff schools: The case for financial incentives.* Arlington, VA: American Association of School Administrators.

Public Advocates. (2007, August 21). *U.S. Department of Education waters down teacher quality, NCLB lawsuit charges: Major loophole in defining "highly qualified teacher" defies will of Congress, harms students* [Press release]. San Francisco: Author.

Rabkin, J. (1980). Office for civil rights. In J. Q. Wilson (Ed.), *The politics of regulation*. New York: Basic Books.

Ramey, S. L., & Ramey, C. T. (2000). Early childhood experiences and developmental competence. In J. Waldfogel & S. Danziger (Eds.), *Securing the future: Investing in children from birth to college* (pp. 122–150). New York: Russell Sage Foundation.

Ravitch, D. (1983). *The troubled crusade: American education, 1945–1980*. New York: Basic Books.

Raymond, M., Fletcher, S., & Luque, L. (2001). *Teach for America: An evaluation of teacher differences and student outcomes in Houston, Texas*. Stanford, CA: Hoover Institute, Center for Research on Education Outcomes.

Rebell, M. A. (1989). Testing, public policy, and the courts. In B. R. Gifford (Ed.), *Testing and the allocation of opportunity* (pp. 135–162). Boston, MA: Kluwer Academic.

Rebell, M. A. (2002). Education adequacy, democracy, and the courts. In T. Reading, C. Eley, Jr., & C. E. Snow (Eds.), *Achieving high educational standards for all*. Washington, DC: National Academy Press.

Rebell, M. A. (2004). Adequacy litigations: A new path to equity? In J. Petrovich & A. S. Wells (Eds.), *Bringing equity back* (pp. 291–327). New York: Teachers College Press.

Rebell, M. A. (2007a). Professional rigor, public engagement and judicial review: A proposal for enhancing the validity of education adequacy studies. *Teachers College Record, 109*(6), 1303–1373.

Rebell, M. A. (2007b). Poverty, "meaningful" educational opportunity and the necessary role of the courts. *North Carolina Law Review, 85*(102), 1467–1543.

Rebell, M. A., & Block, A. (1985). *Equality and education: Federal civil rights enforcement in the New York City school system*. Princeton, NJ: Princeton University Press.

Rebell, M. A., & Wolff, J. R. (2006). *Opportunity knocks: Applying lessons from the education adequacy movement to reform the No Child Left Behind Act* (Policy Paper No. 1). New York: Campaign for Educational Equity.

Reville, P., Coggins, C. T., Schaefer, B., & Candon, J. (2004). *Examining state intervention capacity*. Boston, MA: The Rennie Center for Education Research and Policy.

Riddle, W. C. (2006a). *Adequate yearly progress (AYP): Implementation of the No Child Left Behind Act* (No. RL32495). Washington, DC: Congressional Research Service.

Riddle, W. C. (2006b). *The No Child Left Behind Act: An overview of reauthorization issues for the 110th Congress* (No. RL33749). Washington, DC: Congressional Research Service.

Rivkin, S. G., Hanushek, E. A., & Kain, J. F. (2000). Teachers, schools, and academic achievement. *NBER Working Paper No. 6691 (revised)*. Cambridge, MA: National Bureau of Economic Research.

Robelen, E. W. (2002, June). *Taking on the gap*. Naperville, IL: North Central Regional Educational Laboratory (NCREL). Retrieved April 13, 2006, from www.ncrel.org/gap/takeon/toc.htm

Roosevelt Elementary School District No. 66 v. Bishop, 877 P.2d 806, 817 (Ariz. 1994).

Rose v. Council for Better Education, 790 S.W.2d 186, 211 (KY 1989).

Rosenholtz, S. J. (1989). *Teachers' workplace: The social organization of schools.* New York: Longman.

Rotherham, A. J. (2006, July). *Making the cut: How states set passing scores on standardized tests.* Washington, DC: Education Sector.

Rothman, R. (1993). "Delivery" standards for schools at heart of new policy debate [Electronic Version]. *Education Week.* Retrieved May 30, 2007, from http://lnk.edweek.org/edweek/index.html?url=/ew/articles/1993/04/07/28deli.h12.html&tkn=Mj03Y3HvmOoETXKjfGAINNxJtQ%2FrsW4%2B

Rothman, R. (1995). *Measuring up: Standards, assessment, and school reform.* San Francisco: Jossey-Bass.

Rothman, R. (2004). Benchmarking and alignment of state standards and assessments. In S. H. Fuhrman & R. F. Elmore (Eds.), *Redesigning accountability systems for education* (pp. 96–114). New York: Teachers College Press.

Rothstein, R. (2004). *Class and schools: Using social, economic, and educational reform to close the Black-White achievement gap.* Washington, DC: Economic Policy Institute.

Rothstein, R., Jacobsen, R., & Wilder, T. (2006, November 13–14). *"Proficiency for all"—An oxymoron.* Paper presented at the Examining America's Commitment to Closing Achievement Gaps—NCLB and Its Alternatives, Teachers College, Columbia University.

Rothstein, R., & Wilder, T. (2005, October 24–25). *The many dimensions of racial inequality.* Paper presented at the Social Costs of Inadequate Education Symposium, Teachers College, Columbia University.

Rothstein, R., Wilder, T., & Jacobsen, R. (2007). Balance in the balance. *Educational Leadership, 64*(8), 8–14.

Rouse, C. (2005, October 24–25). *The labor market consequences of an inadequate education.* Paper presented at the Social Costs of Inadequate Education Symposium, Teachers College, Columbia University.

Rumberger, R. W. (2007). Parsing the data on student achievement in high-poverty schools. *North Carolina Law Review, 85*(5), 1293.

Ryan, J. E. (1999). Schools, race and money. *Yale Law Journal, 109*, 249–316.

Ryan, J. E. (2004). The perverse incentives of the No Child Left Behind Act. *New York University Law Review, 79*(3), 932–989.

Sack, J. (2005, May 11). State agencies juggle NCLB work, staffing woes. *Education Week*, p. 25.

San Antonio Independent School District v. Rodriguez, 411 U.S. 1 (1973).

Sanders, W., & Rivers, J. (1996, November). *Cumulative and residual effects of teachers on future student academic achievement.* Knoxville: University of Tennessee Value-Added Research and Assessment Center.

Schemo, D. (2007, March 26). Failing schools see a solution in longer day [Electronic Version]. *The New York Times.* Retrieved June 28, 2007, from http://select.nytimes.com/search/restricted/article?res=F10813FA39540C758EDDAA0894DF404482

Schrag, P. (2003). *The final test: The battle for adequacy in America's schools*. New York: The New Press.

Schuck, P. H., & Zeckhauser, R. J. (2006). *Targeting in social programs: Avoiding bad bets, removing bad apples*. Washington, DC: Brookings Institution Press.

Schwartz, R. (2006, November 13–14). *Standards, tests, and NCLB: What might come next*. Paper presented at the second annual Equity Symposium, Examining America's Commitment to Closing Achievement Gaps—NCLB and Its Alternatives, Teachers College, Columbia University.

Slavin, R. E. (1999). How can funding equity ensure enhanced achievement? *Journal of Education Finance, 24*(4), 519–528.

Smylie, M. A., Allensworth, E., Greenberg, R. C., Harris, R., & Luppescu, S. (2001). *Teacher professional development in Chicago: Supporting effective practice*. Chicago: Consortium on Chicago School Research.

Snipes, J., Williams, A., Horwitz, A., Soga, K., & Casserly, M. (2007, April). *Beating the odds: A city-by-city analysis of student performance and achievement gaps on state assessments. Results from the 2005–2006 school year*. Washington, DC: Council for Great City Schools.

Sobol, T. (2004, November 12). *School improvement*. Presentation at the conference, NCLB: Developing a Common Agenda for Reform, Pocantico, New York.

Soler, M., & Shauffer, C. (1990). Fighting fragmentation: Coordination of services for children and families [Special issue]. *Nebraska Law Review, 69*(2), 278–297.

Southeast Center for Teacher Quality. (2004). *Unfulfilled promise: Ensuring high quality teachers for our nation's students*. Hillsborough, NC: Southeast Center for Teacher Quality.

Spellings, M. (2006, September 5). Letter from the Secretary of Education to Chief State School Officers. Retrieved May 30, 2007, from www.ed.gov/policy/elsec/guid/secletter/060905.html

Spellings, M. (2007, May 22). Speech at the Manhattan Institute. New York.

Sunderman, G. L. (2006). *The unraveling of No Child Left Behind: How negotiated changes transform the law*. Cambridge, MA: Harvard Civil Rights Project.

Sunderman, G. L., & Orfield, G. (2006, September). *Domesticating a revolution: No Child Left Behind reforms and state administrative response*. Cambridge, MA: The Civil Rights Project at Harvard University.

Swann v. Charlotte-Mecklenburg Board of Education, 402 U.S. 1, 3 (1971).

The Teaching Commission. (2004). *Teaching at risk: A call to action*. Retrieved June 29, 2007, from http://www.ecs.org/html/Document.asp?chouseid=4993

Tucker, M. S., & Toch, T. (2004, March). The secret to making Bush's school reform law work? More bureaucrats [electronic version]. *Washington Monthly*. Retrieved May 30, 2007, from http://findarticles.com/p/articles/mi_m1316/is_3_36/ai_114477542

Tyack, D. B. (1974). *The one best system: A history of American urban education*. Cambridge, MA: Harvard University Press.

Tyack, D., & Cuban, L. (1995). *Tinkering toward Utopia: A century of public school reform*. Cambridge, MA: Harvard University Press.

U.N. Food and Agriculture Organization. (2000). *The state of food insecurity in the world*. Rome, Italy: Author.

UNICEF. (2005). *Child poverty in rich countries, 2005*. Innocenti Report Card No. 6. Florence, Italy: UNICEF Innocenti Research Center. Retrieved November 16, 2006, from http://www.unicef-icdc.org/publications/pdf/repcard6e.pdf

U.S. Department of Education. (2002). *Meeting the highly qualified teachers challenge: The secretary's annual report on teacher quality*. Retrieved May 30, 2007, from http://www.title2.org/ADATitleIIReport2002.pdf

U.S. Department of Education. (2004). *Guidance on the transferability authority*. Retrieved March 21, 2007, from http://www.ed.gov/programs/transferability/legislation.html

U.S. Department of Education. (2005). *A highly qualified teacher in every classroom: The secretary's fourth annual report on teacher quality*. Retrieved May 30, 2007, from http://www.title2.org/TitleIIReport05.pdf

U.S. Department of Education. (2006a). *A highly qualified teacher in every classroom: The secretary's fifth annual report on teacher quality*. Retrieved May 30, 2007, from http://www.title2.org/secReport06.asp

U.S Department of Education. (2006b). *No Child Left Behind. Growth models: Ensuring grade-level proficiency for all students by 2014*. Retrieved April 15, 2007, from www.ed.gov/admins/lead/account/growthmodel/proficiency.pdf

U.S. Department of Education. (2007a). *Measuring the achievement of students with disabilities*. Retrieved April 9, 2007, from http://www.ed.gov/parents/needs/speced/twopercent.html

U.S. Department of Education (2007b, May). *Update on state standards and assessments systems*. Retrieved July 30, 2007, from http://www.ed.gov/admins/lead/account/statesystems.html

U.S. Department of Labor Bureau of Labor Statistics. (2005, March). *A profile of the working poor, 2003*. Report 983. Retrieved December 5, 2006, from http://www.bls.gov/cps/cpswp2003.pdf

U.S. General Accounting Office. (1995). *School facilities: Condition of America's schools*. GAO/HEHS-95-61. Washington, DC: Author.

U.S. General Accounting Office. (2003). *Title I: Characteristics of tests will influence expenses; Information sharing may help states realize efficiencies* (No. GAO-03-389). Washington, DC: Author.

U.S. House of Representatives, 1st Session, 107th Cong. (2001, December 13). *No Child Left Behind of 2001 conference report*. Report 107-334. Washington, DC: U.S. Government Printing Office.

Varenne, H., & McDermott, R. (1998). *Successful failure*. Boulder: CO: Westview.

Von Zastrow, C., & Janc, H. (2004). *Academic atrophy: The condition of liberal arts in America's public schools*. Washington, DC: Council for Basic Education.

Waldfogel, J., Garfinkel, I., & Kelly, B. (2005, October 24–25). *Diversity and the demographic dividend: Achieving educational equity in an aging White society*.

Paper presented at the Social Costs of Inadequate Education Symposium, Teachers College, Columbia University.

Washington Area School Study Council. (2003). *Improving accountability for limited English proficient and special education students under the No Child Left Behind Act.* Washington, DC: Author.

Weiner, R. (2006, October). *Confounding evidence on achievement gaps: Understanding opportunity gaps that undermine the school success of students from poverty.* Prepared for the UNC Symposium on High Poverty Schooling in America.

Wells, A. S. (2006, November 14–15). *Our children's burden: A history of federal education policies that ask (now require) our public schools to solve societal inequality.* Paper presented at the Examining America's Commitment to Closing Achievement Gaps—NCLB and Its Alternatives, Teachers College, Columbia University.

Wells, A. S., Holme, J. J., & Duran, J. (2006, April). *A spatial understanding of the schools left behind: Scapegoating poor schools in an era of accountability and school choice.* Paper presented at the annual meeting of the American Educational Research Association, San Francisco.

WestEd. (2000). *Teachers who learn, kids who achieve: A look at schools with model professional development.* San Francisco, CA: Author.

Wilkerson, D. (Ed.). (1979). *Educating all our children: An imperative for democracy.* Westport, CT: Mediax.

Wolf, R. M. (1966). The measurements of environments. In A. Anastasi (Ed.), *Testing problems in perspective.* Washington, DC: American Council on Education.

Wolff, J. R. (2001, December). *In evidence: Policy reports from the CFE trial. Vol. 4. Teacher quality matters.* New York: Campaign for Fiscal Equity.

Zabala, D., & Minnici, A. (2007). *"It's different now": How exit exams are affecting teaching and learning in Jackson and Austin.* Washington, DC: Center on Education Policy.

Zehr, M. A. (2005). State testing of English-language learners scrutinized. *Education Week*, pp. 3, 12.

Zimmer, R., Gill, B., Razquin, P., Booker, K., & Lockwood, J. R. (2007, July). *State and local implementation of the No Child Left Behind Act: Vol. 1. Title 1 school choice, supplemental educational services, and student achievement.* Washington, DC: U.S. Department of Education.

Index

About the Authors

Michael A. Rebell is executive director of the Campaign for Educational Equity and professor of law and educational practice at Teachers College, Columbia University. He is also a lecturer in law at Columbia Law School, a visiting professor at Harvard Law School, and previously taught for many years at Yale Law School. Mr. Rebell co-founded and served as executive director and counsel of the Campaign for Fiscal Equity (CFE), which won a major constitutional ruling that entitles all children in New York State to the opportunity for a sound basic education. He is one of the nation's foremost authorities on fiscal issues in education and has pioneered the legal theory and strategy of educational adequacy. Mr. Rebell has also litigated numerous class-action lawsuits on a variety of issues involving law and education, including *Jose P. v. Mills*, the landmark New York State case establishing the legal rights of students with disabilities. He served as special master in the Boston Special Education litigation, *Allen v. Parks*. He has co-authored two books *(Equity and Education* and *Education Policymaking and the Courts)* and has written several dozen articles on a wide range of education issues. Mr. Rebell is a graduate of Harvard College and Yale Law School.

Jessica R. Wolff is the policy director of the Campaign for Educational Equity at Teachers College, Columbia University, and conducts research in educational accountability and comprehensive approaches to educational opportunity. She served as director of policy development of the Campaign for Fiscal Equity (CFE) from 2000–2005, where she played a critical role in bringing the public voice into policy development through the conversation series, "Accountable Schools, Accountable Public (ASAP)," "Making the Money Matter: A Community Dialogue," and other public engagement projects. Her work with the Sound Basic Education Task Force on Accountability helped guide school funding legislation in New York State. Among other works, she is author of the series, *In Evidence: Policy Reports from the CFE Trial*. Prior to CFE, she wrote widely on public school issues for the Public Education Association and, for many years, authored a monthly column on public education for the award-winning online news journal *Gotham Gazette*. Ms. Wolff has a B.A. from Brown University and an M.A. from New York University.